A SMALL BAND OF MEN

An Englishman's Adventures
in the Hong Kong
Marine Police

Les Bird

A Small Band of Men

By Les Bird

ISBN-13: 978-988-8552-51-1

2nd edition-2020

BIOGRAPHY & AUTOBIOGRAPHY

EB120

Published by Earnshaw Books Ltd. (Hong Kong)

The stories in the book reflect the author's recollections of events. Some names and identifying characteristics have been changed to protect the privacy of those depicted. The dialogue has been re-created from memory.

Contents

1. A SMALL BAND OF MEN   1
   精選小隊

2. IT'S ALL HERE IN HONG KONG   6
   香港錦囊

3. DOING BRICK HILL   14
   跑磚山

4. A REAL GWAILO   23
   正牌鬼佬

5. HIGH JINKS   35
   惡作劇

6. DIAMOND DON BISHOP   46
   钻石

7. THE MARINER, THE HANGMAN, AND THE PRIEST   57
   海員、劊子手、傳教士

8. OTTO THE AUTO   68
   老闆的車

9. GHOST SHIP   79
   鬼船

10. FRIGHTFULLY MAULED   100
    可怖咬噬

11. BLACKBEARD THE PIRATE   127
    黑鬍子海盜

12. A VERY LARGE COSSACK FUR HAT   138
    哥薩克式皮草帽

13. TAI O   149
大澳

14. AM I UNDER ARREST, INSPECTOR?   163
幫辦，係唔係拉咗我

15. PORT OF FIRST ASYLUM   185
第一收容港

16. WE ARE GOING TO NEED REINFORCEMENTS   194
極待增援

17. LOSING THE 'ROYAL' TITLE   203
皇家不再

18. HARBOR AIR CRASH   213
港內墜機

19. FORGOTTEN ISLAND   226
被遺忘的小島

20. IT WAS AN ARSE OF A DAY   239
狼狽的一天

21. OPERATION SEAGULL   252
海鷗行動

22. DEADLY GAME   275
亡命遊戲

23. THE HANDOVER BEGINS   228
回歸序幕拉開

24. GOODBYE AND ALL THAT 1997   302
再見亦是朋友

1

A SMALL BAND OF MEN
精選小隊

OVERWHELMED — that was the only way to describe how I was feeling. Why on earth had it taken me so long? As the taxi weaved its way through the neon blur of north Kowloon I sat in the back and worried. It had been twenty years since I had seen anyone from the unit. I'd been invited, every year, to the annual reunion, but I always found an excuse. There were phone calls and requests to attend but I never felt the need.

I was their longest-serving commanding officer and the only one to command the Marine Police fast pursuit unit on more than one occasion. The first time was in the 1980s as an inspector, and then again during the unit's heyday in the early 1990s as chief inspector. So many memories, and so much time had passed.

There would be almost three hundred at the dinner that night, a huge Chinese banquet in a private function room decked out in celebratory red and gold. White linens covering round tables, and the room overflowing with the men I once knew so well. A sensory overload of food, noise, and booze. Reminiscing with laughter, handshakes, and back-slapping. Legends would be recalled, and inevitably there would be the singing, the same drinking songs we all sang after a big case. All the aged, wannabe Canto pop singers once more performing in full force and into the night. They were ready to sing their hearts out because they still cared about those days, they still cared about what they had done. It's comforting to know that some things don't change. It was their time; it was our unit.

I first became involved just five years after arriving in Hong Kong. "A small band of men," ordered Geoff Hodges, the head of Marine Police. "Find me fifty of our best men. Form a unit, train them in covert ops." That's when things got interesting.

In just ten months we intercepted, arrested and repatriated over ten thousand illegal immigrants from across the border in the People's Republic of China. The results shocked everyone, including Hodges and the Police Commissioner.

"The government had no idea so many illegals were breaching the fence," said the Commissioner.

"Neither did I," replied Hodges.

Hardly anyone ever left the unit of their own volition, and as we expanded and moved into counter-terrorist operations, we evolved into one huge family, a mix of young and not-so-young alike. And they were all here tonight, with a few exceptions. Young Billy Lee would not be here. In ceremonial uniform, we slow-marched behind his coffin through the streets of Kowloon, behind his mother and sisters and buried him with full force honors. He was killed in the darkness of the Tolo Channel during a night-time op, cut to pieces by the bows of an armor-plated smuggler's speedboat tearing across the dark waters at ninety mph. It was the deliberate murder of a young officer. But his memory, his presence, would certainly be felt tonight.

I looked out of the taxi window once more, catching my own reflection. Men who were the backbone of the unit all those years ago, who put themselves in physical danger day after day, would be there. Joe Poon, my trusty second-in-command for so many years. The same Joe Poon who went off into the darkness of the

Tolo Channel, alone, to find the men who killed Billy Lee. And Kwan, the unit's senior sergeant and the uncle of the bunch who never got flustered. The young lads admired and feared him in equal amounts. He seemed indestructible back then.

I wondered if the men had changed, faded with the years, all of us now old and retired. I wanted my memories intact, to be the only memories of these men. That's probably why I had stayed away all these years.

The taxi pulled up outside the restaurant. I was deliberately late as there would be several hours of *mahjong* before dinner, and I had no interest in that. As I climbed out, a man who had been leaning against a nearby road sign smoking glared at me. He screwed up his eyes in concentration.

"Bird!" he shouted and pointed, "*Ah* Bird, sir, *ho loi mo gin!* Long time no see!"

An image from years ago, I recognized that grin, "*On Jai?*" I asked. The grin widened and he began to laugh. I shook his outstretched hand. "It has been a long time. How are you?"

"*Jung mei sei* – not dead yet," laughed the man who had once been one of my senior patrol NCOs. "Come," he said, "I'll take you up."

He grabbed my arm and escorted me towards the restaurant doors. We jabbered away in Cantonese, climbing the steps towards the noise. The dinner was already in full swing.

Together we shoved open the double doors. The noise was deafening with large groups of men drinking, laughing and arguing. It was what I expected. One by one, they turned to stare in my direction and I was quickly surrounded by a sea of half-familiar faces, old faces. People who looked like the men I once knew. There were lots of *jung mei sei*, "not dead yet" comments.

"Good evening, sir," said Kwan, pushing his way through. I recognized him immediately. He was tall for a Cantonese, over six feet and powerfully built. The years had been kind, he still looked superbly fit. True, his hair had turned silver-grey, but it was all there. He reached forward and we shook hands.

"Good evening Mr Kwan, how are you?" I said.

"I am fine, sir. Welcome. Come."

Kwan turned and the sea of faces parted. I followed, shaking hands as I went. There were "good evenings" from every direction. I spotted *Din Gau*, Mad Dog, one of our senior coxswains. Now an old man, he was standing at attention on the far side of the room, his chest stuck out. He threw me a mock salute and I saluted back, then gave him a thumbs-up.

We arrived at the head table to be met by the other senior ranks. I was struck by how our former rank structure remained in place. As a group of retired officers, we still maintained the line of command, each one falling into place within that structure. Everyone was comfortable playing out their former roles. It was their way of not letting go. Certainly no one in the room would have had it any other way.

As I sat there listening to my oldest NCOs relating stories and squabbling over who had said this or who had done that all those years ago, others, men now in their sixties who once had been juniors in the unit, approached the head table and waited to be called forward by Kwan to speak.

I scanned the room, everyone looked genuinely happy to be at the reunion, to be back in amongst their memories.

"Where's Joe?" I asked Kwan.

He nodded, "Here comes your former partner in crime now."

Joe Poon edged his way through a group towards us. "Ah, you are finally here," he smiled.

"Indeed I am, Joe," I said standing up and shaking his hand. "It's good to see you again."

The scar running across his upper lip and down his chin was

4

as prominent as it always had been. He had been thrown from his fast pursuit craft during a chase and while underwater had been struck on the face by the hull of another of our pursuit craft. Joe called the scar his "lucky cut." He said it made him look more interesting. He claimed it was why so many girls were attracted to him.

Joe still looked fit. His hair showed a few flecks of grey but otherwise he didn't look that much older than the last time I'd seen him.

"Here, have a beer." He thrust a large bottle of Tsing Tao in my direction. "We were wondering if we would ever see you again."

"I know, my apologies. It's been far too long."

"Never mind, you here are now. That's what matters."

I recalled the first time we'd met in the police training school, back in 1976. We had been squad mates. Little did we know at the time how our careers would entwine.

There was a pause for a moment as I poured the beer. It had been so long since I'd seen him. Twenty-five years. I had so much to say, yet now, in front of everyone, it wasn't the time.

Joe caught on. "Let's catch up a little later tonight? After the ruckus dies down?" he said smiling and nodding towards the noisy drinking game that had started between a group of engineers at the next table.

Joe turned and went off to join another group. He had done his duty for now, anyway, done what was required of him. He had been seen by everyone to formally greet me. So now he was no longer the senior man in the room. And I was officially back.

2

IT'S ALL HERE IN HONG KONG
香港錦囊

I LEFT SCHOOL at the age of eighteen armed with average examination results. With the ignorance of youth, I believed I was ready to take on the world. But in the early 1970s, the United Kingdom was far from united and was going downhill rapidly, particularly where gainful employment for young people with average exam results was concerned.

It was the beginning of a recession, with an oil crisis, miners' strike and a three-day working week. The dire situation in which the country found itself eventually prompted the government to declare a state of emergency. I guess it was this economic gloom and doom that helped me make my decision. If ever there was a time to put my boyhood master plan into action, it was now.

From an early age I'd had a burning desire to travel the world, and as I grew older this desire became an obsession. The passion for adventure stemmed mostly from hearing my father's stories of his teenage years, which were spent fighting the Imperial Japanese forces in the Pacific during World War II. In 1940 my father, who was aged sixteen at the time, had attempted to enlist in the Royal Navy, only to be told to go away and come back when he was eighteen. He tried again a year later and this time was accepted. "We were running out of men," was his explanation for his success at the second attempt. For the next four years he was in the thick of the fighting, both at sea in the Pacific and on land throughout Southeast Asia. He came home in 1946, a five-year war veteran. He was twenty-two years old.

Like most men of his generation, Dad hardly ever spoke of the war. I learnt about what he did by eavesdropping on conversations he had with his three brothers, all of whom saw active service in the Royal Navy. But while my father was mostly silent about his war years, my mother simply never spoke about it, ever. And it never occurred to me to wonder why. After all, she was a housewife, what could she have to say about armed conflict? That is until one day I came home from school and noticed what looked like a jewelry box on a side table. I took a peek inside and found a set of World War II medals. They were not my father's. I asked my mother what they were.

"Oh, those," she replied, "I was just sorting out the dresser drawers and found them. They are mine."

I was shocked. How did she get medals during the war? Did they just give medals out to people for staying calm?

"Oh no," she replied, "I was in the army, you know."

"Oh?" I said, while marshaling about one thousand questions. The army? How would I have known? I'd never heard any stories. I'd never seen any photographs of her in uniform or doing anything war-like. I had never known my mother in any role other than being my mother. No, I didn't know.

"Yes. It wasn't just men who were conscripted. Women were too. Most went into factories, but I volunteered and saw active service as an anti-aircraft gunner on the south coast, overlooking the English Channel. I was part of an all-girl unit that became very well-known. The press called us Ack-Ack Girls. Mr Churchill said we were vital to the defense of our nation. Our job was to shoot down the Luftwaffe planes that were on their way to bomb London. The Ack-Ack Girls name came from the sound our anti-aircraft guns made when we fired at them."

I studied my mother as she continued folding laundry. She recounted this story as though she was telling me about what to pick up at the shops in the High Street.

"Ack-Ack Girls? Churchill? You shot at bombers?" I asked, my disbelief now harder to contain. I half-expected her to say something like, "No, I'm just joking." But she didn't.

"It was the bombers, and the Messerschmitts. They were a nuisance."

"A nuisance? You mean fighter aircraft?"

"Yes, they used to fly low so they could fire their machine guns at us, providing cover for their bombers."

Who was this woman? She looked like my mother and she sounded like my mother, but she was not the mother I knew. I thought about this for some time. I began to imagine her, young and in uniform, in her gun crew, taking fire, shooting at enemy aircraft.

"Mum, can I ask, when you fired the anti-aircraft gun, did you ever hit anything?"

She continued to fold freshly-ironed shirts. "Well, yes. You see they were shooting at us, weren't they? So it was our duty to shoot at them, wasn't it?"

Incredible. My mother had actually been in gunfights. She may have actually killed someone. I never knew any of this. However, on reflection, this was typical of my mother, and typical of those who lived through World War II. In 1939, with the outbreak of war, the British government told the country to 'Keep Calm and Carry On.' And that is precisely what my mother had done. No fuss, no bother, as soon as she was old enough, she joined-up and did what was required.

In comparison, I'd never done anything. Here I was, eighteen years old and living at home with my parents. Parents, who by the time they were teenagers had seen action in the Pacific or been in gun battles with the Luftwaffe. I felt inadequate. I felt as though somehow I was getting left behind, letting life slip by. I needed to get my plan up and running.

Calling upon all I had been taught during A-level math, I worked out that if I sold my Ford Escort for £400 I'd have enough cash to buy a one-way ticket on a ship to Australia. The ticket price was listed in a Sunday newspaper at £310 'including all meals on board but excluding alcoholic beverages.' And I would have enough left over, £90, to start a new life.

A Greek ship, the RHMS *Ellines,* was scheduled to sail for Fremantle from Southampton on January 3, 1971. I first sold the Escort, then bought the ticket to Australia, then told my mother. Her reaction was not favorable.

"That's a long way," she said in her usual unflappable way tinged with concern. "That's the other side of the world," she added.

I understood. In those days, if people left Britain to places like Australia or New Zealand, they never came back. My mother was worried that she would never see me again. My father's response was a little different. He was sitting in his armchair reading his newspaper.

"Dad, I have sold my car and bought a one-way ticket to Australia. I am leaving in three weeks."

For a second he didn't move, he seemed not to have heard me. Then he looked up and stared at me for what seemed like quite a long time. He raised both eyebrows, just for a second, then went back to reading his paper. He never said a word.

I went and didn't return for four years, drifting around the world, failing to find a future. The first thing my father said to me upon my arrival back home was, "What are you doing back here?"

It was harsh, but with no brothers or sisters, my Dad's hopes were on me and me alone. I knew what he meant. He was disappointed that I hadn't made a go of it in Australia, and returned with no more than I had left with. It was now 1976, Britain was still in turmoil, the IRA was bombing London, decent jobs were still scarce. And to top it all, at twenty-two I was still not qualified to do anything after 'gallivanting around the world,' as my father so accurately put it. I began scanning the job vacancy pages, but day after day I could find nothing I was qualified to do or wanted to do. There seemed to be a choice between manual labor or utter boredom in a dead-end office where I knew I wouldn't last until the end of the first week. I could see no clear path ahead. I was getting frustrated.

"Any ideas yet?" asked my father.

"Still looking," I muttered and scurried off.

But then, a lifeline. There it was, at the bottom of an inside page of the *Daily Telegraph*:

> Variety, Action, Comradeship, Command — It's all here in Hong Kong. . .
> In a Colony where ninety-eight percent of the population is Chinese. . .
> Going anywhere special in the next three years?
> We'll ask you to be a Lawyer, Welfare Officer, Diplomat, Commander. . .
> We are an armed force, which adds an extra dimension to a police officer's responsibilities. . .
> If you are aged 19–30 and have some decent A-levels. . .'

The Royal Hong Kong Police were recruiting probationary inspectors on three-year contracts.

Hong Kong, the Far East, a disciplined service, adventure, a different culture, danger... My imagination ran wild. My father had been a member of the British task force that liberated Hong Kong from the Japanese in 1945. This, then, could be my chance to do something that really mattered, just as my father had done.

I applied that same day and, a couple of weeks later, was called for an interview at the Hong Kong government offices in London. As I knew very little about Hong Kong at that time, or indeed about police work, I decided to do some preparation prior to the interview. I went to our local library where I found (amazingly) the Hong Kong Government Yearbook for 1974. This hard-cover reference book was packed with information about the British Crown Colony, giving an overview of all aspects of government administration, the legal system, commerce, education and transport. I pored over every paragraph, fascinated by the photographs, maps and statistics. I read the whole thing, cover to cover, twice.

There was a chapter on public order. It recounted the politically-fueled 1967 riots, when pro-communist leftists turned a Hong Kong labor dispute into large-scale demonstrations in defiance of British colonial rule. Violent clashes escalated into terrorist attacks and bombings. With the mainland in turmoil, there were rumors that China was preparing to take control of the colony, and the Chinese government put pressure on the Chinese Hong Kong police officers, encouraging them to rebel against the British colonial administration, but the officers refused to turn. As a result of their handling of the riots, Queen Elizabeth granted a Royal Charter to the force, making it the Royal Hong Kong Police.

I decided that if I was successful with my application, I would volunteer to be assigned to the Marine Police, which would not only give me the chance to work in a disciplined service, but also to work at sea and learn all things maritime. With my father's naval background, I knew this would please him.

There were a few pages in the book on current issues facing the Marine Police. Illegal immigration from China was a primary cause for concern in Hong Kong at the time. They were arriving by the thousands and the Marine Police were tasked with intercepting them before they could infiltrate Hong Kong. This was sometimes a grisly job. Many illegal immigrants died trying to make the swim across the bays and inlets that separated Hong Kong from mainland China. I also scanned newspapers for anything about Hong Kong, and read about growing numbers of refugees from war-torn Vietnam arriving at the colony's sea borders. I made copious notes and memorized great chunks from the yearbook.

The interview in London was pretty straightforward. The interview panel comprised two senior RHKP officers and a chap from the Foreign and Commonwealth Office who fired questions at me for about thirty minutes. I regurgitated paragraph after paragraph from the yearbook. There were a few nods from the panel. Then one of them asked, "If you were required to do so, would you shoot someone?" I guess what the panel did not want to hear was, "Oh no, I could never do anything like that." Or worse, "Shoot someone? You bet I would! That's why I want to join! Just give me a gun!" I think my "If it was absolutely necessary, to save life?" was well received as there were more nods from the two police officers, but I caught the Foreign and Commonwealth chap giving me a suspicious look.

At the end of the interview, I was told that I would be informed in writing as to the result and was free to leave. My thoughts then turned to my girlfriend, Olivia – I had yet to tell her about my plan. Olivia and I had had an on-off relationship since we were at school together. I'd left her behind once already to go to

Australia. On that occasion I promised to write every week while I was away, not realizing it would be four years before I came back. Not surprisingly, our exchange of letters eventually dried up, and we lost touch. But after my return home, we got back together. Poor Olivia, she knew I was still frustrated about the lack of career opportunities in England, and she also knew that my thirst for adventure had by no means diminished. In the pit of my stomach I felt bad that I was now planning on leaving her for a second time.

Two weeks later, a letter from London arrived. I tore it open. Pending a medical examination, I was in. I had been accepted into the Royal Hong Kong Police as a probationary inspector for a three-year tour of duty. My starting salary was HK$2,400 (£275) per month and my flight to Hong Kong was booked for 3 September 1976.

When I told Olivia that I was off to Hong Kong, all she could do was shake her head in disbelief. Once more, I promised to write.

I tried to imagine how the next three years of my life would turn out. Asia, a disciplined service, public order, illegal immigration, crime, refugees. Things were certainly going to be different. I reread the letter from London. My successful application to join the Royal Hong Kong Police left me feeling that here was my chance to do something useful, something important. I was fired up and raring to go.

3

DOING BRICK HILL
跑磚山

THE HONG KONG POLICE is a paramilitary force where its officers are armed. While the thought of joining a disciplined service in an Asian environment was certainly intriguing, in all honesty, I didn't fully comprehend what I was getting myself into. The information I was given at the Hong Kong government offices in London amounted to a couple of pages of facts and figures that I'd already read in the Yearbook. Then there was the information I'd received in the post after I had been accepted. This was predominantly advice about traveling to Hong Kong, police pay scales, and a few lines about government accommodation. Other books I found in the local library didn't offer much more, just a few statistics and black and white photographs of busy streets and boats in the harbor.

But what exactly was I in for? I imagined working in difficult circumstances. I assumed physical challenges, and there probably would be danger. How was I going to fit into a Chinese environment? In terms of crime, I could not even imagine how I would be involved. I thought back to a Bruce Lee film I'd seen where the bad guys were the Chinese secret societies, the triads. Would I be dealing with them? In that film, some poor wretch was subjected to a 'death by a thousand cuts.' Death by a thousand cuts! Shit.

But I was determined to make the most of it. A three-year tour in the Royal Hong Kong Police was the opportunity I'd been looking for. No more drifting aimlessly around the world, taking jobs here and there, this was serious stuff that could, eventually, turn into a worthwhile career. It would also be a chance to test myself, and I liked that idea. I felt that in Hong Kong, I would have an opportunity to do something that mattered.

The Royal Hong Kong Police Training School (PTS) was not so much a school as a sprawling camp located on the south side of Hong Kong Island. Inside the grounds, there were a dozen or so buildings that housed the classrooms, accommodation blocks (all recruits live-in), several sports fields, a couple of gymnasiums, two live-firing ranges, an assault course, an officers' mess, and the place for which recruits had little affection — the drill square.

'Marching,' I read in my personal-issue drill manual, 'instills discipline into untrained civilians. It teaches them to obey orders without question,' and, 'it promotes smartness of dress and pride in appearance.' The manual came with grainy black-and-white photographs of police officers demonstrating how to march properly. Then came a more interesting statement. 'Drill can be utilized as a form of punishment. Marking time, or marching on the spot, in extreme cold or very hot conditions is a particularly good way to ensure a recruit does not repeat mistakes.' Our drill instructors had obviously read every word in this manual and were intent on delivering its directives to the letter.

For the next nine months, I would spend every day with my squad. We would eat, sleep, drink, study, run, climb, shoot, grovel, salute, and march our way to becoming senior police officers, or so we hoped. And all this under the watchful eye of the school's conspicuous Chief Drill and Musketry Instructor and his team.

Back in 1976, there were about two hundred recruit inspectors under training at any one time. In addition, there were also some eight hundred junior recruits training to become police constables. New squads, or intakes, arrived every two months to coincide with the graduation of those who had successfully completed their training and were ready to fight crime in the real world. The cultural mix of each inspectorate squad was always about 50-50, local to expat officers. For some, life at the training school, or indeed in Hong Kong, was not to their liking. Of the thirty expatriate recruit officers who arrived in my intake, five disappeared within the first week. Some underestimated what was expected of them in terms of the physical training and resigned. Others were upset by the discipline and resigned. Some found the heat and stifling humidity unbearable, and then there were those who simply disappeared. One day, they were marching on the drill square, next day they were nowhere to be seen. When I asked the course instructor what had happened to the recruit inspector who had up until that day stood next to me during the morning parade, he replied, "Mr Bird, I advise you to mind your own business and get on with it." I had visions of this poor chap being driven to the airport with his suitcase, his recently acquired PTS short back and sides, a huge amount of disappointment, and a one-way air ticket home.

I found that I actually enjoyed early life at the training school. Every day there was a new challenge. After all, this was why I had joined. When I found the going getting tough, I thought back to my mother's World War II advice of 'Keep calm and carry on,' or my instructor's frequently heard version of the same thing, 'Just stop complaining, Bird, and get on with it.'

This advice was all well and good, and designed, I suppose, to help everyone through their nine months at the training school. But there was one thing our instructors could not help us with

– female company. Or rather, the lack thereof. After the first few weeks at the school, a celibate lifestyle was becoming a bit of a problem for many of the young recruits, including me. I wrote every week to Olivia, and she replied, but that didn't really deal with my immediate needs. What compounded the matter was that shortly after arriving in Hong Kong, I had discovered that the city had more beautiful women than I'd ever seen before in my life. So, I, with others, decided to dedicate what little free time we had to meeting as many of these shy young women as we could. There was, however, a problem for young foreign probationary police inspectors. Mixed-race relationships were rare in the 1970s. They attracted attention. In public, people stared at a white man in the company of a Chinese girl. Some pointed, and some felt the need to make crude comments, which I soon learned to understand. This scared many young Chinese girls away from any fraternization with foreign men. But, of course, we persisted.

The window of opportunity for us recruits came on Saturdays after the weekly parade when we were free to leave camp to go into town and escape our regimental lifestyle. As we were not required to return until the following evening, this gave us a whole thirty-six hours. For most, this meant going in search of whatever female company we could find.

Our first attempts to meet girls in town involved going to our favorite pub or bar and drinking copious amounts of beer in the hope that a pretty girl would approach us and start a conversation. Unsurprisingly, this strategy did not meet with great success. Some did their homework and scoped out new entertainment establishments called discotheques that were springing up around Hong Kong at the time. Then, dressed in the ridiculous disco uniform of flared trousers and bright, colorful, large-collared shirts, unbuttoned down to the belt buckle, they would go along to try their chances.

This disco look on a shaven-headed probationary police inspectors just didn't look right. Nevertheless, each Sunday evening, recruits would gather in the Officers' Mess at the training school to welcome home the budding John Travoltas and to listen to their previous night's exploits in the hope of catching a lifeline, which never came.

But it really was the lack of hair that set us recruits apart from other 'normal' young men in Hong Kong. Men's fashion in the 1970s included long, flowing locks. Abba and Saturday Night Fever (a somewhat ironic title for us) were all the rage, whereas the standard training-school shaven head was not. This being the case many, faced with no choice, and in abject desperation, resorted to the obvious route, that of the red-light district of Wanchai. In the grubby, dimly-lit, bars of Lockhart Road, with names such as Club Pussy Cat, Crazy Horse and Club Venus, men could, for the price of a lady's drink (a small glass of scented water), secure the temporary attention of one of the bar girls. But only for the time it took the girl to finish her drink. After which the *mamasan* appeared out of nowhere demanding that if the conversation was to continue then more drinks were required.

The bars were generally humorless places. Bored girls listening to the same old stories, *mamasans* hovering. Catching a glimpse of oneself in the large mirror at the back of the bar, just as the girl delivered the well-worn line, 'I like you so much, can I have another drink?' was a stark check on reality. It was a finely balanced performance by all involved. But for some, this weekend visit to Wanchai, dubbed by recruits as the Forlorn Hope, proved the lifeline that made the next week's training just about bearable.

Of course, the fact that organized prostitution was illegal in Hong Kong wasn't lost on us probationary police inspectors. It was interesting, therefore, when the time came to study the laws pertaining to vice that, just by glancing around the classroom and noting the sly grins and nervous glances, it was easy to identify which among us were members of the Forlorn Hope.

We were required to march everywhere at PTS. Every ten yards we saluted or were saluted. Salutes at the training school were acknowledged as smartly as they were given, 'longest way up, shortest way down,' with the palm of the right hand displayed open, and the fingertips one inch above the right eye, almost touching the peak of the cap. The junior officer always salutes his superior first, and the senior officer must return the salute to acknowledge the respect accorded.

In addition to two daily sessions of drill, there was also one of physical fitness and one on the firing range. Most looked forward to the firing range as we got to fire live rounds, usually at a paper target, a silhouette of a stout-looking man. The drill was run, draw and shoot. During one of the first sessions, Probationary Inspector Dakers ran up to the mark, drew his revolver, pulled the trigger too soon, and shot the ground immediately in front of him. The bullet ricocheted off a stone, flew back and took a piece out of his course instructor's clipboard. The instructor, quite understandably, vehemently produced the longest stream of obscenities I'd ever heard. Although Dakers received extra training for months after that, and eventually became quite adept in the handling of firearms, the spaces next to him on the range were always unpopular.

All PT sessions at the school were led by the head of physical training, Chief Inspector Bob Crist. Crist was a short muscular Welshman aged about forty. He was highly skilled in all martial arts, with a specialty in unarmed combat. It was Crist's job to teach us the art of self-defense, but his methods were baffling. He would begin every gym session by asking for a volunteer.

"Okay," he would announce, once the volunteer, or victim, was lined up. "Come at me from behind, attack me and hit me as hard as you can," he would say, turning his back on the recruit. The volunteers would ultimately try punching, diving, rugby tackles, and even a casual saunter followed by a sudden leap, with all methods proving practically hopeless. The end result was always the same. The 'attack' recruit would inevitably be skillfully grabbed, turned upside down, and slammed with enormous force onto the mat. Why there was always a volunteer willing and stupid enough to take him on was beyond me. If Crist was in a particularly vicious mood that day, he would follow up the body slam with some swiftly applied arm and wrist-twisting that produced screams for mercy from the volunteer. Invariably, the volunteer-victim would then be classified as 'injured on duty' and be carted off for medical treatment.

Once Crist was done crippling recruits in the gym, those of us still standing would be marched double-time to the assault course where a team of physical training instructors, or PTIs, would put us through our paces. Crawling under barbed wire, climbing over wooden walls, carrying logs above our heads, swinging via ropes over ditches would all be accompanied by verbal abuse from the PTIs.

I wondered what made an officer want to become a PTI. I watched Crist work, but only when I was sure he wasn't watching me. As an officer, out in the streets, I felt he would fail. There would be no place for him in the world outside. There would be no place for him in a police division. Men would not follow Crist.

Once a week, we got a break from the assault course, and in its place we got to 'Do Brick Hill.' To the rear of the training school is the 750-foot-high peak Nam Long Shan, or Brick Hill. Doing Brick Hill was a timed run that all recruits were required to complete once a week. Everyone was expected to improve on their previous week's time, every week.

"On my word, you will set off through the school grounds and out of the East Gate," announced Crist, after he had lined us up near the drill square. Crist pointed with his clipboard towards the gate. "Then you will turn right and run up Brick Hill," he pointed again, this time towards the tree-covered mountain about half a mile away to the rear of the school grounds. "You will then run down the other side of the hill and enter the school via the West Gate, finishing here, on this very spot." There was yet more pointing.

"Right, got it? Any questions? Good. Go!"

It was always a scramble, as thirty recruits tried to push and shove their way free of the pack and sprint off. Fallers were ignored. It was every man for himself.

For those who eventually made it back, Crist was on hand, with his stopwatch, clipboard and a question or two for the exhausted finishers.

"Ah, congratulations, very well done," he said, on one occasion, to the recruit who had arrived just ahead of me, and who looked to be in a state of collapse.

The recruit's thoughts also must have been a little befuddled as he fell into Crist's trap. "Yes, sir, thank you, sir, it wasn't too bad this week," he replied.

"Oh, enjoy the run, did we?" smirked Crist, "Okay then, off you go. Do it again."

As the horrified recruit set off back up Brick Hill for the second time, this time with his own personal PTI in tow to let him know what an idiot he was, Crist added, "And if you don't beat your previous time, you will be going around once more."

In addition to all the drill, physical training and weapons training, there were several hours a day of classroom work. For the expats, the first two months were dedicated to learning the basics of the Cantonese language. If I thought sprinting to the top of Brick Hill was tough, I was in for a surprise on day-one in the language lab.

4

A REAL GWAILO
正牌鬼佬

LEARNING TO SPEAK Cantonese was one way in which we had a chance to bridge the invisible gap between locals and expats. Prior to traveling to Hong Kong, I'd read in one of the pamphlets I had been given at my interview that outside of the upper echelons of local government and business leaders, virtually no one in Hong Kong spoke any English, certainly no one I would be dealing with. Therefore it was imperative for all expat police officers to become fluent in the local language. The pamphlet went on to say that after passing out from PTS, not only would I be expected to converse with members of the public in Cantonese, I would also need to communicate with the officers under my command.

The first two months of training for the expats included eight hours a day, Monday to Friday, in the language lab. At first, I couldn't figure out how I was going to get to grips with the language sufficiently to even get by. How was I going to learn Cantonese properly, in just two months?

Our language instructors at the training school were civilians, and they had the patience of Job.

"Cantonese is a tonal language," announced Mr Wong, our teacher, on the first day. "Before we teach you any vocabulary or grammar, you must first learn these tones." There were puzzled looks around the classroom.

"There are ten tones in Cantonese," continued Mr Wong, with a smile. "But don't worry, we are only going to concentrate on the six basic ones."

"Ten? Six?" I thought. I glanced at the recruit to my left who raised his eyebrows and shrugged.

"Cantonese words have many different meanings, and if you use the wrong tone you'll only make a fool of yourself." Mr Wong proceeded to demonstrate all six tones. Unfortunately, to me, it all sounded the same. Then it got worse.

"The best way to learn these tones is to sing them."

Was this a set-up? An initiation for new recruits? It appeared not.

"Like this." Mr Wong burst into song. Then, satisfied he had clearly demonstrated how to sing in Cantonese, Mr Wong announced, "Now it's your turn."

Most of those in the language lab that first morning were young British or Australian men who had been soldiers or police officers in their home countries before coming to Hong Kong. The tonal singing exercise therefore quickly disintegrated into complete chaos. It sounded like feeding time at the zoo.

During that first week, all we did was sing the six tones, and by the end of it, we were all still completely tone deaf and very confused. But Mr Wong remained upbeat.

"The tones will come in time," he told us.

If we doubted him, we shouldn't have. He really knew his stuff and by the end of the course, most of us had a grasp of the basics of the language. We didn't, as yet, have sufficient skill to command a platoon of Cantonese police officers, but if we used our remaining seven months at PTS wisely, remembering that many of our new squad mates were local lads, then by the time we graduated, it certainly would be possible to attain a reasonable level of spoken Cantonese.

Once the formal language training was over, the expat and local officers came together as one to study the laws of Hong Kong. I found that my Chinese squad mates mostly came from two different backgrounds. There were those who had arrived at PTS straight from university and had no work experience whatsoever, then there were those who already had five or six years of service as junior police officers in Hong Kong and had recently been promoted to the inspectorate. Many of the latter were a little older than the rest of us, and most had been streetwise NCOs prior to promotion. Joe Poon was such an officer. Not only was he assigned to my squad, he also was billeted in the room next to mine in the accommodation block.

Joe had, until his promotion, been a beat patrol sergeant in the densely-populated and notoriously dangerous district of Mongkok. One of the course instructors told me that Mongkok had, for decades, been controlled by the triads and was awash with drugs, prostitution, illegal gambling dens and corruption. The instructor went on to say that some months before we began our training, a number of the senior and middle-ranking police officers from Mongkok had been called in for questioning by the newly-formed Independent Commission Against Corruption, with some subsequently arrested and charged with corruption-related offenses. Joe Poon, on the other hand, was promoted.

Joe was a twenty-seven-year-old stocky man. He had studied kung fu since childhood and possessed surprisingly quick reflexes. One Saturday after the weekly formal parade, he and I decided to go for a few drinks in Wanchai. It also happened to be when the U.S. fleet was in town. Some of the senior recruits warned us about the Pacific Fleet — their ships visited Hong Kong every few months and their servicemen were allowed ashore for a few days of R&R. The Americans were mostly a good bunch and well-behaved when in Hong Kong, but as their ships were 'dry,' the young sailors tended to make up for lost time when ashore and things sometimes got out of hand. The group of U.S. Navy guys who came into the same bar as Joe and I that evening had certainly been making up for several weeks at sea without a drink. They were all in good spirits and very noisy. They took up a position next to where I was sitting at the bar and it wasn't long before the horseplay began. There was a bit of friendly pushing and shoving between them until one toppled backwards and knocked over my beer. The beer glass rolled off the bar and smashed on the floor. Customers and staff stopped what they were doing and stared at the scene. The music stopped.

I stood up, primarily to avoid being covered in beer, but it seemed that some of the navy boys thought I was making something of their friend's clumsy actions.

"You got a problem, buddy?" asked one of the larger Americans. Before I could speak, or even think for that matter, Joe stepped forward and stood between me and the group. He was by far the smallest man in the bar, about a foot shorter and fifty pounds lighter than the towering American. But this was not the same man who moments before had been talking to me about his family in China. His whole demeanor had changed. His face was hard, eyes piercing. He rocked slowly on the balls of his feet. His hands relaxed at his side. For a moment there was only silence.

Joe's move took the sailors by surprise. The larger of the Americans swayed a little. He'd obviously had a lot to drink and was now a little uncertain as to his options.

"Hey, sorry fella," said one of the others from the rear, jerking his drunken buddy back. "Here, let us get you a round. Barman," he called, "get my two friends here some beers."

The incident was over. Joe had said nothing. He simply moved back to his seat and we continued our evening. Throughout our training, it was obvious to me that Joe Poon was streetwise — clearly not a man to mess with.

It was during those first few months at the training school that I discovered that prior to joining the police it was rare for any of the Chinese officers to have had any dealings with foreigners. And, of course, for us the expat officers, our time at the training school was our first exposure to anything Chinese. This made for a tentative start for everyone.

"You are the first *gwailo* I have ever had a real conversation with," said Joe as he sat in my room one evening.

"*Gwailo*. Joe, isn't that a derogatory term?"

Joe nodded. "Well, yes, it can be. It means 'ghost man' or 'foreign devil.'"

Slightly annoyed at the connotation, I asked, "And that's me, is it?"

"I said, 'can be'. We locals often refer to non-Chinese by their ethnicity and, you are right, historically the term *gwailo* was considered racist. But most now use it to refer to Westerners in a non-derogatory way. You will find that many of our British course instructors use it themselves. These days it's used in joking more than anything."

Since arriving at PTS, I'd found that local officers, while friendly towards myself and the other expats, were very reserved in their manner and wouldn't open up on anything remotely controversial. Yet Joe seemed quite the opposite. "So I am the first *gwailo* you have had a conversation with? What about your previous police service? Surely you have spoken with foreigners before?"

"In Mongkok, there were a couple of British officers but they were very senior, a chief inspector and a superintendent. They never spoke to the juniors. Have you seen this?" Joe held up a book titled *The History of Hong Kong*.

"I don't think so. Why?"

He opened the book and flicked through a couple of pages. "It has some interesting things about nineteenth-century Hong Kong. It calls it 'no more than a rough-and-tumble port where opium dens and grog shops shared doorways with reputable commercial businesses.'"

"Sounds a bit like Wanchai today."

"Yeah, I know, but listen, it talks about the beginnings of the police force and the racial segregation." He glanced up. "It explains how the Hong Kong Police Force was 'made up largely of suspect individuals – European constables and sergeants, who were mostly seconded army privates and navy sailors, and whose grasp on law enforcement was limited, to say the least.'"

"I guess they almost press-ganged the soldiers?"

"Well, they couldn't have done a good job of it, as at one point more soldiers — veterans from the Bombay Native Infantry — were shipped in to strengthen police numbers. But, here's the bit that I found interesting, in those early days, policemen were assigned a letter before their police identification number. The letter told you to which ethnic group they belonged." Joe looked up, to make sure I was listening. He was coming to the part he wanted me to take in. "'A' was for Europeans, 'B' for Indians, 'C' for local Chinese who spoke Cantonese, 'D' for Chinese recruited from Shandong Province, and 'E' was assigned to White Russians, who arrived from Siberia after the Russian Civil War. What do you think of that?"

"You mean the letters identifying their race?"

"Exactly."

"It was probably just a way of keeping track of everyone. As you said, it was a rough-and-tumble place. I'll bet police records were not up to much."

"Yes, but the letter, telling you the officer's race, it was accepted." He looked at the book again. "I still think there's something like that today. Do you know that it wasn't until after World War II that locals were recruited directly at officer level? Before that, only expats could join as officers."

I actually hadn't realized until now that racial inequality was still an issue. Did my local squad mates still hold us expats responsible for what went on a century before? Joe sensed my curiosity.

"Don't worry, Les, it's not all bad. I just want you to be aware of the background, the history. You know, when my father came to Hong Kong from China in 1948, the civil war was spreading south, towards Canton. The communists were winning and it was obvious that they would eventually rule China. My father didn't like that. He preferred the British version." Joe smiled. "So my parents escaped across the border into Hong Kong. They swam across Mirs Bay and arrived here as illegal immigrants. My father knew they were coming to a place run by the British, and that all the manual work here was done by mostly Chinese. But they just accepted it: they accepted how things were between the British and the Chinese. They enjoyed the security of Hong Kong."

"Okay, that's the past." I sat up. "What about the present? What about you, Joe Poon? How do you feel about Hong Kong being run by a British administration? Here at the training school, how do you feel about most of the instructors being British, the portrait of the Queen hanging in pride of place in the Officers' Mess, how we all stand and toast Queen Elizabeth at Mess nights? And that the police force is now recruiting so many expats?"

Joe stood up and looked out of the window. "Everybody here

at PTS has sworn allegiance to the British Crown." Joe pointed to the insignia on his shirt. "We wear the Royal RHKP title on our uniforms. It would be hypocritical to hold any sort of resentment towards the administration. But. . ." He paused in thought. "But honestly, in the police there's sometimes a feeling of unfairness and, in some cases, mistrust. You expats have a backup plan should things not work out in Hong Kong. You have a passport out. You can always go somewhere else. Of course, that's okay for you, we don't mind that. But what really pisses me off is the way some expats act as though they are on holiday here and don't pull their weight, abusing their position. You can tell that some in our squad are using their time in the Hong Kong Police as a stepping stone to other things. That's what gets to us. We work hard to get this far. If you *gwailos* are here for the long haul, then fine. But if you are here on a holiday then we have no time for you. If you want respect from the people who call Hong Kong home, then you need to earn it."

"So we are guilty until proven innocent?"

"If you want to put it that way, then yes."

I could see Joe's point. The local officers saw Hong Kong as their home, a home that their parents had risked all to help to build, and by joining the public service, they were continuing that work. If any of the expat officers were freeloading in some way, the locals had the right to be annoyed. In some ways, it made me feel like an outsider. Maybe some of the locals looked at all expats in this way?

"Do you know about the 1997 issue?" asked Joe. I shook my head.

"Well, here's some history for you, then." Joe sat down on my only other chair and launched into a lecture "Back in the 1800s, after the local Chinese viceroy up in Canton seized much of the opium from foreign traders, the British sent their Royal Navy ships to 'rectify the imbalance,' as they put it. The British had been trading the opium they had purchased in India for Chinese tea, porcelain, and silks that were in demand in Europe. The Chinese Emperor wanted to stop the importation of the opium as it was becoming increasingly popular throughout southern China. So when the British ships arrived off Canton, they were met by a Chinese fleet, there to defend the opium-seizing actions. The British defeated the Chinese in what we call The First Opium War."

I'd read about the Opium Wars and their eventual impact on Hong Kong, but I also knew it was important to Joe; he needed to tell me all this in order to make his point.

"It was at the end of this war, and in order to secure a ceasefire agreement, that the Chinese ceded Hong Kong Island to the British, so that they could continue their opium business." Joe smiled and held up the book. "There's some more," he said. "About twenty years later, in 1860 I think, there was more trouble, which saw the start of the Second Opium War, which the British also won. The prize this time was the Kowloon peninsula, which was also ceded to Britain." Joe stood up, placed his hands on his hips and stared out of the window again. "Some years later, in 1898, the British decided that the colony of Hong Kong needed larger rural areas, I guess in order to become more self-sufficient. So they managed to negotiate a land lease of ninety-nine years over the area to the north of Kowloon that became known as the New Territories and the Outlying Islands. But, now here's the interesting part. When this extra land was granted, the British agreed to return it to China after ninety-nine years, that's in 1997."

"Ah, yes," I said, "I do know about the lease, but that's the first time I have heard it referred to as 'the 1997 issue'. But why is it an issue? Why would China take back the New Territories in 1997? What good would it do them? China is a vast country, what's a small piece of land like the New Territories and a few islands to them?"

Joe sat back down again and folded his arms, "On its own, nothing. But look at it another way. What's Hong Kong going to do without the New Territories and the Outlying Islands?"

"What, you think China would intentionally disrupt Hong Kong, by insisting on taking back the NT? Why? What's the point?"

"Face maybe?"

"Face?"

"Look, losing bits of your country to foreigners, and losing it by force, is a loss of face. The Chinese in Beijing think in centuries rather than decades. To them the seizure of Hong Kong in the 1800s is recent news. The Chinese are a patient lot, you know."

"They think nothing of waiting a hundred years?"

Joe nodded. "In 1997, I'll be forty-eight, and you are younger than me. It'll be an interesting time in our careers. If we are still here, of course."

"Don't know about that, Joe. Personally, I'll be happy to get through next Friday's stage exams."

One of the first things that struck me about the local officers was how diligent they were in their studies. Every day, upon the conclusion of our lectures, the locals would head off back to their rooms to study law late into the night. This contrasted with most of the expats who, after an hour or so of revision, preferred to wander down to the Officers' Mess for a few drinks. It seemed as though the local boys were studying twice as hard as we were. One of the reasons was later explained to me by Joe. One day in class I happened to glance over at the law books spread open on his desk. The pages were covered with what at first looked like the footprints of a very small chicken. They were in fact hand-written Chinese characters, scribbled in pencil all over the pages.

"Why are you writing all over your textbooks, Joe?" I asked, pointing at his scrawl.

He looked up at me, "What, this?" he replied, looking surprised that I'd asked. "Just like all the other guys, I need to translate the legal terms and the formal English phrases into Chinese so that I can properly understand and remember them. That's why I have this." He held up an English-to-Chinese dictionary. "It's the only way I can remember things." He smiled and went back to his studies.

If I thought studying law was tough, I now realized how arduous it was for the local officers. We were taught law in English, their second language. Afterwards, they translated the day's lessons into Chinese and restudied it so that they were confident they had got things right. Once they had done that, they then translated the whole thing back into English in preparation for the next round of exams, which were, of course, in English.

Basically, for the next six months, the local officers had twice the workload that we had.

It was at this time that I wrote my first letter home to Mum and Dad. I told them about Joe Poon and that we had become friends. I didn't even try to explain the underlying racial divide that Joe and I had discussed, or the '1997 issue' as Joe had called it. Dad would have understood, but Mother would have worried. I told them about the heat and the humidity and how some (not me) had found it too much to handle. Being British, it was compulsory to cover the subject of the weather in all letters home but, for my mother's benefit, I made a point of adding, that I was well and that I was looking after myself. I told them about life at the training school, about the discipline and regimentation. I knew this bit would please my father. I could just hear him thinking to himself, *it's about time he had some common sense knocked into him.*

5

HIGH JINKS
惡作劇

THE LONG, HOT DAYS of marching, physical fitness and weapons training continued, while in a classroom ventilated only by slow-turning ceiling fans and the occasional breath of wind through open windows, we studied the laws of Hong Kong.

In the evenings, the officers would eat dinner together, then we were free to have a drink in the bar afterwards. But with the local officers setting an example, and as the law exams twice a month required high marks to pass, many spent their free time studying. Of course, during nine months of this routine, with two hundred young men living in close proximity to each other, there was bound to be the occasional distraction.

It was rumored that one recruit, Christopher Hammond, kept a live snake in his room. Hammond was a strange character who didn't mix well. He was one of those people you meet from time to time who has an air of entitlement and never seems interested in what others have to say. He was young, and at nineteen, was one of the youngest at PTS. Possibly this is why the staff tolerated him. But it was well known that certain instructors, particularly Chief Inspector Peter Crotty, didn't care for Hammond at all.

Some believed this snake story had been started by Hammond himself, in the hope of enhancing his own notoriety amongst us recruits. This certainly was in keeping with Hammond's character. But the question still remained, did he actually keep a snake in his room? Pets of any kind were forbidden and, if it were true, he would certainly be up before the commandant and possibly face dismissal from the force. So, with a story like this going around it wasn't long before word reached the ears of the senior teaching staff (CI Crotty), who decided to investigate.

It was a Saturday afternoon and we had just finished the morning parade. I was sitting on my bed unbuckling my anklets when I heard the loud clack-clack of metal-studded boots coming down the tiled corridor. It sounded like two or three officers marching in step, so I got up and went to the door, curious to find out what was going on. The marching belonged to a stern-faced Peter Crotty and two equally hard-nosed-looking drill instructors. They went past my open door at pace. The sight of senior teaching staff in the accommodation blocks on the weekend was rare. I had the distinct feeling that something was wrong.

As I peeked out to see what was going on, the three-man posse came to a halt outside Hammond's room, and paused while one of the drill instructors checked some papers on a clipboard. Crotty then rapped on Hammond's door with his swagger stick.

"Mr Hammond, open the door. Room inspection."

Crotty's voice echoed along the corridor. More heads appeared. Peter Crotty was a powerfully-built man. The peak of his uniform cap was pulled down low over his eyes. As he faced Hammond's door, the muscles in his neck were tense. He had a look of determination. He was ready for action. I figured this must be about Hammond's snake. If Hammond was indeed keeping a snake in his room, he would be crucified for sure.

Hammond's door opened. "Yes, sir, can I help you?" I could just hear him say.

"Room inspection," bellowed Crotty once more. He sounded seriously pissed off. Some recruits ducked back into their rooms, not wanting to be part of this. I watched as Crotty pushed past a surprised Hammond.

Once they were inside, I quickly kicked off my boots and tiptoed down the corridor. I was keen to see whatever drama was about to unfold. A few others did the same. We congregated outside so that we could hear what was going on while keeping out of Crotty's line of sight.

Hammond's room, like all the others, was a 12' by 10' shoebox. Walls painted throughout in cream, with a brown-tiled floor. The standard single bed ran along one side, with a desk and bookcase on the other. Open law books were scattered across Hammond's desk. A large window at the rear of the room overlooked one of the school gardens. The rays of the afternoon sun shone in from between a row of leafy trees.

"Are you keeping any livestock in your room, Inspector Hammond?" demanded Crotty, looking around. Hammond was standing rigidly to attention, "Livestock, sir? No, sir."

Crotty scanned the room. He had one hand tucked into the small of his back as he prodded at things with his swagger stick, jabbing at the bed, then the pillows. "You won't mind if we take a look around then, will you?"

"Er, no, sir," stammered an apprehensive-looking Hammond.

Crotty gave a nod to the two instructors who began rummaging through a chest of drawers. One of them dropped to the floor and looked under the bed. He scrambled back to his feet. "Nothing."

Crotty studied Hammond closely, then he pointed at the built-in wardrobe. "Open those doors."

Outside, the group of eavesdroppers was growing. "Have they found a snake?"

One of the instructors opened the wardrobe and took a step back. He shook his head, "Only clothes, uniforms and civvies." But now Crotty was looking up at a smaller cupboard above the wardrobe.

"What's up there?"

"Nothing, sir," Hammond fired back.

"Nothing?" said Crotty, sensing Hammond's urgency. "Really? You won't mind if we take a look then?"

Hammond shuffled around a bit. Now he was not looking his usual cocky self.

Crotty dropped his swagger stick on the bed and dragged Hammond's study chair across the room. He climbed up and grabbed the two cupboard door handles.

"I wouldn't open that if I were you, sir," warned Hammond.

Crotty turned and looked down. "Oh, so there is something in here is there? Let's see, shall we?"

Through the large window to the rear of Hammond's room sunlight fell directly onto the cupboard as Crotty threw open the doors. For a second, nothing happened. Outside, we were frozen in suspense. Inside, everyone stared up at the cupboard. Then, the large eagle owl that had been sleeping inside went berserk.

An adult eagle owl has a wingspan of about six feet and weighs as much as ten pounds. The one in Hammond's cupboard was of the larger variety. With the cupboard now flooded with sunlight, the eagle owl's world had changed instantly from one of deep, peaceful sleep to that of blinding sunlight, noise, and the startled face of Chief Inspector Peter Crotty.

The owl's fiery orange eyes focused on Crotty, it puffed out its brown-black barrel-chest and let out a deafening screech.

"Fucking hell!" screamed Crotty in return, but his words were lost in a crescendo of screeches and a flurry of feathers. Crotty toppled backwards off the chair, and as he fell his uniform cap was sent spinning by a powerfully-wielded owl wing.

"Jesus Christ," blurted the chief inspector as he landed, unceremoniously, in a heap on the floor.

With Crotty's head no longer blocking its way, the eagle owl — probably in abject panic — launched itself out of the cupboard. The room was instantly filled with flapping wings, flying feathers and manic screeches, mostly from the owl. Like most wild creatures that find themselves cornered, the eagle owl will fight for survival. Crotty, still on his hands and knees, began to crawl towards Hammond's bed. He later claimed that he was trying to locate his cap and not, as a number of eyewitnesses reported, trying to crawl under Hammond's mattress. The owl, now believing it was in a fight to the death, took the last available course open to it — it went on the attack. The owl pounced, claws first, on Crotty's back and began pecking, furiously, at the top of his head.

"Fer fuck's sake, get that fucker!" cried Crotty, curling into a ball. He took a couple of defensive swipes at the owl, but that just incensed the bird even more. It became obvious to us bystanders that trying to fend off an eagle owl fighting for its life, is not easy.

The two drill instructors backed against the wall, well out of the way. And then, in an attempt to regain some dignity, and possibly deciding this sort of thing was way above their pay grade, edged sideways out of the room to join the ever-growing group of onlookers in the corridor.

Hammond, however, being more familiar with the antics of a berserk owl, and probably wishing to limit the amount of trouble he was already in, made a grab for the bird. But the owl was having none of it, and it flew directly upwards, avoiding Hammond's lunge.

Outside, I and the others remained rooted to the spot, staring in disbelief at the whole performance.

"Will one of you useless bastards shoot that fucking owl?" screamed Crotty, as he once more tried to get to his feet.

"Chief Inspector Crotty has positively identified Hammond's snake as a fucking owl," remarked some joker from the rear of the ever-growing corridor audience.

Crotty was still scrambling around, and the two DMIs were AWOL, so the eagle owl decided it was a good time to make a break for it. With two or three flaps of its incredibly powerful wings, it took off and flew directly into Hammond's closed window. There was an almighty thud as the big bird bounced off the glass. This produced more screeches, more feathers, and more mayhem.

The whole incident was getting ridiculous and something had to be done. Joe Poon ran into Hammond's room, and for some unknown reason, I followed. I had absolutely no idea what to do about a berserk eagle owl, certainly one that was making repeated attempts to fly through a closed window. But Joe did. He subdued the bird from behind with his arms, pinning the wings close to its body.

"Throw that towel over its head," he said calmly, while holding the bird still.

I quickly did as he said, grabbing one of Hammond's towels from a rail and slinging it over the owl. Suddenly, with daylight removed from its world, the owl stopped struggling.

"Jesus H. Christ," growled Crotty, freeing himself from under Hammond's bed, and slowly getting to his feet. "I'm going to have his balls on a plate for this," he muttered.

I assumed Crotty was referring to Hammond's balls rather than the eagle owl's, but thought it best not to ask. I picked up Crotty's cap and swagger stick and held them out for him. He snatched them from me. "Bastards," he muttered.

Joe Poon was now up on the chair and putting the terrified

owl back inside the cupboard. "Best place for it until we can find a cage and a home for it," he said.

A disheveled Crotty turned and looked down at Hammond.

"You are in big trouble," he said, waving his swagger stick in Hammond's face. "My office, 0800, Monday."

And with that, Crotty put on his cap and marched out, straightening his uniform and brushing off owl feathers as he went.

"I wonder what happened to the two instructors?" said Joe. "They are going to be in trouble, too, for doing a runner."

Poor Hammond sat down on the bed, his head buried in his hands.

"Do you have a snake as well?" asked one of the onlookers from the corridor.

Hammond stood up. "Fuck off," he said, and slammed his door.

We later learnt that Christopher Hammond was charged with breaking a number of training school rules, not least of which was keeping an eagle owl in his cupboard. In the following days, after facing a disciplinary hearing, he received a written warning for dismissal, which put him on probation for the remainder of his training. The general opinion amongst us recruits was that Hammond was lucky to have escaped summary dismissal. But he never kept a snake or any other living creature in his room again. The two drill instructors who had 'taken their leave' during the heat of battle were spotted the following Monday morning, in full dress uniform, standing nervously outside Crotty's office. Their fate was kept confidential from us, but a severe bollocking was the general consensus as to their just desserts. As for Chief Inspector Crotty, he never quite recovered from being attacked by Hammond's eagle owl. Whenever Crotty saw any one of us around the school grounds, he would immediately become angry and give us some unsavory task or other. These unreasonable orders became known as Crotty's Revenge.

Mischievous recruits weren't the only ones responsible for the high jinks at the training school; on occasions the staff were too, even the commandant himself.

During formal Mess dinners, held once every two months to celebrate the senior squad's graduation and passing-out, recruits were required to be on their very best behavior. That is, until the conclusion of port and cigars when, from the top table, the school commandant would announce a game of Mess rugby football as a conclusion to the evening. Upon this order being given, all furniture would be dragged to the side of the dining room, leaving the bar and sitting areas clear as the playing field. Teams would be selected, with half those present sent to one end of the dining room, and the other half sent to the other. Everyone was expected to take part, both staff and recruits alike, with the commandant himself acting as referee. A ball was then produced. The ball was, on occasions, a real leather rugby ball. On other occasions, a wicker waste basket made do. The rules of the game were never explained to anyone. In fact, I don't think there were any, as once the commandant blew the whistle both teams rushed at each other with gusto, the ball ignored. Some of the collisions were enormous. Some saw the match as a chance to settle old scores, even if the person requiring a smack was on the same team. Some of the course instructors, silly or drunk enough to get involved, often ended the evening with a few more cuts and bruises than they had started with, while spilt blood, ripped Mess jackets and torn shirts were the norm.

During my first fixture I was lucky to avoid a tackle involving five large recruits who managed to collide into each other all at the same time. Collectively they became one out-of-control drunken wrecking ball that careered across the room directly into a display cabinet containing the Mess silverware. In a crescendo of splintered wood, smashed glass and inebriated officers, the whole thing collapsed. The game continued regardless, with the flattened silver dragged to one side, the five semi-conscious drunks ignored and the debris kicked into a corner.

I never saw anyone score a point, and as far as I am aware no one cared, and no one ever won. At the conclusion, those still able to stand adjourned to the bar for liquid refreshments, while others were helped to one side to rest and tend to their injuries. The broken furniture was left where it had fallen for the cleaners to deal with. At the bar table napkins were issued as tourniquets, and in one case the curtains were pulled down to cover a recruit who the commandant had pronounced dead. This dead recruit was later miraculously brought back to life by one of his team mates who poured a pint of reviving beer over his head.

Some pushed high jinks to an even more dangerous level. RI Swift was quite a controversial and outspoken young man. He had a habit of opening his mouth before he'd thought through what he was going to say. Some didn't take to Swift from the word go and decided he needed to be taught a lesson.

One day, when Swift was in class, someone entered his room in the accommodation block and laced every pair of his underpants with Tiger Balm ointment. Tiger Balm is a popular camphor and menthol-based liniment that brings heat to sore muscles. When in contact with certain sensitive areas, Tiger Balm can cause a really annoying burning and itchy sensation. When applied in large quantities to certain areas of the male anatomy, it causes mind-numbing discomfort.

Next morning on parade, those in-the-know waited as the squad stood at attention in the heat. As the temperature rose and the humidity gradually increased, thoughts were, generally, of Swift's baking nether regions. It must have taken enormous restraint and self-control to remain motionless on the square as Swift did that day. Throughout the parade he sweated from head to foot and his face turned a deep shade of purple. He looked as though he was about to explode. But he didn't move. Later, as we marched off the square, those unaware of what was going on could have been forgiven for thinking that Swift's testicles had expanded to the size of footballs. He marched as though his genitals were on fire. As the squad reached the steps leading up to our quarters, Swift finally broke into a sprint and, more than likely, went directly into the showers.

The Tiger Balm group then retired to the Officers' Mess to congratulate themselves on a job well done. Unbeknownst to them, Swift, convinced the unbearable sensation was the result of an incurable sexually transmitted disease contracted during the previous weekend's Forlorn Hope excursion, decided to take the man's way out. He hobbled down to the armory to withdraw a revolver and end it all right there and then. Fortunately, the duty armorer, seeing the state Swift was in, refused the request and reported him to the staff. After questioning by his course instructor, and with no such thing as psychological counseling in those days, Swift was simply told to 'grow up, take a cold shower and stop being such a fool.' He was also banned from carrying a firearm for two months. This whole episode was chalked up as a victory by the Tiger Balm group who also agreed that in the future they needed to tread very carefully when pulling stunts on Recruit Inspector Swift.

After nine months under training at PTS, despite the various diversions, I sat and passed my final law, drill, and firearms exams. Nine months living and training at the Police Training School had been quite an experience. It had fluctuated between a regimental life of uniforms, discipline, drill, and examinations, and games of Mess rugby and a string of practical jokes. I was certainly a different person at the completion of the training to the one who had arrived. While I was happy and relieved to have graduated, I was still, in a small way, sad to be leaving. But I was now a probationary inspector of police in the Royal Hong Kong Police Force and about to be assigned to the Marine District. Of course, there would be much more training ahead, mostly of a maritime nature, and I was relishing starting work in earnest. True, I was right at the bottom of the officer cadre, but life was exciting and enjoyable. And just over the horizon change was coming. Change in the form of one man: Don Bishop, also known as Diamond Don.

6

DIAMOND DON BISHOP
钻石

DON BISHOP. People weren't just afraid of him, they were terrified; and not just a few people either, everyone. As Chief Inspector and Sector Commander of East Sector of the Marine Police, Bishop was in charge of ten vessels and four hundred officers and crew. He was a bull of a man and a legend in his own right.

Don Bishop wasn't tall, no more than five-ten; but he was almost as wide as he was high, practically a cube. It wasn't just his gorilla-like frame and his barrel chest that set him apart from the average man. There was also his impressive head. Large and hairless, it sat on top of his huge, stocky body like a polished bowling ball. Everything about him was thick and disproportionate, right down to his tree-trunk calves and formidable feet.

The Chinese had their own name for Don: *Gwong Tao Daan*, The Baldheaded Egg. For brevity, junior officers simply called him, *Ah Daan*, The Egg.

His reputation preceded him. He was respected for how he had handled difficult and dangerous situations during his long career in the Hong Kong Marine Police. But there was also a dark side to Donald Bishop — his fierce, volatile, temper. He didn't suffer fools lightly and if someone screwed up, or if things just didn't go his way, he was prone to outbursts that bordered on violence. Some officers dreaded the mere sight of him, to the extent that if they saw him coming their way, they would instinctively turn and head in the opposite direction.

It was well past midnight and Marine Police Inspector Dougie Kerr was on his sixth, maybe seventh, beer. The next morning would be my first with the Marine Police. I really should have been getting an early night, but instead I was in the Bull and Bear getting the lowdown on Don from my soon-to-be colleague ,while he got more and more wasted.

"Diamond Don Bishop was born two hundred years too late," Dougie said, his Glaswegian drawl becoming more pronounced with each swig of San Miguel.

"I can just see him on the forecastle of a four-masted galleon, off Port o' Spain, cutlass in one hand, rum in t'other, barkin' orders at the crew. He's a law unto himself. He could get away wi' murder if he wanted because the senior officers at headquarters are all terrified o' the man."

I could see Dougie was in the mood for more beers and rambling, so I made my excuses and tried to head out.

"Rubbish, Bird, I've ordered more pish. Have one fer the road then you can get yer beauty sleep."

He signaled to the barman who placed two cold beers on the bar. He picked one up and studied the label.

"Rumor has it that you'll be posted to Police Launch 1 in East Sector, so you are going to experience life wi' Don and his tempestuous seas firsthand. And you mark my words, laddie, life will never be the same again."

I couldn't figure out how Dougie knew my posting before I'd officially been told. I reckoned he was trying to wind me up. "Come on Dougie, how many beers have you had? Anyway, what's the big deal about East Sector?"

Dougie drew a deep breath, straightened himself up and looked me up and down. "East Sector!" he began. "For a start, young Leslie, East has the roughest waters in Hong Kong. The whole of the south-east corner of the colony is exposed tae huge rollers comin' in from the South China Sea and the Pacific Ocean." Dougie waved a hand above his head. "Most of the duties out east are search and rescue, for ships in distress, particularly during typhoon season. It can get seriously rough out there. That's why Don Bishop has been the commander there for so many years." Dougie took another mouthful of beer.

"You wouldn't be exaggerating by any chance would you, Dougie? Just for my benefit? Don Bishop could well have his own reasons for working in East, reasons you are not aware of?"

Dougie pointed the neck of his bottle at me. "You mark my words Leslie-boy, Bishop is there because it suits his character. He's the only senior officer in the force who thrives in that kind of environment, that kind of shite weather, day-in and day-out. For all his faults, he really is the most capable seaman in Marine. Do you know, back in 1971, he was awarded a commendation for saving the lives of sixteen crewmen from a sinking ship during Typhoon Rose?"

"Really. . .?"

"It was before my time." Dougie placed his beer on the bar and made himself comfortable. "But the crew on PL 1 told me the story. Rose was the biggest typhoon to hit Hong Kong since the great storm of 1937 when over eleven thousand people lost their lives. In 1971, as Typhoon Rose was approaching Hong Kong, Don was out on patrol in East Sector on PL 1. He was doin' a final sweep along the coast, looking for vessels in distress. It was then that PL 1 received a Mayday radio call from a freighter that had been thrown against the rocks off Tung Lung Chau. The ship was sinking."

"Tung Lung Chau, the big island outside Tathong Channel?"

Dougie nodded and took a swig of beer. Some of it dribbled down his chin.

"Apparently..." Dougie looked around the empty bar and lowered his voice, "...apparently, after considerin' the situation for no more than a few seconds, Don gave the order to turn PL 1 around and go back out to sea to effect a rescue. It was a tough call t'make as in those severe conditions he was about to put PL 1 and the lives of her crew in great danger."

I could almost see the raging ocean in Dougie's wide, staring, eyes.

"But search and rescue is a part of the job."

"Aye, it is, young Leslie. But remember, as the commander he's also responsible for the lives of his own men. By turning PL 1 around he was puttin' over twenty of his own officers into a highly dangerous and precarious situation."

"So what happened?"

"He rescued the entire crew, just before the ship sank." Dougie picked up his beer. "I kid you not, it was a major achievement just to hold PL 1 steady enough in those seas to get everyone safely off that freighter."

"And he got a gallantry award?"

"Aye. I looked it up in Headquarter Orders. 'For courage, leadership and professional ability of an exceptionally high order during the rescue of sixteen crewmen from a stricken vessel.'" Dougie looked down at his empty glass, then turned. "Hey, barman, two more," he said, waving his glass.

"Dougie, I need to push off, I need to be up bright and early."

"Oh, no, no, no," Dougie held up a hand. "You ain't heard the half of it yet. You just sit yerself back down." He pointed at me again with the neck of his bottle. "You are going to thank me in the morning for this."

As Dougie took a long swig of his beer, I shook my head and sat down, hoping this wasn't all a waste of time. As I watched him drink, something he had mentioned earlier came to mind. "You said Bishop was a law unto himself... that he could get away with murder. What's that about?"

"You have no bloody idea," said Dougie, spraying spittle across the bar. "There is another side to Diamond Don Bishop. Trust me on this one. He's a volatile fucker is that one, and the strongest man I've ever met. You don't really know when he's going to turn, what he's going to do next, or when he will lose his temper. He operates on fear."

Dougie belched and thumped his chest a couple of times.

"Fear?" I asked.

Dougie practically exploded. "Aye, bloody fear!" More spittle erupted from his mouth, flying further this time. I took a step back, out of spittle-range.

"You never know when he's going to switch from professional leader of men to marauding psychopath."

I looked at Dougie as he swayed around and wondered how much of this was the booze talking?

"You mentioned earlier something about Bishop being violent?" I said.

Dougie settled back in his seat and regained his composure, out of breath after delivering his last discourse.

"Well, I've never seen him clobber anyone," he said scratching his head. "Although he has threatened me on more than one occasion. But, a couple of years ago, Freddie Kwok told me that Don just lost it with Mr Chan, the cook." Dougie smiled at the thought, then began to chuckle.

"And?" I asked.

"Ah, yes. You see Freddie was working on PL 1 before me, and Mr Chan is Don's cook. This Mr Chan has been a fixture on the command launch fer yonks, and he's about a hundred years old. Anyway, one day Mr Chan screws up in the galley and he serves Don something he hates; not sure why, maybe it's on purpose. So, Don, on seeing his grub, picks up his plate and goes into PL 1's galley t'give Mr Chan a dressing down."

Dougie started laughing again, then took another swig.

"So, an argument starts, during which Don loses his temper, picks up a meat cleaver and takes a swipe at the old cook." Dougie chuckled on seeing the look on my face. He held up his hand. "It's okay, the old Chinaman was quick on his feet, and he knows all about Don's temper too, so he was ready for him. Mr Chan takes off at about fifty knots through the hatchway and out onto the open deck, and Don lunges after him, calling him all sorts of names as he goes. So the chase is on, see. Picture it."

Dougie could hardly get his words out. "There's this little old Chinaman, dressed in his chef's whites and cook's hat, screaming obscenities in Cantonese, followed by this crazy gorilla of a *gwailo*, who just happens to be the sector commander, in uniform, waving a meat axe above his head. And they are running around the upper deck of the East Sector Marine Police command launch while it's on patrol."

Dougie was now laughing so much he started to slip off his stool.

"What about this Freddie, and the crew? Didn't they try and stop him?"

"That's just the point," said Dougie, hauling himself upright. "Everyone is afraid of Don. He is indestructible. Honestly, it's amazin' how no one has never drawn a gun and shot the bastard."

"So. . . what happened?"

"Oh, nothin'."

"Nothing?"

"Nothin' ever happens. Don eventually ran out of puff and gave up the chase. Mr Chan disappeared down some hatch or other, so Don threw the meat cleaver overboard. Later that night, Mr Chan cooked Don's dinner, as usual, and nothin' more was said about the matter. It's always like that. Don loses it, there's mayhem, then it's forgotten and everyone carries on. Waiting for the next outburst, of course."

"You're pulling my leg, aren't you?"

Dougie drew a deep breath, and regained his composure. "Freddie and quite a few of the crew have told me the same tale."

I sat down on the bar stool next to Dougie. "Bloody hell, it sounds awful."

I began to worry now. Even factoring in fifty percent for booze-fueled exaggeration, there must be something to Bishop's reputation. What was I getting into? For nine months at the training school I'd had discipline and professionalism morning, noon, and night, and now there's this Long John Silver character rumored to be my new commanding officer.

"Also," mumbled Dougie after a few seconds, "to compound matters, those pencil-pushing wasters at Marine HQ are scared of Don. To catch him out, they would need to get off their fat backsides and get on a boat and go out there to see for themselves what he gets up to."

Dougie leant back against the bar, rubbed his forehead and gathered his thoughts, which were obviously a bit cloudy. He struggled to his feet again. There was more.

"It's a classic case of *saan go, wong daai yuen*, that's what it is. *Saan go, wong daai yuen*, Les. Do you ken what that means?"

"No idea."

"It means 'tall mountains, king far away.' It means that with Don on the other side of the colony, the senior officers at MHQ here in town haven't a clue what Don's up to out there. He can operate without fear of being caught for whatever he wants to get up to."

"So what does he get up to? Are you talking corruption?"

"Jesus no!" Dougie almost lost his balance, grabbing the bar in to stay upright. "Not Bishop. He's a rogue and a bully all right, a hell-raiser for sure, and as mad as a March hare, but he'd strangle the life out of any man in his sector he found on the take." He took a deep breath. "Don operates under his own set of rules. He's not bent, just unorthodox. Oh, and damn frightening, don't forget frightening. You just be very careful what he asks you to get into."

"What's with this Diamond nickname anyway? I've ask a few people about it, but couldn't get a straight answer. Is there something I should know if I'm going to work for him, as you seem to think?"

Dougie went silent once more, taking a long drink of his beer.

"Dougie?" I asked again.

"Oh aye, the diamond," he said. "I was there that day. You see, a few years ago, Don got into the habit of taking PL 1 into the Western Quarantine Anchorage, at the entrance to Victoria Harbor. It's where incoming freighters wait for clearance from the Immigration and Customs Departments before being allowed into the port to offload their cargo. Some are kept waiting there for two or three days. Don was always trying to get invites from captains to go aboard their ships, bullying his way in so he could drink their whisky, or whatever hooch they kept in their ward rooms. One night, we found a Panamanian-registered freighter at anchor off Stonecutters Island. The crew were mostly Filipino, but the captain was a Honduran national. He invited Don on board for a game of poker. Personally, I thought Don would be taken to the cleaners by an organized group of card sharks, and I told him so. But he just told me to shut up and mind my own business. Don fancies himself as a good poker player. So, he went on board the freighter with a pocket full of cash. He also went alone and unarmed."

Dougie took another slug from his beer. He was getting quite animated once more, enjoying his own story. "About two hours later Don came back onto PL 1. He was furious. His face was an off-shade of purple and the veins in his head were bulging. He barged through the Mess without a word and went down below to his cabin, then a minute later he was back up with his wallet. I asked him what was going on but all he said was, 'I'll teach that fucking Spaniard,' then he was gone."

"At about midnight, we were still alongside the freighter and it was obvious we were not going anywhere fast. I went up to the bridge and checked on our launch deployment. Everything was in order, not much happening, so I went down below to my cabin for a kip. With the launch stationary, I slept like a log. The following morning, I was woken by PL 1's engines turning over and the movement of the launch, so I quickly got up, not knowing what to expect. I found Don alone in the Mess, drinking coffee."

Kerr stopped again, lost in thought for a moment, then, "When I walked into the Mess, Don put a paper bag on the table and pushed it towards me. 'What's this?' I asked. 'Take a look,' replied Don sipping from his mug. Inside the bag was money, lots of it — US dollars, Hong Kong dollars, Filipino pesos and some other South American currencies, thousands. 'Told you I would take the bastards,' he said. 'Cleaned 'em out, the whole lot.' He sat back and grinned at the look on my face. Then he fumbled around in his pocket and pulled out a bloody great diamond and pushed it across the table towards me. 'The Spaniard staked this on his last hand... one less tooth for that bugger,' said Don. I picked up the stone and held it up to the light. I don't know anything about precious stones but it was beautiful, the mornin' sunlight refracted through the stone when I held it up. Aye, it was amazing."

"Once off duty, he took it to a pawn shop in the back streets of Western District. They gave him, wait for it—" Dougie held up his hand "—HK$68,000 for the stone. Which was, in those days, about a year's salary." He sat back and smiled at the what-the-hell expression on my face.

"My God," I said.

"My God, indeed. Once the story got out," he continued, "people began referring to Don as Diamond Don. But then the powers-that-be got to hear something about it and Don was called into Marine HQ to explain. Of course he denied the whole thing in fear of a charge being laid against him for one of a dozen things, gambling on duty being just one. But by that time nothin' could be proven as the ship had already off-loaded its cargo and left Hong Kong. Don just stonewalled them, so that was the end of the matter. These days, it is considered taboo to talk about it. Oh, by the way, he hates the name Diamond Don, so whatever you do, don't call him that to his face. He claims the whole incident never happened. Anyway, that's the sort of thing I am talking about when I say unorthodox. So watch yourself with Diamond Don Bishop."

Dougie took another long drink of his beer.

"Anyway, you will be able to ask him about his past yourself soon."

"Dougie, what makes you so certain I will be posted to PL 1?"

"Ah, that's an easy one," he said, leaning forward. I could smell the beer on his breath. "Don needs two inspectors on the command launch. One Chinese officer to relay his orders to the crew, to act as his local adviser and be his interpreter, his comprador, plus..." Dougie prodded me in the chest "...a second-in-command, an expat officer, a bagman, a native English speaker, to listen to all his rantings and ravings, do all the jobs he doesn't like doing himself and go on the pish wi' him when he feels like it. That, Inspector Leslie Bird of the Royal Hong Kong Marine Police, as of tomorrow, will be you. I did my bit for six months. Now I am in charge of Police Launch 53, which, I admit, is still on Don's patch, still under his command. But at least I am out of direct contact with him. Now it's your turn, Leslie boy, and guess what?"

"What, there's more?"

"No, that's all about Don for now. I am going for a slash, so watch my beer and don't let that old fart of a barman take it."

7

THE MARINER, THE HANGMAN, AND THE PRIEST
海員、劊子手、傳教士

THE FOLLOWING MORNING I arrived at Marine Police Headquarters. My uniform was immaculate, but underneath I was sweating profusely, alcohol seeping from my skin. I cursed Dougie Kerr and his two-for-the-road, and I cursed myself for listening to him and not leaving when I was ready. *I'll never do that again,* I thought, knowing immediately that that wouldn't be the case. At the top of the ramp, at the entrance to the headquarters compound, I could see Joe Poon waiting for me. Just why Joe and I were the only two officers accepted into Marine from our PTS squad was a mystery to the both of us. There were several former Royal Naval officers in our intake, all of whom were pretty confident they would get a Marine posting. But only Joe and I had made it. It was baffling. I had no military experience whatsoever, while Joe's six years as a junior police officer had been spent in Mongkok District. He had no maritime experience either. "Maybe they want people with no experience, so they can train us the way they want, rather than taking RN officers who think they know it all?" speculated Joe after we had been told of our postings by our course instructor.

I reached the top of the ramp and looked at the impressive

headquarters building. Located on a hill overlooking Victoria Harbor, Marine Police Headquarters was one of the first structures built by the colonial British administration on the Kowloon peninsula a century before. This palatial pile first opened for business in 1884 and had since then, apart from a brief visit by the Japanese during their occupation of Hong Kong in the 1940s, been the home of Hong Kong's Water Police.

"You ready?" asked Joe.

"Ready as ever," I replied. We straightened our uniforms and went in.

Most of that first day in Marine was spent in the company of the barrack sergeant in the Marine stores office in the quadrangle. The barrack sergeant controlled everything that moved in and out of Marine. He recorded the existence, position, condition, movement, and even the destruction of every item of equipment in a set of enormous desk ledgers.

By late afternoon, Joe and I had accumulated kit bags full of gear, some of which was maritime paraphernalia I had never seen before and had been offered no word of explanation as to why I had been given it. I caught Joe looking puzzled, too, as he packed his bag.

The barrack sergeant signed-off Joe's gear first. "Okay sir, you have drawn stores, you can leave."

Joe set off to look for the deployment officer, to find out where he would be working. "See you later," he said disappearing out the door, dragging his sack of kit after him. Half an hour later, after receiving the same all-clear from the barrack sergeant, I tied up my bag and lumbered off through headquarters carrying my stash. As I went, the only sound was that of the metal studs on the soles of my uniform boots as they click-clacked on the corridor floors. I felt incredibly new. I knew that everything about me reeked of 'junior inspector on his first day.' What was it that the

Chinese called first-tour inspectors? *Bomban jais*, little inspectors. Even my uniform, only days old, was a slightly different shade to everyone else's. I stuck out like a sore thumb. I quickened my step.

I eventually found the office I was looking for. On the whitewashed stone walls, a dark blue hand-painted sign read: Chief Staff Inspector Marine. C.M. Harrison CIP. I straightened up, tugged at my tunic, checked my cap was on straight and knocked on the open door.

"Ah, you must be Bird," said Harrison, looking up from his desk. "Come in, come in, please have a seat."

Harrison had more than thirty years of police experience in Asia. He first signed up with the Colonial Police Service at the end of World War II, joining the Federation of Malaya Police as a sergeant. He helped deal with the Malayan Emergency, then later saw action in the Brunei Revolt. After Malaya, he arrived in Hong Kong, sometime in the mid-1960s.

"Well, you have drawn stores, collected your kit then?" he asked, nodding at my bag.

"Yes, sir, all done, thank you."

"Good. I have just seen your friend, what's his name?" Harrison looked at his file. "Poon," he said, looking up. "Now, let's see, your Marine posting." Harrison studied the file on his desk once more.

"It says here you will be going to East Sector, working on board Police Launch 1."

He looked up for a reaction, but I just nodded in agreement. Lowering his voice, Harrison leant forward and added, "You realize that's Don Bishop's sector, don't you?"

"Yes, sir."

Harrison studied me for a second. "Good, that's settled then." He actually looked relieved. "You are to report at East Sector

Base at 0800 Monday."

Harrison pushed a couple of sheets of paper across his desk. I noticed the dark sun freckles on the back of his scrawny hands. He had skinny, skeletal fingers.

"Sign both copies of this order, would you? It's your posting directive. Return one to me, for the file, and keep the other. It's your orders. Now," he said, suddenly sounding quite chirpy, "what do you say we pop along to the Mess?" He smiled for the first time. "It's five o'clock, after all."

As I followed Harrison out of his office and down the corridor, I wondered if I should have objected to being posted to Don Bishop's sector. Could I have objected? On what grounds? What if Bishop later heard that I'd objected? What would have been his reaction? It was too late now. I stuffed the order memo into my tunic pocket and followed Harrison.

The Marine Police Officers' Mess, the Mariners Rest, occupied the southeast quarter of the first floor of MHQ. Its French windows and balconies gave the Mess sweeping views over Victoria Harbor. High ceilings, a long polished wood bar, louvered shutters, ceiling fans, and a fireplace for those cold winter evenings made the Mariners a favorite watering hole for officers.

Most evenings, the Mess was busy with a mishmash of off-duty Marine Police, senior officers from land divisions, government officials from the Public Works Department, and a smattering of civilians. Some journalists would also stop by for a beer and a chat in the hope of picking up a story.

The Mariners on this particular evening was bursting at the seams, or as the Cantonese would say, *bau paang*, exploding bamboo, chockablock with a firecracker atmosphere. Harrison and I edged our way through the crowd to the bar where Joe was standing alone, beer in hand.

"What you get?" asked Joe quickly.

"East Sector. You?"

"North," replied Joe.

"This is Tony Choi," interrupted Harrison, nodding towards the barman.

The barman, a thickset little man with stern features and a surly expression, opened a leather-bound book on the bar and waved a pen in front of my face, signaling for me to use it.

"This is Inspector Bird," Harrison continued. "He has been posted to East Sector. And that's Inspector Poon, who you have met already. Now, let them sign for their first case of beers."

Choi grunted in response. "We send you bill on launch. At end of month. You come here, Mariners, you pay me, okay." It wasn't a question.

Beer in hand, Joe and I followed Harrison through a crowd of officers to where a huge brass bell hung over the bar. Harrison gave the bell a resounding clang. Everyone stopped what they were doing and turned. A sea of faces.

"Gentlemen, thank you for your attention, this will only take a minute. I would like to introduce Inspectors Joe Poon and Leslie Bird, who have today transferred to Marine from the training school. Inspectors Poon and Bird have just opened their Mess accounts and signed for twenty-four large ones, so please help yourselves. And also please welcome them to Marine, and to the Mariners Rest. Thank you, gentlemen."

There were a few cheers from the back of the room and several people came over and shook our hands.

A group of young inspectors gathered around and started the getting-to-know-you chat. After a second beer, I was beginning to relax, even enjoy myself. Harrison had already made his excuses and moved off, leaving us junior officers in a cluster under the brass bell.

"Junior officer present," came a growl from behind. The words rippled across the back of my neck. The other officers fell silent. I turned to face the voice.

"Donald Bishop."

He reached out his bloated mitt and we shook. At first, Bishop offered no more than a firm grip, which I matched, but then a smile formed on his face, followed by the gradual tightening of the grip. Not one to shrink from a challenge, I equaled the tension, but it was too late, my hand was turning a shade of violet and the pain caused my voice to turn into that embarrassing high-pitch that every man has experienced from a direct hit to the balls.

"You are posted to East Sector, I hear?" he said, still holding fast.

"Yes, er, yes, I am, sir."

"Good, grab your beer, and come and join me over here," he said as he released my crippled hand, turned and pushed his way towards a group seated at a table near open bay windows. I looked down at my mangled hand, shook it a couple of times, picked up my beer, and followed my new boss to where three men sat in armchairs around a coffee table littered with empty bottles.

"This here is Father Dominic," Bishop said, pointing to an elderly man who smiled and gave a nod.

"He's French, but he can't help that. The father likes a drop of the hard stuff, and he's partial to altar wine, too, provided he doesn't have to pay for it. Tight as a gnome's foreskin."

Bishop introduced the men as though he was delivering an operational briefing.

"And this gentleman to my left..." Bishop pointed to a small man with grey hair sunk deep into his armchair "...last killed a man in 1966." Bishop looked at me for a reaction.

"Don't worry, young Leslie, there's no need to put the cuffs on him. He was only doing his job. Ex-Prisons Department. He was Hong Kong's last hangman, prior to the suspension of the death penalty. Did quite a bit of neck-stretching back in those days, didn't you, Lucas? This is Lucas Remington, by the way. Doesn't look like he could strangle a cat now."

The former hangman strained a tired smile.

"And seated there is my old chum George Perkins, Marine Department. We don't usually lower our standards in the Mariners and allow Marine Department lowlifes in here, but we make an exception for George, although he can be a bit of a pain in the backside at times. But he once saved my bacon, so I suppose he can stay."

Perkins faked a smile and nodded. I didn't know it at the time but I was experiencing my first, and certainly not my last, Don Bishop drinking session — a booze-up in which Don typically surrounds himself with oddball characters who he can dominate. He turned to me. "And this young chap has just joined Marine." He flicked a thumb in my direction. "His name is Leslie Bird, that's Inspector Bird to you lot. He is coming out East, aren't you, lad? He'll be with me on PL 1 for a spot of crime fighting and adventures on the high seas."

Bishop dropped down into an armchair and motioned for me to do the same.

"So, your first day in Marine, young Leslie," he said, picking up his beer. "What have you been up to?"

"I spent most of the day drawing stores, then I went to see Mr Harrison to be told that my posting was East Sector." I was still rubbing my sore hand.

"Ah, Harrison." Bishop smiled, topping up his glass from a large bottle of Tsing Tao beer. "Didn't make any inappropriate suggestions, I hope? He got chucked out of the Malayan police many years back. Became too attached to his house boy, if you get my drift." He winked and took a long pull of his beer. "I'd watch that old bugger if I were you, pardon my French." Bishop laughed at his own joke then nudged the old French priest, who almost fell off his chair. Bishop ignored him. "Do you know what this is, Leslie?" asked Bishop, as he placed a silver badge on the table in amongst the bottles.

"It's a police cap badge, isn't it?"

"Indeed it is, but it's more," he said, pushing the badge across the table towards me. "It's also the official crest of the Royal Hong Kong Police. There's a bit of history here if you look closely."

I'd studied the police crest before. It was an interesting badge and every policeman seemed to have his own story as to its origins. In the center was a very small carving of what appeared to be three men standing on a beach. The men were so tiny they were only just distinguishable. Behind them were what looked to be two sailing ships, one of British design, and the other a Chinese junk. The peaks of Hong Kong Island completed the backdrop.

I looked up, suspecting Bishop was about to enlighten me on the history of the badge.

"That was once the governor of Hong Kong's official seal," he said pointing at the silver crest. "Referred to as the Flag Badge of the Crown Colony. The scene depicts the birth of Hong Kong under British colonial rule. It signifies how and why Hong Kong became a British colony, initially a trading port in the mid-nineteenth century. But there's something else, something far more interesting in this little scene. If you look very closely, you will see that one of the figures is wearing Western clothes, a tailcoat and a top hat, and the other two are dressed in traditional Chinese dress, with one wearing a conical hat. And, now here's the bit that most people fail to see, can you see what's on the beach next to the men?"

"Looks like some square objects, boxes?"

"Correct, boxes they are. But it's what's in the boxes that is really interesting. Any ideas?"

"Tea?"

"Good guess, but wrong. Would you believe opium?"

"Opium?" Joe Poon's story of the Opium Wars sprang to mind.

"Yes, opium, or *foreign mud* as the Chinese referred to it. Hong Kong was founded on a tea-for-opium trade between the Chinese and the British. This carving in the center of our official police crest depicts the British shipping opium into China. All this trade, as we liked to call it, led to the First Opium War. We wanted their tea in exchange for the opium we had picked up in India."

This was Joe's Opium War story and, according to Don Bishop, it was all here on the police cap badge. I examined the badge more closely, but Bishop hadn't finished.

"The Chinese emperor in the south didn't want this opium spread through his province. The whole thing was concluded in 1841, when Britain sent a gunboat up the Pearl River and blew the Chinese fleet to matchwood. A year later, the Chinese were forced to sign the Treaty of Nanking," Don said, as he pointed out of the French windows towards Victoria Harbor. "So all you see before you became a British Crown possession. In other words, China ceded Hong Kong to Britain as part of the deal. So, the birth of Hong Kong is right there on our cap badge. What do you think of that?"

"I had no idea," I said, intrigued by Bishop's cap-badge connection to a piece of colonial history. I recalled how Joe had linked all this history to the future, to the expiry of the ninety-nine-year lease on the New Territories. "What's your feeling about 1997 and the expiry of the lease on the NT, sir?" I asked.

Bishop stared back, a blank expression. "1997, what are you talking about?"

"The ninety-nine-year lease on the New Territories. It's got just over twenty years left. What happens after it expires?"

Bishop's eyes narrowed and he fixed me with a stare. I felt the sweat form in my palms. Had I asked the wrong thing? Interrupted his lecture with a question he didn't like?

"Ah, that," he exclaimed, sitting back and smiling. "Why, nothing of course. Nothing will happen. The NT is of no use to China. Hong Kong, as it is now under British rule, is far too useful to the Chinese." Bishop pointed out of the window once more. "I expect the British government will just tear the lease up. Hong Kong Island and the Kowloon peninsula are ours for good anyway, so there's no point in fannying around with some old lease."

Bishop sat back in his armchair and took another swig of beer. I figured this wasn't the time to push my new boss on something he had declared a non-issue, but I couldn't help thinking a discussion on this between Don Bishop and Joe Poon would prove very interesting.

"You married, Leslie?" Bishop asked, changing the topic. He eyeballed me over the top of his glass. George Perkins leant forward. I noted his deep-set eyes fixed upon me, he seemed overly interested in the question. "I'm still single actually, sir."

My answer was met with silent stares. "But I have a girlfriend back in the UK," I quickly added. Perkins sat back in his seat and sighed.

"Can I ask a question about next week's duties?" I added, trying to interest my new commander in the subject of present-day matters.

"What do you want to know?" Bishop snapped.

"I will be working on Police Launch 1. Is that a three-day

patrol?"

"Yes, it is. You will be working three days on, three days off, that's how the duty system works on the East Sector command launch. You, me and the crew. About twenty-five of us altogether make up the A Crew on PL 1. We are at sea, on patrol, for three days. Under my command, I also have another five major patrol launches, plus some other smaller ones. All up, we have about four hundred men in East Sector. Your job will be to help me run the show. I warn you, after three days working on PL 1, all you will want to do on your first day off is sleep. Mark my words, boy, it gets rough out there."

With that statement he drained his glass, rammed it down on the table, and stood up.

"Right, I'm off. Good evening to you all."

He gave a cursory nod to the group, turned and stomped off in the direction of the door, shoving officers out the way as he went. I turned back to face the other three, who were all silently staring at me, expressionless. I looked at these three old men. The mariner, the hangman, and the priest. I felt like the prisoner who had just finished his last supper.

8

OTTO THE AUTO
老闆的車

THE FOLLOWING MONDAY MORNING, I arrived at the Marine East Sector Base in Aberdeen Harbor on the south side of Hong Kong Island. As I placed my gear in the inspector's office, my thoughts were mostly on what my first day with Don Bishop would have in store. After that first meeting with Don and his three strange friends, I really didn't know what to make of my new commanding officer. Since seeing him storm out of the Officers' Mess, I had received a number of other warnings about his unpredictable temper from Marine officers. I was told that I needed to watch myself, and 'watch your back.' When I asked for clarification, all I got in return were either crafty winks or a need-to-know tap on the side of the nose. I wasn't sure if these were genuine warnings or if they were winding me up. I hoped my first day would shed more light on the matter.

I found Bishop down on the jetty barking orders to everyone in sight. Police Launch 1 was alongside and the crew were busy washing her down. Others were carrying supplies and personal gear onto the launch, while a major refueling operation was going on at the stern.

"Good morning, sir," I said snapping off a salute.

"Ah, Bird, good," replied Don flicking the peak of his cap

with one finger. "Follow me, we have a lot to cover." He marched off down the steps.

We spent most of that first day inspecting PL 1, which served as the operational command of the sector. I was introduced to the crew and had my responsibilities explained. That was all fine and Don was actually quite pleasant. We would be starting our first three-day patrol together the next morning and Don gave me a thorough briefing on what to expect and what specialist kit I would need to bring along.

"Write this down," he ordered, pointing at the left breast pocket of my tunic in which I kept my notebook.

"A set of waterproof overalls," he fired off before I could find my pen, "a heavy-duty duffel coat, a pair of rubber-soled deck boots, a pair of wool gloves — military, one webbing belt — black, one holster, a lanyard..." The list went on, ending with, "and don't forget your Marine beret." He gave me one of his infamous stares, then added, "or you will look like a complete arse." With that, he marched off pointing at things while I tried to keep up and complete my list.

This was the first time I had seen Don in his own environment. He certainly had a good rapport with the men under his command but were these men seem happy in their work because they genuinely liked their commanding officer, or because they feared him? Maybe a bit of both.

Around six o'clock that evening, Don and I were bumping along a busy street in his car on the way to Tsuen Wan Police Station in the New Territories. We were finally off-duty and heading back for a drink at his quarters, which were situated above a police station. As he put it, we were going to 'celebrate our new partnership with a little drink.' I recalled one of the warnings I'd received in the Mariners Rest: 'If you want to avoid trouble from Bishop, never refuse an invitation for a drink. He doesn't like that.' I had a suspicion that Don's 'little drink' was going to be anything but.

Don's car was a battered old Mercedes Benz saloon, the one with big bulbous headlights and a heavy-set steering wheel. It had seen better days, but he seemed very fond of his faithful chariot.

"This is a 1965 W108," said Don with an air of authority. "The car's name is Otto by the way. That's Otto the Auto to give it its full handle."

He chuckled to himself. I looked around the interior of the car feigning admiration for what was obviously Don's pride and joy. Otto's front seat was a leather-bound sofa-style affair that didn't inhibit Don's hefty frame. I slid over towards my side a little more to give Don the room he needed now that he had turned on the cassette recorder and had begun thumping the steering wheel and waving his hands around in time with the German or Russian concerto that was blasting out. He began to hum cheerfully as he drove.

"One of Otto's faults is the braking system," Don suddenly announced during a lull in the music.

"Braking system?" I asked, glancing at the speedometer which was reading fifty miles per hour.

"Yes," he said ramming his huge foot down on the brake pedal, which did nothing to slow the car down. "Sometimes it doesn't work, see?"

For a second I thought he was joking.

"I sometimes need to give it a good kick, like this." He rammed his foot down on the pedal two or three more times before Otto began to slow down a bit.

"Why don't you get it fixed?" I asked, looking ahead to see if we were going to hit anything.

"Bah, no need. Why waste the money? It works, just needs a

firm hand. Or boot, bah!" He slammed his foot down a couple more times and Otto's speed reduced to the legal thirty miles per hour. I closed my eyes, put my head back. This would all be over soon.

"This girlfriend of yours, Leslie," Don broke the silence and I was dragged from my half-conscious state.

"What, sorry, girlfriend?" I asked coming too and rubbing my eyes.

Don was looking directly at me, his eyebrows knotted in curiosity. "Yes, girlfriend. The one you mentioned in the Mariners. Are you going to bring her out to Hong Kong or are you planning to find a new one here? Three years is a long time."

"Oh, well, yes, she is still in England. I mentioned it in the Mess the other night, didn't I? Well. In Hong Kong? I don't know. I haven't met anyone yet."

Don stared straight ahead. He didn't seem happy. I thought I'd better elaborate.

"While at the training school I didn't get much of an opportunity, all that studying for exams. And, of course, being confined to camp during the week didn't help, and living in a communal block, and the rules about bringing in guests."

I glanced across at Don again, wondering if any of my answers had been acceptable. He seemed deep in thought.

"You must meet the Lady Angelique," he announced suddenly. Don was now grinning to himself as he drove.

"Lady Angelique?" I asked.

"Yes, she is my — how shall I put it — my little friend, bah." Don chuckled to himself once more. So Don had a lady friend! This news took me aback a little. I knew he didn't have a wife, but for some reason I'd never imagined him having a girlfriend. I envisaged him married to his work, or a bottle of single malt, or both. I was surprised to hear about a little friend.

"She works at the Rose and Crown, the English pub in Nathan Road," he continued.

"Rose and Crown?"

"Yes, the bloody Rose and Crown!" he exclaimed, turning and giving me a look as though I'd just queried the existence of the Queen of England. "In Nathan Road," he repeated. "They serve the best rare roast beef in the colony."

He looked away, back at the road and smiled to himself once more. I pictured his thoughts, the Lady Angelique serving rare roast beef in the Rose and Crown. Heaven.

"You must come with me next time we are off duty. I'll introduce you to her."

With that, he inserted another cassette into Otto's player and a rousing concerto filled the car once more. Don began tapping the steering wheel again and humming along to the music. But just as I relaxed back on my side of Otto, Don turned towards me, this time with a scowl plastered across his face. "But you keep your hands off her, understand?"

I tried to imagine this woman, Don's woman. I shuddered. I felt for sure she would be of no interest to me. I snuck a look at Don. There was a reflection of his massive bald head in the car's side window. Two Don Bishops. Don's thick, muscular neck was tense as he moved his jaw, refocusing on his driving. His giant powerful hands looked as though they could snap the steering wheel from its housing with one twist of the wrists. What on earth did the Lady Angelique see in Diamond Don Bishop?

In the 1970s, some single expatriate police inspectors, such as Don, were housed in residential quarters above police stations around the colony. Of course, in Don's case, he didn't actually work at Tsuen Wan police station, but because Marine Police bases didn't have inspectorate quarters of their own, he chose to live there. The upper floor of the Tsuen Wan police station housed half a dozen or so officers' quarters, and an officers' mess, where the inspectors had their meals and a drink in the evenings. Police messes became popular hangouts for single officers posted around the district. The beer was cheap, the food was generally good and officers could sign for food or drinks and then settle up at the end of the month. The mess was also private, where shop could be discussed without fear of eavesdropping.

As we drove through Tsuen Wan, Don suddenly veered towards the pavement, rammed his foot down a few times on the brake pedal, knocked over a dustbin and finally brought Otto to a complete stop by jamming the car's nearside front wheel into the curb. We shuddered to a halt.

"Jump out and buy me a box of cigars will you, Leslie old boy," Don said, handing me a hundred-dollar note. "That shop is the only place in Hong Kong that stocks the ones I like." He pointed out of the car window. "Just tell the old git in there they are for Chief Inspector Bishop and he will give you what I want."

I stared at the money Don was waving in front of my face.

"Go on lad, hurry up, if we stay here any longer I'll get a parking ticket from one of the local coppers." Don made a shooing motion in front of my face with his hand so I clambered out of the car.

"I'll see you in the Officers' Mess. The station is just a bit further down the road. You'll find it," shouted Don, and with that he crunched Otto's gears and took off, almost knocking a man off a bicycle as he went.

Along the brightly-lit main street of Tsuen Wan, every neon sign was in Chinese. There was not a word in English. The shop that Don had pointed out was a typical Hong Kong shop, open-fronted, brightly lit, and crammed with goods. It didn't seem to specialize in anything in particular. Then it occurred to me. How was I going to ask in Chinese for a box of cigars for Chief

Inspector Bishop? I was sure that no one in this remote village would understand much English. What the hell was Chinese for cigars? How did I refer to Don in Chinese? Should I call him by his nickname? *Gwong Tau Daan*, The Bald Egg? Would the shopkeeper know what I was talking about?

I walked into the shop clutching the hundred-dollar note. An old Chinese man, dressed in a grubby white vest was sitting behind a glass-topped counter. He looked up from his newspaper and we stared at each other for a second before he turned, selected a box from the shelf and placed it on the countertop. A box of cigars. Damn, Don had done this before. The shopkeeper knew why a young *gwailo* was standing in his shop looking lost. Dougie Kerr's words echoed around in my head, 'You'll be his bag-man.' I wondered how many other junior inspectors before me had been sent on personal errands by Don Bishop. I was getting the feeling that Don was a throwback to old colonial times, where the commander literally owned his subordinates both professionally and personally. I paid for the cigars, tucked the box under my arm and made for the police station at the far end of the street. The words, 'You'll be his bag-man,' continued to rattle through my head as I went.

The Officers' Mess was packed that evening. Everyone was in good spirits. I found Don holding forth with some older-looking officers. I handed him his cigars and shifted around the bar to where I'd spotted a couple of inspectors I knew. After a few beers, I was in a jovial mood and recalling Dougie's stories about Don with more skepticism. Maybe he wasn't that bad. A bit rough around the edges and a bully for sure, but this was a British colonial Hong Kong police force. I expected old-fashioned ways, and I also expected to come across the occasional eccentric. It made life more interesting. Unpredictable, but interesting. I figured I could handle my new predicament.

We were in the Mess for hours. A large group of CID officers had gathered after they had cracked a big case. I got talking to one of them, and he was keen to tell me all about Diamond Don Bishop.

"If you take a look out of the rear windows at the station car park you will see that the compound is quite small, hardly enough space for all the police vehicles," said the CID man. "And Bishop is the only copper allowed to park his private car inside, even though he doesn't work here."

"Why is that?" I asked

"He commandeered a space by scaring the hell out of the report room staff every time he came back to the station. Don's intimidation eventually led to him being assigned a permanent space for his beloved old Merc, just to stop him from bothering everyone."

I went over to the windows and took a look. It was pretty dark down in the car park and I couldn't make out one vehicle from another, but the compound was full of cars with some blocking others in.

By midnight the place was still buzzing, and I noticed that Don had been on the hard stuff in a big way. He had gone bright red in the face and he was becoming quite animated. But he seemed in good spirits, laughing and joking with the CID officers. With a tumbler of scotch in his hand, I watched him sway over to the balcony to get some air. The party at the bar continued for a minute or so until the whole group was interrupted by a manic scream.

"Some fucker's parked in my spot," shouted Don, who was now pointing down at the car park. Everyone in the Mess remained motionless, frozen by the ferocity of Don's outburst.

Don lurched back towards the bar, cursing under his breath. The assembled crowd parted to let him though. Those too slow to move were pushed out of the way. He then disappeared behind the bar into the pantry, only to come charging back out, this time carrying a crate of large empty beer bottles. Don pushed his way back through the crowd and hauled the crate over towards the balcony doors. Arming himself with a handful of empties he hurled one with as much force as he could muster at the offending vehicle.

"Asshole! I'll teach that bastard to park in my spot!" he yelled, shaking a fist at the offending car. There was stunned silence throughout the room followed by a loud crash of broken glass from down in the yard. Someone suggested going over and taking Don to one side, as he had actually committed a criminal offense, but no one dared. I looked on in disbelief. There was no way I was going to try and stop him. He looked completely out of control, shouting obscenities down at the carpark. Then he stopped, breathing heavily. He grabbed hold of the balcony rail, steadying himself, dropping his remaining arsenal of bottles on the floor next to his feet. He shook his head, huffed, turned and staggered back to the bar where he poured himself a reviving whisky, which he downed in one gulp.

"That'll teach the bastard to park in my space," he muttered. "An empty beer bottle from fifty paces, direct hit on the windscreen and bonnet, bloody good shot, even if I do say so myself."

Don seemed satisfied justice had been done. The other policemen gradually began to drift out of the Mess leaving Don to himself as he continued to chunter, "Lack of respect, that's what it is, no respect for rank. What a bloody cheek."

That night, I slept on Don's sofa as I had no way of getting home. Don had staggered to his bed and snored loudly all night. The following morning, I woke early to find the apartment empty. Don was out somewhere so I took a look in the Mess.

The place had been cleaned up overnight, the day's newspapers were spread across a coffee table and the dining table was laid for the first meal of the day. But there was no sign of Don. It was then I heard a sound from outside. It was the sound of broken glass being swept up, so I went out onto the balcony and looked down at the carpark. There, in amongst the parked cars, Don and another man, a uniformed police officer, were standing talking. Don was waving his arms around, pointing in various directions. I could hear his voice, he was agitated and angry, but I couldn't make out what was being said. I thought I'd better go down.

"Well, I don't know!"

I could hear Don's voice from the opposite end of the carpark as I stepped outside. I could see his massive head over the top of the cars. The police officer standing next to Don, an expat, looked bemused and was shaking his head. Their attention was on something on the ground. I walked over.

"I want this investigated," Don demanded. "It's outrageous."

"It is very odd," replied the uniformed officer. "We have never had an act of vandalism in the compound before."

Next to Don's feet was a pile of broken glass, a broken beer bottle.

"Good morning, sirs," I said. "What's happened?"

Don turned and looked at me. I could tell he was still a bit befuddled from the previous evening's session.

"What?" he exclaimed, looking up. "Oh it's you, Leslie," he said. He moved to one side so that I could see Otto the Auto's cracked windscreen and dented bonnet.

"Oh," I exclaimed upon seeing the damage to Don's beloved Merc. Then, without thinking, I asked, "Is this by any chance your parking space, sir?"

Don stared back at me, as though I'd asked him something totally ridiculous. "Of course it's my space," he snapped back.

"And what the bloody hell has that got to do with anything?"

9

GHOST SHIP
鬼船

HUNDREDS OF SHIPS enter and leave Hong Kong waters every day. Around the clock, these enormous vessels, piled skyscraper-high with containers, maneuver their way along the designated shipping lanes. Weaving in between these ships is a non-stop procession of small coastal freighters originating, mostly, from mainland China, Indonesia and Vietnam. The standard of seamanship on many of these smaller traders can only be described as varied. Many of the captains of what can be described as "rust buckets" have scant regard for maritime rules as they pick their way in and out of port. Collisions and groundings, particularly when the visibility is restricted, are not uncommon. And when the fog was as dense as it was on this particular April morning, it's a case of when, rather than if, something will happen.

It was day-two of my first three-day sea patrol. Don had recovered from his eventful night in the Officers' Mess, while Otto the Auto was temporarily out of action due to 'a long-needed wash and brush-up.' There'd also been no further mention of the Lady Angelique so, with all that seemingly behind us, we were now very much in work mode.

Throughout my training, I had been looking forward to starting work with the Marine Police, but now I found myself a little anxious about my new environment on Police Launch 1. I was very much the new man on board. The thought of embarrassing myself in front of twenty highly experienced mariners produced some anxiety, and this, coupled with Don's recent off-duty performance, left me with a feeling of trepidation about what I was doing here.

A blanket of fog had covered the South China Sea for almost a week, shrouding everything in a white veil. We'd spent the night edging our way through the eastern waters looking for vessels in difficulty. Fog horns sounded from varying distances across the flat steel-grey sea, dull groans through the gloom. I was on the bridge watching Don navigate from the radar. It was 0530 and the morning had an eerie feel to it.

Being as inexperienced as I was, I had difficulty putting my entire faith in the small electronic radar screen as we moved around the ocean with zero real-time visibility. What made matters worse was Don's flow of crazy stories about collisions at sea, 'with ships dashed on the rocks and all hands lost.' He'd been going on in this way for most of the night. I assumed the whole performance was just to unnerve me, the new boy. It was Don's idea of fun.

"You're a *Hak Jai,* young Bird," he declared, looking up from the radar.

"Excuse me, sir, a what?"

"A *Hak Jai.* You are bad luck. It's your first patrol in East Sector and the fog is heavier than I've seen it in years. You bring bad luck." He gave me a sly grin.

Don had been hunched over the radar for the better part of an hour. Occasionally he would lean in closer, peering at a cluster of bright specks on the screen. When he did so, the glare from the radar lit up his face. On the darkened bridge, the glow made Don look almost supernatural.

"This really is very strange," he muttered after a while. "This looks like a ship, and it hasn't moved for more than fifteen minutes. Come and see." He motioned me over, moving to one side.

"That, there." Don jabbed a finger at one of the dozens of identical bright specks. "That's a ship, it's bigger than PL 1, it's in the middle of Tathong Channel and it's not moving."

I looked at the speck, unsure what to make of it.

"The ship is stationary in the middle of one of the world's busiest shipping lanes," he explained. "When the visibility is poor, like it is today, it's not safe for the ship in question." He pointed again at the speck. "And it's certainly not safe for other ships passing through the channel." He looked up at me. "A collision waiting to happen. Let's go."

I took another look at the screen and finally registered what Don saw. The bright yellow dot that he was referring to certainly wasn't moving. But Don was.

"Set a course for Tathong Channel. Five knots."

Our position at dawn was east of Cape D'Aguilar, just outside the main shipping lanes into Victoria Harbor. Don had decided earlier that this was the best place for us. If there was an accident at the narrow harbor entrance, we would be in position to get to the scene quickly.

I went outside onto the bridge wing to see if I could see anything. The fog suffocated every inch of the launch. Beyond the bows, there was nothing but fog. The only sound on PL 1 was the gentle lapping ocean against the hull. The distant warning signals at Tathong Point and on Waglan Rock resounded through the morning brume.

"By the size of the radar image, I'd estimate the length of the ship to be three hundred feet," said Don, "which means it's a large coastal freighter."

"Slow. Gear engage," he called out as we got closer to the ship and the speck grew in size on the radar screen. "Port thirty degrees."

We moved gently forward through the fog, waiting for a first glimpse of the ship. There was total silence from everyone on the bridge as we all peered directly ahead. I looked at Kwan, PL 1's senior deck sergeant, who had been plotting positions on an Admiralty chart. He stopped what he was doing and stared ahead too, holding his pencil and calipers up in front of him as though frozen in time. I gripped the edge of the chart table in anticipation of an impact.

"Full astern," shouted Don.

Everyone jumped, in particular the sergeant standing next to him, who slammed the telegraph into reverse. There was a violent chopping sound from our propellers as they churned up water and we came to a dead stop just twenty feet from the ship's black hull that now towered above us.

"Blast," muttered Don to no one in particular.

I stepped out onto the bridge wing and looked up at the rusty hull plates of the ship. We had come very close to ramming it. Don came out and looked up, too.

"Bloody hell, that was close." He put his hands on his hips and stared at the ship. "Where are their lookouts? They have the biggest patrol launch in the Marine Police fleet right next to them and they don't even know it."

"Can't we call them on the radio?" I asked.

"We have no call-sign for this ship as yet, and an open broadcast has so far resulted in no response." Don huffed and wiped the perspiration from the top of his bald head with the small white towel he always seemed to have at hand.

"Give them a blast on the loud hailer," he shouted back into the wheelhouse. "Let's wake 'em up and wish them a very good morning."

The initial screech from the Tannoy was deafening. It splintered and crackled through the fog.

"Attention, this is the Royal Hong Kong Police. You are in breach of maritime regulations."

Sergeant Kwan's voice reverberated and echoed off the ship's hull. We all waited, looking up at the ship. Nothing happened.

"Damn," said Don stepping back inside and taking over control. "We are going to find out what this blighter's up to."

Don maneuvered PL 1 along the side of the ship towards her bow section. As we passed, the name ORIENTAL CRYSTAL appeared, painted in large white letters.

Our radio operator began transmitting the ship's details back to the Marine Command and Control Centre. Don stuck his head inside the radio operator's cubical.

"We need more information about this ship, its movements, its cargo, also the date and time of arrival in Hong Kong. We need crew details and copies of any recent radio messages."

"What do you think has happened, sir?" I asked Don.

"I'm not sure. But there is something seriously wrong here."

The radio crackled to life as the Marine Controller came on. "Last message received from Oriental Crystal was at 0327 today as she entered Hong Kong waters. The ship has not radioed in since, and has not responded to any calls from us. Her last port of call was Kabil Batam. We have no information regarding her current cargo or crew. I will update you as soon as I have more, over."

Don grabbed the microphone. "Marine Control, this is PL 1, this ship is not at anchor, it is drifting in the Tathong Channel. It's high tide and the current is slight. We need to take action immediately before the conditions change and she ends up on the rocks or another ship appears out of the fog and we have a collision on our hands." Don looked up. "We are going to board her, over."

Upon hearing these words Sergeant Kwan stopped what he was doing and stared in surprise at Don. The sight of Kwan looking worried gave me cause for concern. Together we watched Don as he handed the microphone to the radio operator.

"Find out where PL 53 is," he instructed. "Mr Kerr is on board. Tell him to come here now. We need two police launches to control this situation." Don turned to Kwan.

"Unlock the armory."

At the training school my instructor told me that ninety-nine percent of my on-duty time would comprise of routine tasks, paperwork, writing reports, and just waiting around for something to happen. The remaining one percent would be manic, unplanned and could well be dangerous. And here I was on my very first patrol about to take part in an armed assault on a foreign freighter that appeared to have sailed into Hong Kong without a crew. Perhaps Don was right, I was a *Hak Jai*.

Kwan began handing out weapons: shotguns, machine guns, and clips of ammunition. One by one, designated officers came forward to receive their equipment. Everyone went about their task with a minimum of fuss. I was handed a revolver and a pouch full of bullets. I had fired a gun many times before, but that was under training, and at a paper target. This was for real.

I carefully loaded my revolver, a .38 caliber Mark IV Webley, and placed the gun into my side holster, adjusted its position then clipped it shut. I pressed the clip a second time, just for good measure.

While all this was going on, Don's 'unlock the armory' had transformed PL 1 from a ship half asleep into a hive of activity. Below decks, I could hear NCOs barking orders while junior officers were busy carrying all sorts of gear in different directions.

Everyone had a specific job. Everyone knew what to do. I stood to one side and checked my revolver once more.

"Every man will be armed," Don instructed. "I will lead the party from PL 1, boarding via the ship's port side." Don turned to me. "Bird."

My heart missed a beat. "Yes, sir."

"Inspector Bird, you will transfer to PL 53 when she arrives. You will support Dougie Kerr and board the ship from the starboard side, then secure 53 to the ship. Understood?" He fixed me with that brutish look I'd seen a couple of times before.

"Yes, sir," I replied in a firm voice. Don took a step forward and raised a podgy finger to within an inch of my nose. "Listen, Bird, don't screw this up," he growled. His face was so close I could smell his sweat. "Boarding this ship could be highly dangerous. Do you understand?"

"Yes, sir."

"You are going to back up Inspector Kerr. Understand?"

"Yes, sir."

Don lowered his voice even more, "Now, I know you are fresh out of PTS, lad, but you are well-trained. I'm putting my faith in you. Stay close to Kerr and don't do anything rash. And look after yourself. You got that?"

I nodded again, staring directly into his unblinking blue eyes. "Yes. Yes, sir."

Don gave a grunt, stepped back and turned to face the others. I wiped the sweat from my palms down the side of my uniform trousers. The personal warning from Don had come as a bit of a surprise, but I understood why he had done it. In a potentially dangerous situation, it's vital to work as a team. Every man has to put his trust in the others. Once on board the freighter, we needed to back each other up. This was, as Don said, no longer the training school.

"Both boarding parties will be armed with a Sterling submachine gun and a Remington shotgun," Don shouted at those issued with weapons. "All officers will carry side arms and long batons. All understood?"

"Yes, sir."

"We take no chances here. We have no idea what's happened on this ship. Now, get the portable radios checked out." He marched off carrying a submachine gun.

Within minutes, PL 53 arrived. I heard Dougie Kerr's heavy boots slamming down on the metal steps as he climbed up to PL 1's bridge.

"Is this fer real?" he asked when he saw me. Dougie's hair was a mess and he needed a shave. He looked like he'd been up all night.

"Yes, it is," replied Don emerging from the radio cubicle. "That ship has not responded to any calls. We have been here for almost an hour and we still have yet to see a living soul. It's as though the ship has been abandoned."

"What, no one?" asked Dougie, turning and studying our position on the chart. "This is serious. We got'a get this ship out of here before it gets rammed up the chuff."

"Precisely, and thank you for putting it so eloquently," said Don. "Now, get back onto your launch and moor up alongside the ship's starboard side, then board her from that side. And take Bird and Sergeant Kwan with you."

"Yes, sir," replied Dougie, turning. "Follow me."

There were four men in our boarding party. Dougie led, I followed, Kwan was designated as number three on the ladder, while Dougie's radio operator would bring up the rear. Looking up from the deck of PL 53, I estimated the vertical climb up the side of the Oriental Crystal to be about thirty feet.

Climbing up a rope ladder is not easy, especially when you

have a Remington shotgun or a Motorola radio pack set strapped
to your back. While I was thankful for all of the PTS assault
course training, doing this for real seemed a lot harder.

"Jesus, this Remington weighs a ton," gasped Dougie. The
nails in the soles of his black uniform boots scratched and scored
into the wooden rungs just above my head as we climbed. I
looked down at the two men below who were waiting for their
turn on the ladder. Further down, the dark green sea sloshed
around as the gap between the two ships widened and closed.
As I turned to look back up, the freighter suddenly rolled
outwards in the swell and our ladder swung away from the
ship's side. Dougie and I were, momentarily, airborne on the
ladder. Immediately I tightened my grip on the ropes and dug
my boots into the corners of the rungs to stop myself slipping off
as we were tossed through the air like a couple of trapeze artists.
Dougie managed to hold on too. As the ship rolled in the other
direction, the ladder, Dougie and I came clattering back against
the metal hull with an almighty crash. The impact knocked the
breath out of me and I felt a sharp pain in my shoulder.

"Jesus Christ," screamed Dougie. I glanced up. He looked
hurt.

"You all right?" I shouted out. There was no reply. He didn't
move. Below I could see Kwan and the radio man staring up
at us from the deck of PL 53. Dougie shook his head and took
another step up. "Yeah, I'm okay," he mumbled and continued
the climb. As he got to the top, I shouted, "Dougie, what can you
see?"

He didn't answer or turn around. Instead he made a grab
for the ship's balustrade and hauled himself over and onto the
freighter. I took the last few rungs as quickly as I could. My
shoulder was killing me but I just wanted to get off the ladder.

Over the side, the first thing I saw was a tall steel gantry towering above the center of the ship's main deck. The top of the gantry disappeared into the fog. The deck surface was a chipped, grimy green, peppered with rust. Bits of wood, flat broken pieces that looked like a smashed crate, were strewn everywhere. Other than Dougie, there was no sign of life.

"Blast, I really didna need that," cursed Dougie. He was standing near the gantry and rubbing his hand. He looked shaken. As I dropped onto the deck, he straightened himself up.

"You okay?" I asked again.

"Yeah, yeah, just winded. Let's get on with it. We need to secure PL 53 ta this ship, fore and aft. When Kwan gets up here, you two go to the stern and I will go to the bows. Once you have the ropes attached, meet back here."

Seconds later, Kwan and our radio man appeared over the side and lowered themselves down next to us. Kwan swung the Sterling submachine gun off his back and checked the mechanism. The fog now was so thick that once Kwan and I had taken a few steps towards the stern, we completely lost sight of the others. The only sounds were the occasional thud of the police launches buffeting against the freighter's hull. The question still remained, where was everyone?

After securing PL 53 to the ship, we found Don near the gantry. He was inserting a full clip of thirty-four rounds into the black metal body of his submachine gun. He pointed the barrel upwards and cocked the firing mechanism. The loud click-clack of the spring was a sharp reminder that we really were in the middle of a serious operation. He raised a hand.

"Listen up," he began. "So far we have found no one on this ship, but by securing the two police launches on either side we have at least prevented it from drifting further. Now let's find out what's happened." Don looked around at the group, his face hardening as he spoke. "First place is the ship's bridge. Kerr,

Bird, you two come with me up top. Maintain total silence, and keep your eyes and ears open."

This was the first time I'd seen Don like this. He was now totally professional, calm, confident. His crazy side seemed to have evaporated. Now I'm with the big boys, I thought, checking my revolver yet again.

Don stepped through the hatchway into the bridge tower and began to climb the steps. Dougie followed. The stairway was steep, narrow and poorly lit. Condensation covered the grimy walls. We climbed in silence. At the top, Don stopped and looked back, his large frame obscuring the door to the bridge proper. I was glad he was leading.

He tried the door. It seemed locked but he gave it an almighty shove with his shoulder and it flew open and crashed against the bulkhead. Dougie flinched.

"Steady, Mr Kerr," I whispered from behind.

Dougie looked back. "Fuck, off," he mouthed.

By now, Don was inside, scanning the bridge with the Sterling, moving slowly forwards. Dougie and I followed, fanning out left and right, Dougie with his shotgun, me with my service revolver drawn and held up at arm's length. Running through my head were all the regulations about when it is and isn't lawful to open fire. Now was not the time to screw up.

Towards the rear of the bridge there was a small cabin whose entrance was covered by a heavy black curtain. Don pointed at the curtain and nodded, Dougie tore it open to reveal the radio room — a bank of dials and lights, a desk, and an empty chair. A set of headphones dangled from the back of the chair. On the desk was a large book — the ship's log. Don went inside and sat down, placing his gun on the desk. He opened the book and began to read.

I continued to look around the bridge. A couple of half-empty tea cups had been left on the console near the ship's wheel. I touched them. They were cold.

"There's nothing here. There's nothing in the log we don't know already," declared Don. "Back down to the main deck."

I couldn't help thinking of all those months under training. What had I learnt that was relevant to what I was doing here, now? The discipline? The teamwork, perhaps? One thing was for sure, in a situation such as the one we were in, I felt comfort that I knew how to use a gun.

"We will split into two four-man search parties from here," Don announced once back on deck. "I will take the port side. Kerr, you and Bird take the starboard. We will each take an NCO and a radio man. Keep in frequent comms." Don marched off into the fog. His search team followed.

"Right," said Dougie. "Bird, Kwan, let's go." We moved off in single file along the starboard side walkway, guns at the ready.

The first door we found was a metal watertight hatchway with a heavy central wheel-lock release in the middle. Once through, I shone my torch directly in. The beam lit up a dingy set of steps leading down below decks. The whole place was damp, it stank of rotting fruit. A dim ceiling light was of little help. Dougie stepped in and edged sideways down the steps. As the ship shifted position in the swell, the hull creaked and groaned. The only sounds, other than our breathing, were from the deep structural ache of this old ship.

The cabins below had a recently "lived-in" feel. Civilian clothes were tossed over wooden bunks, while a few books were scattered here and there. On a desk there was an old copy of *The Straits Times* newspaper. A stale odor of fried food and tobacco smoke permeated the air.

"Where the hell is everyone?" I asked as we all moved back out into the corridor.

"Get the handle of this next door," said Dougie. He backed into the wall opposite and raised his shotgun. I looked at the gun barrel, then at Dougie.

"Go on," he nodded. "I'm not going to shoot you."

I tried the door, it swung open at the first push.

"It's the galley," I said, peering inside.

The galley was considerably bigger than the cabins. At its center was a long dining table surrounded by eight heavy wooden chairs. Cupboards lined both sides, while a cast-iron cooker ran along the far end. Pots and pans of varying sizes hung above the cooker. On the dining table, there were a few dirty plates and a couple of mugs. Again, the whole place was completely devoid of life.

I picked up a packet from the center of the table. "Fortified biscuits."

"Not exactly the Mandarin Grill, then. What's on the stove?" asked Dougie as he began to open the cupboards.

"There's water in this saucepan," I said touching the handle, "and it's still warm."

"Warm?" He stopped rummaging and came over to check for himself. "So it is."

"The switch to this burner is still in the ON position. Someone left in a hurry."

As I spoke, a loud clanging noise from further down below resonated through the ship. Dougie froze. "What in God's name was that?" he said, looking back towards the passageway. A shiver ran through me and I felt sweat in the small of my back.

We moved back into the passageway, to where another stairway led down into the bowels of the ship, where the sound had originated. Kwan shone his torch and I caught a glimpse of a metal staircase and yet more darkness.

One by one, we crabbed down the narrow stairway. We were

now well below the waterline, going down to the lowest part of the ship.

At the bottom, opening up in front of us, and filling most of the compartment, were the ship's main engines — two pieces of machinery, each the size of large passenger cars. Overhead, there were a myriad levers, gauges and pipes of varying thickness connecting the whole system. At the far end, about thirty feet from where we stood, there was a work surface, covered with papers and books. Other than the steps we had climbed down, there didn't appear to be another way in or out of the engine room.

"Whatever made that noise is still down here," said Dougie raising his gun. "We are the Royal Hong Kong Police!" he shouted. "Come out with your hands raised above your head." He glanced over at Kwan who repeated the order in Mandarin.

For a moment there was only silence. But then, a sound. A scraping noise from the far end of the room. I raised my revolver, adjusting the grip, keeping my sights directly down the barrel, finger slightly off the trigger. I took a deep breath. Standing next to me I could hear Dougie doing the same.

In the shadows behind the engineer's table at the far end of the room, a man stood up. He was tall, dark-skinned, and bearded. He was dressed in a navy-blue boiler suit. In silence, he raised both hands above his head.

Before we could do or say anything, a second man appeared next to the first, slowly climbing to his feet, also with hands raised. Both men were young, Asian.

I snuck a glance at Dougie, waiting for his lead. But before he could speak, more men appeared, this time from behind the long table at the far end. Six, seven, now eight men, they shuffled sideways with their hands raised and stood beside the others.

"Bloody hell," muttered Dougie as he adjusted his grip on the shotgun. "I think we have found the crew."

We kept our guns leveled. I counted them, twelve in all, mostly Southeast Asian in appearance. A couple looked Indian. One older man, with a greying mustache, was certainly Chinese. Some were wearing bright orange life jackets. All twelve stood in a line with their hands raised and stared back through wide, frightened eyes.

"We are the Hong Kong Police," repeated Dougie. "Do not move or we will open fire. Get down on your knees, hands on your heads, now!"

As the men did as they were told, I lowered my revolver slightly.

"English! Who speaks English?" demanded Dougie.

The men glanced at each other. "Yes, English," said one of the younger ones. "We speak English."

"You are Filipino?"

"Yes, Filipino." He glanced along the line. Some of the others were nodding.

"What are you doing down here?" asked Dougie.

"It's the captain, Captain Hendrik," said the young spokesman. "He's got a gun, he said he was going to kill us all."

"He went crazy," said one of the others.

"He was drinking," said another. They all began to chatter at once.

"Wait! Wait!" ordered Dougie lowering his shotgun. "This Captain Hendrik, is the ship's captain?"

"Yes, he has a shotgun, just like yours. He said he was going to kill us. Kill us all."

"Where is he now?"

"He chased us around the ship. He was screaming at us and shooting his gun, we all ran down here to hide. I don't know where he is now."

"How long have you been down here?"

"Since five o'clock this morning. We were too scared to go back up."

Dougie glanced at his watch. "0745, almost three hours?"

"Was anyone hurt during the shooting?" I asked.

"No," said one. "We are all here, the whole crew, except for Captain Hendrik."

"Kwan, search these guys for weapons," said Dougie, turning to the group. "All of you, stand up, turn around, and place your hands flat against the wall. Feet apart. Come on, jump to it!"

The only weapons found were two short wooden batons that had been dropped by the men as they got to their feet. Kwan kicked them across the floor into a corner.

"Kwan, you keep an eye on this lot," said Dougie. "Bird, you come with me. Seems we have a heavily-armed, crazed drunk on our hands."

"Hendrik, our own ancient mariner," muttered Dougie as we climbed back up the steps. "I wonder if he's Dutch. That would be appropriate, wouldn't it? The Flying Dutchman, the legendary ghost ship that can never make port and is doomed to sail the oceans forever."

I knew Dougie loved his poetry. I'd heard him spout Coleridge two or three times in the past. But now he was serious. We had to warn the others about the captain.

"That figures," replied Don, after Dougie had briefed him back up on the main deck. "We found the captain's cabin, it was wrecked, smashed chairs, a couple of empty whisky bottles, broken glasses, and a locker door had been ripped off its hinges. And there was a large hole in a plywood partition, almost certainly the result of gunfire. And we found these." Don took three spent shotgun cartridges out if his pocket.

"The crew referred to him as Captain Hendrik," I said.

Don pulled a battered dark blue passport from his uniform breast pocket, "Hendrik Van Bueren, Dutch national. We found it in his cabin."

The photograph was of a man in his late fifties with a round, rosy, fat face, piggy blue eyes, cropped greying beard, and thinning hair combed across a large forehead.

"The date of birth puts him at fifty-eight years old."

"So where is he now?" asked Dougie.

"I have no idea," said Don. "For all we know, the crew could have murdered him and thrown the body overboard, and this crazed drunk tale is just part of their cover story. I have called for reinforcements. Two more patrol launches will be with us shortly and a team of CID officers are on their way... "

An enormous explosion reverberating from the bows of the ship stopped Don in mid-sentence. We all froze.

"Gunfire," exclaimed Don, swinging his Sterling around. "Take cover!" he ordered.

I was actually so shocked by the ferocity of the blast that for a few seconds I remained motionless, staring towards the bows.

"Take cover!" Don screamed again and I quickly dropped behind a metal deck winch. Drawing my revolver once more, I peered forward into the fog, expecting a crazed, shotgun-wielding Dutchman to come charging out of the gloom.

For what seemed like the longest minute of my life, we stared directly ahead, guns at the ready, waiting.

Don broke the silence. "Dougie," he whispered from behind the gantry, "you and Bird go starboard side and around towards the bow." He pointed forward with the barrel of his machine gun. "I will go forward along the port side. We'll meet, bow section, front of the bridge tower. Stay close to cover. If you see Hendrik and he is armed..." he paused, considering his options "...if he hesitates when told to lay down the shotgun, even for a split second, shoot him." With that, Don stepped out from behind the winch and moved slowly along the ship's port-side walkway towards the fog-engulfed bows.

"You ready?" asked Dougie, looking my way. I was surprised by Don's order to shoot but I nodded. I knew that a couple of direct hits to the chest from my .38 caliber handgun would not have an immediate stopping effect on a large and determined man. To stop him dead in his tracks, the shots would need to be to the head. And a moving head-shot in a manic situation is a difficult ask. But at least I had Dougie and his shotgun.

As we inched our way towards the ship's bows, I strained to see into the fog ahead. If Van Bueren appeared, as Don had said, we first needed to ascertain if he was armed. If he was, we were then required, under law, to order him to put down his gun, warning him of the consequences if he didn't. All this before we could use force. "The odds are always with the nutter," mumbled Dougie, who seemed to know what I was thinking.

"Kerr, Bird, over here." As we came around the front of the bridge section we found Don crouched by the port side rail, he was pointing his Sterling at the bows. "I just caught a glimpse of the forward deck through a break in the fog. A hatchway is propped open."

"That would probably be the anchor chain locker?" asked Dougie.

"Let's find out," said Don standing up and walking slowly into the fog.

Dougie glanced at me, nodded and moved forward taking the middle line. I moved over to the starboard side. We walked in line with our guns directed at the open hatch. Don stopped a couple of feet before the hatchway and raised a hand. Then he pulled a torch out of his pocket and aimed it inside.

We waited. There was no movement, no sound.

Don took one step nearer, craning his neck to get a clearer look. "Van Bueren!" shouted Don. I flinched at the sound of Don's voice. "Van Bueren," he repeated. "We are the Hong Kong Police, drop your weapon and come out."

There was no response.

Don took another step closer. "Ah, bugger," he sighed as he reached the lip of the chain locker. Don relaxed his hunched shoulders and lowered the Sterling.

"That was the gunshot."

He pointed his torch into the hatchway and knelt down. Dougie and I stepped forward and peered in. There, lying on a pile of chunky anchor chains, was the body of Captain Hendrik Van Bueren. He was on his back, slightly twisted to one side. The shotgun lay next to him and looked to have fallen from his hands. The collar and shoulders of Van Bueren's once white shirt were sodden black with blood. Immediately behind the torso, scattered across the wall of the chain locker, was a large crimson spray. The face, and most of the top of Hendrik Van Bueren's head, was missing.

"Looks like the good captain has successfully blown his own brains out," declared Don standing up and removing the clip from his machine gun.

"He didn't miss, did he?" said Dougie staring at the body.

I had seen dead bodies before. During training, we were taken to the mortuary to witness an autopsy. Seeing a human body dissected for evidence for scientific reasons is one thing, but seeing what was left of Captain Hendrick Van Bueren in the chain locker that morning was something entirely different. Van Bueren had been alive just seconds before. A desperate man. A troubled man. Someone in need of help. I looked at the others. Dougie was wiping sweat from around his mouth. Don remained stony-faced. There really was nothing we could have done.

The subsequent search of the ship, carried out by over thirty police officers, took the remainder of that day. In the captain's cabin, the CID uncovered a packet of papers and letters. In one, dated just weeks before, there was news of the tragic death of Van Bueren's son, killed in a motorcycle accident in Holland.

"Enough to drive a lonely man to drink?" queried Dougie.

"And possibly push him over the edge," said Don.

Later that evening, the crew were taken ashore to Marine HQ for further questioning by CID. And, after two days, and with no evidence to implicate them in any criminal activity, police handed them over to Hong Kong's Immigration Department and representatives of the shipping company. They all eventually left Hong Kong as crew on other ships. The *Oriental Crystal* was towed to a government mooring near the western approaches to the harbor where it remained until the forensic investigation was complete. Three weeks later, standing at the bar in the Mariners Rest, Dougie asked me what my opinion was of the case.

"It was quite an introduction to life in the Marine Police," I said. "I certainly didn't expect to be involved in such a dramatic incident on my first patrol."

The thought occurred to me that only ten months ago I had been at my parents' house in England packing my suitcase to come to Hong Kong for the first time. At that time I'd never even seen a real gun. Now I was standing in the Marine Police Officers' Mess discussing a case, our case, in which a man had blown his own head off with a shotgun.

"Things happen quickly around here," I added.

Dougie remained silent, deep in thought. I asked him, "What about you, you must have seen things like this before? What do you think about it all?"

As soon as I'd put the question, I knew I'd fallen into Dougie's ever-present Coleridge trap. He stepped away from the bar and

LES BIRD

raised his beer:

> Alone, alone, all, all alone,
> Alone on a wide wide sea!
> And never a saint took pity on
> My soul in agony.

> I looked upon the rotting sea,
> And drew my eyes away;
> I looked upon the rotting deck,
> And there the dead men lay.

Dougie took a swig of beer, wiped his mouth and smiled.

10

FRIGHTFULLY MAULED
可怖咬噬

DURING THE NEXT five months, Don's eccentricity aside, our patrols on PL 1 were relatively quiet. Certainly, since my baptism of fire with our Flying Dutchman case there had been nothing much of note to report. Our days were filled with routine border patrols, searching fishing vessels for anything untoward, and visiting the remote villages on the islands along the eastern coastline. There'd been plenty of downtime too, during which I had gotten to know a little bit more about my commanding officer. Once, when off duty, I'd *had the honor*, as Don put it, of being his guest for Sunday lunch at the Rose and Crown, where I was introduced to their rare roast beef and to his 'little friend' — the Lady Angelique.

Upon meeting Angel, which was her actual name, I was quite surprised. She was a far cry from what I'd imagined. For some reason I had pictured Don's confidante-to-be as a large, brash woman in her mid-forties, a barmaid displaying lots of cleavage. I had expected the Lady Angelique to be a tart whose voice could be heard from all points west. But Angel was just the opposite. She was a small, plain Chinese girl in her mid-twenties. She was quiet, had a pleasant and ready smile, and went about her waitressing effortlessly and efficiently. I found myself liking her from the word go, and I could see why Don was attracted to her.

But what did she see in him?

Angel had been waitressing at the Rose and Crown for several years. From our brief exchanges that Sunday, I gathered she had spent most of these years being pursued and pestered by Don, and that she had become his 'little friend,' not by choice but by lassitude – after years of badgering she eventually just gave up and succumbed.

As we were shown to our table on that particular Sunday, Don took great pride in pointing out that we were being seated at 'his' table. The waiter removed the reserved sign as we approached. The sign read RESERVED FOR CHIEF INSPECTOR D. BISHOP, ROYAL HONG KONG POLICE. It was like a warning to other diners to keep clear. Don's table was positioned on a slightly raised area of the restaurant, I assumed so that Don could look down on everyone else.

"It keeps us away from the riff-raff," he said, confirming my theory. Don then aimed a thumb at the people on the next table, just in case I was unsure who the riff-raff were.

After downing his first cold beer of the day, it didn't take long for Don to assume the role of ringmaster for the entire restaurant. He began by telling staff what to do and how to do it.

"Bring me a bottle of bold red," he demanded across the dining room.

The young expat couple at the next table looked surprised as Don barked his orders. I had an inkling their quiet Sunday lunch was in for a bit of a jolt.

Don, noticing that the man had looked our way, leant across and nodded.

"Good afternoon," he said reaching over and grabbing the couple's wine out of the ice bucket next to their table. The young man looked on in surprise as Don closely examined his wine. "What's this?" queried Don squinting and pulling a face. "Ha, thought so, *Pigalle Brut*. This is rubbish."

The man looked shocked.

"It has the bouquet of a Spaniard's armpit," added Don, ramming the bottle back down into the ice, causing some of the cubes to shoot out and bounce onto the floor.

"What? I'm sorry?" asked the man in surprise.

"What's the matter, sport, you deaf?" replied Don. "Spaniard's armpit."

He turned away, nonchalantly flicking open his napkin and tucking it into the top of his shirt collar.

"Cheap plonk," he whispered and winked. I looked at the couple and smiled. They looked stunned. But before anyone else could speak, Don turned towards the bar.

"Speaking of cheap plonk, where's that bottle of bold red? Angelique, bring *vino collapso*, bah."

One of the things I had discovered in the months I had been working with Don was that this kind of outing was all part and parcel of being his second-in-command. Unless I could come up with a really watertight excuse, I was always going to get press-ganged into some awful outing or other on our first day off duty.

On this particular Sunday, however, with Don well into his second bottle of 'bold red,' I was stuck at his table listening to the same old sea dog tales, the ones I'd heard a dozen times before. Until an angel from heaven intervened.

"I think you have had enough to drink, Don," said Angel appearing at our table. She began clearing our plates away as Don slowly took in what he'd just heard. He looked up at Angel in disbelief. I looked at Don in disbelief. It was the first time I'd ever heard anyone tell Don what to do. And now it was coming from this petite Chinese girl.

"What?" growled Don, tightening his grip around his glass. He looked furious. Now I really didn't want to be there.

Angel stopped what she was doing, put the plates back down and looked at Don. "You don't want the same thing to happen at home tonight as what happened the last time you drank two bottles of wine, do you?"

For a moment there was silence as Don absorbed this. Then, his whole demeanor changed. His shoulders sagged. His face flushed deeper than the bold red. He glanced at me. I faked a cough and covered my mouth with my napkin.

"Well, I, er," he stuttered, "there's no need to, er, bring all that up my dear, not in front of young Leslie here."

Angel began clearing the table in silence. You could have cut the tension with a knife.

I seized my chance, "Oh, is that the time!" I said looking at my watch. "I don't know about you, sir, but I am deadbeat after our past three days. Do you mind if I head off home?"

Don was deep in thought, and seemed mortified by Angel's words. Then he fired back, "No, not at all. Fully understandable. Three hard days, yes, I am sure you are wiped out. Lunch is on me, by the way. I'll sort out the bill, you run along. I'll see you next trip."

He waved me away. I didn't hang around. I gave Angel a quick smile, told her it was nice to meet her and headed for the door. Outside, as I walked along Nathan Road towards the Star Ferry, I tried to figure out what had just happened. Of course, Don had a home life, a private life, just like everyone else. Yet up until now, I'd never considered it. Even imagined it. I had a bet with myself that whatever it was that I had just witnessed between Don and Angel, it would never be spoken of again.

And I was right. It was now 0700 on day-two of our next patrol on board PL 1. I had been in Don's company for a whole twenty-four hours and there'd been no mention of the lunch or of the Lady Angelique. As Don sat in his usual spot in the

Officers' Mess tucking into his customary breakfast of two fried eggs, bacon, sausage, and tomatoes, I thought this was as good a time as any to ask some pressing questions about the contents of a recent report on shark sightings I'd been reading.

"Sir, have you seen this report?" I held the file up for him to see. "Has it really been twenty years since the last shark sightings in Hong Kong?"

He looked up from his breakfast and pointed his fork in my direction.

"That report was put together by an imbecile, some desk jockey who has never been on a patrol launch," he said through a mouthful of food.

He grabbed a bottle of brown sauce from a side table and emptied a dollop onto his plate.

"Sharks regularly migrate through these waters during the summer months. I have seen them myself, caught up in the nets of fishing trawlers just off the coastline."

He continued to munch through a slice of buttered toast.

"You mark my words," he pointed the toast at me, "sharks come close to shore in search of food, attracted by the local fish farms that breed their fish in underwater cages."

I watched him devour his way through a sausage. I wondered if a shark would make as good a job on a swimmer as Don was making on the sausage. I was interested in sharks for one very good reason. As he took another bite I threw caution to the wind and continued.

"Sir, this is interesting," I said, reading from the next page: "'The first-known shark attack victim in the colony was Police Sergeant Herbert W. Jackson who, according to the China Mail on September 24, 1945, was attacked shortly before dusk while bathing off Tweed Beach on the southeast side of Hong Kong Island. He was frightfully mauled and died within a minute of being pulled from the sea by Captain A. M. Braude of the Hong Kong Volunteers.'"

"Mmm, frightfully mauled, eh?" he said, still chewing the remains of his breakfast. "Doesn't sound like a good way to go."

I read on. "'In 1954, two more victims, both Royal Navy servicemen, were killed in separate shark attacks.' Again, these attacks took place in Hong Kong's eastern waters, in Junk Bay. The report goes on to say that these were the last known incidents. That's over twenty years ago."

"Rubbish," he wiped his mouth and tossed his napkin on the table. "Whoever wrote that nonsense has never been to sea around here. I told you. Sharks pass through these waters. End of story."

"But I often go for a swim, when I am off watch," I said, finally getting to the point. "Tweed Beach and Junk Bay are near here, in East Sector. I had no idea sharks came this far north, and this close to shore?"

"So it's probably best for you to stop swimming around here, then, isn't it?" Don chuckled, standing up and pouring himself a mug of coffee. "Last thing I want is my number one to be *frightfully mauled*, bah. Wouldn't be much use to me then, would you?"

With that, he walked out and went up to the bridge.

Bloody hell! Five months working with the man, and I still couldn't decide whether he had a vicious sense of humor or was simply unhinged. He clearly knew there was shark activity around here, and he'd seen me swimming in the mornings, but until I just mentioned it, he never said a word. Yet again, I was left shaking my head in disbelief at Diamond Don Bishop. I picked up my files and headed up to the stern deck.

Recently, when off-watch, I had been studying the basics of marine navigation with Sergeant Kwan, who was a wealth of information on the topic. Kwan joined me a few minutes later, bringing along some charts to work on. We figured we would be pretty safe at the stern. Unfortunately, the peace was short-lived. Half an hour later, Don found us.

"Ah, there you are," he said marching in. "There's nothing going on in East Sector so we are going up to North Sector for an overnight patrol."

I stopped what I was doing and looked up. "Sir?" Kwan looked equally perplexed.

"North Sector is overrun with illegal immigrants crossing Mirs Bay from the Chinese side," continued Don. "Last night, thirty-seven swimmers were plucked out of the water. A few made it and landed on our side. North Sector received a severe ear-bashing from the DS this morning. He said these days, North Sector's so-called Ring of Steel is more like a leaking sieve, so I have offered our services in support. We are going to help plug the gaps."

Before anything further could be said, he simply turned and stomped off towards the bridge.

"That's unusual," said Kwan after Don had left. "A Marine sector commander rarely leaves his own sector to work in another area. It's his job to take charge here. If something happens, it would take us hours to get back."

"Well, Don Bishop does things his own way, doesn't he?" I replied, despairingly. Closing my files I stood up and went off after him; I needed to know more. Kwan followed closely behind.

We caught up with Don poring over maps and charts.

"Leslie, this will be your first venture into the border areas, and your first anti-illegal immigration patrol." He looked up for a response.

"Yes, sir," I replied.

"What do you know about illegal immigration in Hong

Kong?"

"Well, I am pretty clear on recent events. The reasons behind the current exodus from China are mostly down to the Cultural Revolution, which began in the early sixties. The aftermath of it has caused people to flee the country right up until today."

He grunted and raised an eyebrow. "Mmmm, you have been doing your homework, haven't you," he said, with more than a hint of sarcasm. "Now listen up. Everyone on this launch, with the exception of you, has at some time or other been dealing with Hong Kong's illegal immigration problem. It's time to bring you up to scratch. So sit down and pin your ears back."

Classic Don Bishop. Even if I'd rattled off the entire history of Hong Kong word for word, he still would have insisted upon giving me a lecture. I sat down, folded my arms, and waited.

Spreading a large map across the chart table, Don began. "For the first one hundred years after the formation of the colony in 1841, there was little restriction on cross-border movement between China and Hong Kong."

He pointed to the border area. I was obviously going to be treated to the entire history of cross-border activity, from day one. "Hong Kong was a free port and people were, mostly, free to come and go as they pleased," he continued. "Back then, there was no need for immigration restrictions. But in the late 1940s, with a civil war in China and then the establishment of the communist People's Republic, that all changed."

Don had assumed a self-appointed role as professor and China historian. Kwan and I nodded, confirming we were following the lesson.

"In the late forties, migrants at the rate of ten thousand per week began crossing the border into Hong Kong, fleeing drought, famine and the communist regime. So, a 'Frontier Closed Area' was established. Here..." he pointed "...along the border." He drew a line across the map. "Security forces were deployed and a permit system for those wishing to cross legitimately was set up. It was hoped this would stop the influx."

I noticed others on the bridge straining to hear what Don was saying as they went about their routine duties. Don quickly shooed them away. I suspected Don didn't want any of his junior ranks catching him out if he exaggerated a point or quoted a wrong figure.

Sensing I was about to ask a question, he held up a hand. "It was a good idea, and it helped stem the tide, but in the sixties, Mao launched the Cultural Revolution, after which there was another influx."

Don paused to wipe the sweat from the top of his head with his small white towel. "Throughout the late sixties, and continuing through the seventies, hundreds of thousands of people have been fleeing China and entering Hong Kong. Since I arrived, more than ten years ago, the population of Hong Kong has increased from slightly over three million to four and a half million today."

He glared at me for effect, making sure I was appreciating his local knowledge. "The government reckons that about half of those arrivals are illegals from China. The last few years have been frantic for us front-line officers." Don looked at his map again and scribbled a few calculations.

"But there's a slight twist in the tale here," he added looking up at Kwan.

Kwan nodded. "Yes, sir. Many of the older officers now serving in the police force arrived in Hong Kong as illegal immigrants in the forties and fifties. Most of them were young and wanted to come to make a better life for themselves. That's why there's quite a bit of sympathy for the ones we catch these days."

LES BIRD

"Right." Don took back control of his briefing. "When Marine Police officers process illegal immigrants, it's more a case of giving them food and dry clothing before sending them back, rather than arresting them in the formal sense. Many of our boys have been in the same situation."

I decided to interrupt. "You said it's recently been frantic. Is the Touch Base Policy something to do with that?"

"Ah yes. This policy was introduced by the Hong Kong government three years ago. For officers on border patrol, it does not make the job any easier."

"But what is it meant to achieve?"

"It's the government's theory that if an illegal immigrant successfully runs the gauntlet, avoids arrest, and reaches the urban areas, he qualifies for a Hong Kong identity card. It's better to register them as permanent residents rather than have them go underground and exist illegally. The thinking is that this encourages illegals not to turn to a life of crime. I suppose that if you are a civil servant sitting in Government House this makes sense. But..." he pointed out towards the open sea "... if you are out there on the front line, it makes a mockery of our efforts. Basically if an illegal immigrant can out-smart our border patrols, he's in."

"So it's evolved into an incentive to come!" I exclaimed.

"Exactly. This Touch Base Policy is a pain in the neck for those of us who are protecting our border with China. It's just not working. Illegal immigrants just keep on coming." Don shoved the map towards me. "You will see for yourself tonight."

But I hadn't finished.

"Sir," I said before he could get involved in something else, "as we are up in the border area, I wonder if you would mind telling me why you think the ninety-nine-year lease on the NT is a non-issue for Hong Kong?"

109

Don looked at me as though I was a toddler struggling to put on his shoes. He shook his head.

"Because, young Leslie," he began in a condescending manner, "it is in China's interests to ensure the continued prosperity of Hong Kong. Trade, money, it's all that matters. A vast amount of China's trade comes through Hong Kong. It doesn't make sense to tamper with the political and economic equilibrium."

"What about nationalistic pride? What about face? Don't you think that bothers them?"

"Oh, yes, I know all about that. There will be some to-ing and fro-ing, of course. Maybe the lease will not be torn up, maybe it will be extended or something like that, provided, of course, that some bigwig from London comes out and kowtows before whomever is in power at the time. Some rot like that. Just forget it, it's a non-issue, as I said before."

With that Don took over the navigation of PL 1, signaling the end of my personal lecture.

I thought back to what Joe Poon had said at PTS, about how the Chinese think in centuries rather than decades. Joe's and Don's views were diametrically opposite. But we were still twenty years away, and a lot could happen between now and then.

We spent the next few hours cruising northward towards Mirs Point in search of the North Sector command launch. This anti-illegal immigration patrol was intriguing. One reason was the thought of formally meeting the sector commander, known to all as Uncle Daniel. Chief Inspector Daniel Holden-Foster CPM, was the most senior chief inspector in the Marine Police and the commander of Marine North Sector. Also, Joe Poon was working on the North Sector command launch so it would be good to catch up with him. I was yet to see Joe in his Marine working environment. I figured I was going to learn something on this trip. Don began to tell me about Holden-Foster as we set a course north.

"Daniel joined the Hong Kong Police in 1958 after completing two years' national service in England," said Don. "He is now the only sea-going officer senior to me," he chuckled. "But it's odd, even though he is the most senior man, Holden-Foster has complete disregard for rank. He sees himself as everyone's uncle, and everyone refers to him as such, even to the most junior of Chinese constables who speak little English."

"You know," Don continued as he checked the radar scanner, "upon meeting Daniel for the first time one could be forgiven for assuming he was slightly mad."

Now that, I thought, was quite an ironic statement coming from Diamond Don Bishop.

I'd chanced upon Daniel Holden-Foster once before. I guessed him to be in his mid-forties. He was a wiry streak of a man with leathery skin giving the impression he had spent most of his time out on deck. He had silver-grey hair, which he kept razor short at the back and sides, but it was a wild, Einstein-esque cut on top. A sharp contrast to his tanned skin, were his piercing blue eyes.

That first encounter was when I was fresh out of training school. In uniform, I was walking down a corridor at Marine HQ when I spotted him coming in the opposite direction. He was not in uniform but, despite his casual ensemble, I recognized him immediately. The chief inspector was dressed, as usual, in a pair of green uniform shorts, a white short-sleeved shirt, untucked so the tail flapped around, and pair of worn-out hiking boots with no socks. He had his hands in his pockets and was staring at the floor in front of him as he came towards me. Remembering the proprieties we were taught about interacting with senior officers, I quickly put on my cap, came to attention, threw my smartest training school salute and said, confidently, "Good afternoon, sir."

Seeing me for the first time, Uncle Daniel almost toppled over.

"What?" he cried, staggering a little before putting a hand out against the wall to steady himself. "Where?"

"Good afternoon," I repeated, confused but still respectful. "Where what, sir?" I enquired.

"Where is he?" gasped Daniel turning around and looking back down the corridor.

"Excuse me, sir, who?" I asked.

"The senior officer, lad. Where is he?" he replied while fixing me through unblinking pale blue eyes.

No longer confident I said, "I am saluting you, sir."

He sighed and shook his head. "I'm not a senior officer, lad, I am Daniel Holden-Foster. Please stop saluting, you are giving me the shits." He paused and shivered slightly before adding, "Who are you anyway?"

"Bird, sir, Inspector Bird."

Daniel glared at me.

"East Sector," I added, hoping that would mean something to him.

"Ah," he said, as though it did. "Well, bit of advice for you, Inspector Bird."

"Sir?" I looked on, expecting some professional words of wisdom, possibly some advice about working in East.

"Stop going around frightening people, and stop calling me sir." And with that he put his hands back in his pockets and shuffled off down the corridor.

I told Don about the meeting.

"Bah!" he exclaimed. "That's just the way he is. Never wears uniform if he can help it, doesn't like being referred to as sir and doesn't approve of any formal rituals. You really must have startled him."

"Put the shits up him is the way he put it. What's his story, sir? Where's he from, what's his background?"

"Not sure really. Word is he comes from a very wealthy family in the southwest of England, but Daniel was very much the black sheep. He did a runner and came out to Hong Kong as soon as he could get away. Apparently he couldn't stand all the posh formality that came with his family position."

"He seems quite a character."

"His men love him, he treats everyone, no matter what their rank, exactly the same, like a brother, or a nephew. He speaks fluent Cantonese and is one of the best *mahjong* players I have ever seen. During quiet periods on board his launch, he prefers to sit down below decks, in the crew's canteen, chatting with his men."

Since joining Marine, I'd found that many of the expat officers, in particular the older ones, incorporated a form of barrack room, or gallows humor into everything they did or said. Even in major operational situations, it was often difficult to know if these guys were being serious or not. This was certainly the case with Don Bishop. And, from what I'd just heard, it was going to be much of the same with the eccentric Uncle Daniel. I guess it helped everyone deal with what could be difficult or dangerous situations, such as the grey areas around immigration policies and trying to preserve order without a clear mandate, while at the same time retaining one's humanity.

We continued northwards, passing Mirs Point on the Chinese side of the bay. Looking through binoculars, I scanned the long, deserted beaches backed by lush green foliage. How many potential illegal immigrants had made it this far and were waiting for darkness before entering the water? What about the PLA? Were they holed up in the tree line too? Anticipation stirred at the thought of what was required of us tonight. This really was the front line.

An hour later, I spotted the North Sector command launch just west of Tung Peng Chau, an island one mile from the mainland. As we approached, I recognized the figure of Daniel Holden-Foster sitting on the balustrade. The breeze was wreaking havoc with his mop of silver hair and his baggy white shirt flapped in the wind. Don, steering PL 1, brought our launch close in and eventually alongside.

"Kwan, you stay on the bridge," said Don after the two vessels were roped and secured together. "We'll give a full brief when we return. You are in charge while we are away. Call me if needed." He turned to me. "Come on, Leslie, you're with me."

Daniel was waiting for us.

"Don Bishop, you old battle-axe."

"Bah, ah," came the reply. As they shook hands, Daniel glanced over Don's shoulder to where I was standing at a respectful distance.

Glaring at me, he asked, "Who's the young fella?"

"This is Leslie Bird, he's my new number one," replied Don. "I believe you've met him before?"

Daniel examined me a little closer. There was a long silence.

"Really? When?"

"A few months ago at Marine HQ, s…" I quickly stopped, remembering what happened the last time I called him sir.

"Really? Let me think now. He squinted and then he grinned. "Ah, yes!" he exclaimed. "You're the chap who almost gave me a heart attack. Saluting and stamping your feet."

"Yes," I replied, as both CIs gave me the once-over.

Daniel smiled and motioned for us to follow. "Come now, lad, make yourself at home, relax, and no more saluting!"

As we walked towards the bridge, there was activity at the stern. Daniel's men were clearing away what was left of the floatation devices used by illegal immigrants the night before. Pieces of a wooden raft were propped up against the bulkhead while a dozen or so deflated car tire inner tubes were stacked nearby. There was a pile of wet clothes and a couple of sodden shoes thrown on top. Some of the crew were sluicing down the decks with mops and buckets. The aftermath of a busy night.

In the wheelhouse, a map of Mirs Bay had been set up on the chart table. On it were marked the routes illegal immigrants favored when attempting to swim across the bay. Three worn-out North Sector inspectors stood up as we entered. One of them was Joe. I nodded to him and he smiled. He looked knackered.

"I have four patrol launches," Daniel began while Don and I studied the map. "At night, I deploy them in a straight line across the bay, providing blanket radar coverage for the entire border. Tonight, we have the bonus of a Royal Navy ship, one of the Hong Kong Squadron. Their skipper has agreed to cover the eastern side." Daniel pointed at the map. "In theory, between us, we should be able to spot all swimmers as they attempt to cross the bay."

"That's about a three-mile swim?" Don said.

"Yes, most try to cross the bay by swimming as it's very easy to spot a boat on the radar. We call them swimmers but actually they are mostly paddlers or floaters. They use numerous methods to assist them across. Inflated inner tubes are a favorite, or bundles of plastic bags full of air and tied together, that's another. Last night we picked up one on a self-made raft of blue plastic barrels lashed together with bamboo poles. It was quite a work of art, and it must have taken him days to build it. It's still at the stern. Take a look before you leave."

Daniel lit up a roll-your-own, took a puff, and continued.

"Most people who try to cross the bay at night are young — teenagers or in their twenties — mostly male, some young couples. When we catch them, we keep them on board overnight then hand them over to the Chinese military at the border crossing the next morning."

"They must be in poor physical condition by then?" Don said.

"None of them are in any condition to swim in the first place," Daniel said. "Most have trekked for days, weeks even, to reach the coast. They are already pretty exhausted by the time they get into the water. The PLA patrol their coastline with the sole aim of preventing people from leaving their glorious middle kingdom. These poor blighters remain undercover for their entire journey, moving only at night, and eating anything they can find on the way."

"What happens to those who are caught by the PLA before they attempt to swim?" I asked.

"Good question," Daniel said. "Those who are arrested are sent back. Others, well, you might well hear the gunfire yourself tonight. You can draw your own conclusions there. Tonight, you will be policing the maritime equivalent of the Berlin Wall."

I sat back and thought about that. The beach to the north of the bay was China, and we had no jurisdiction there. I felt sorry for these illegal immigrants; on the one hand I wanted them to make it, yet it was my duty to catch them and send them back. It was an odd dynamic, and not one I was entirely comfortable with. I looked out again, across the bay to the deserted beach to the north. In another setting, it would be an idyllic holiday resort.

"We will remain here tonight," said Don. "Our radar is in good nick and we have a couple of night-vision devices. Where should we position ourselves?"

"Here," said Daniel, stabbing at the map. "Middle of the bay. That will allow me to flood the narrower part, to the west, with my smaller launches." Daniel nodded towards his inspectors.

"Good," replied Don. "Is there anything else we can help with?"

Uncle Daniel looked out of the wheelhouse and up at the pale blue sky. "Yes. The sun is over the yardarm. You can help me drink some beer."

I wanted to take a closer look at the floatation devices at the stern, so I motioned to Joe that we should head outside. "You look all-in," I said as we walked along the starboard side walkway.

"This is our patrol's third day," he said, removing his beret and running his hand across the top of his head. "No one has had much sleep. We were working all last night and I have been writing reports for Daniel all day. You probably heard that some illegals breached our cordon and landed Hong Kong side. So there's been bollockings all day."

At the stern, a sergeant was taking Polaroid photos of the illegal immigrant's gear.

"This is Inspector Bird from East Sector. PL 1 will be patrolling up here in North tonight."

The sergeant saluted before carrying on with what he'd been doing. Joe knelt next to where most of last night's paraphernalia was piled up. He pulled at a stack of wooden poles and plastic buckets.

"One man tried to cross the bay on this raft. The radar image was so big that we thought it was another patrol launch. We tracked him from the beach to the middle of the bay before picking him up." Joe shrugged. "He never stood a chance."

"And these clothes," I asked.

"Most of the illegals carry plastic bags with spare clothes. That's what this pile of stuff is. They throw their bags away after we pull them out of the sea."

"All that work, effort, and risk... only to be sent back," I said. Joe nodded in a matter-of-fact way. He looked too tired to chat further.

After returning to the wheelhouse, I picked up a set of binoculars and scanned the coast once more. Nothing was happening. Adjusting the range, I took stock of the geography of the China side, where the illegals would begin their swim. I made a mental note of where the foliage came down to the waterline, providing good cover for anyone not wanting to be seen. Half an hour later, as the sun began to set, Uncle Daniel checked his watch and Don took the hint.

"Right, young Leslie," declared Don as he downed the entire contents of his beer mug. "Time to get to work."

"Stay in touch on channel two," Uncle Daniel said as Don made his way down the hatchway and back onto PL 1. As the launches parted, I turned to thank Uncle Daniel, only to see him standing at attention and throwing a mock salute, with a huge grin on his face.

Once back on PL 1, Don briefed Kwan and the on-watch crew on the overnight duties and our patrol area

"I'd like to remain on-watch tonight if that's okay, sir?" I asked Don after he had finished the briefing.

He stared back at me for a second then shrugged. "Ugh, suit yourself. I'll take the second watch then. You work with Kwan here, and call me if there's a problem or if you come across anything you can't handle." He glared at me as usual for effect, then turned and disappeared down the stairway.

Kwan and I studied the Admiralty chart and fixed our current position.

"First thing is to darken ship," said Kwan, who began dimming the lights on the bridge dials. I turned off all exterior lights, including those on the mast and the stern. Once that was complete, I walked around the decks to make sure all portholes were shuttered. PL 1 could now maneuver covertly across the dark waters of the bay without being seen from the shore. To anyone already in the bay, we were invisible.

Back on the darkened bridge, it took a few seconds for my eyes to get accustomed to what was going on. The coxswain was at the wheel, a sergeant was operating the telegraph while Kwan was hunched over the radar with his face obscured by the screen's anti-glare cover. "I've selected a radar range of one mile," said Kwan looking up and pointing at the screen. "It will give us a picture intensity that will clearly show a person in the water. If we do get a contact, we can then use a night-vision device to examine it further."

By using the little ambient light that exists around the bay, the night vision device, or NVD, produces images in an eerie fluorescent green. It changes a dark environment into a clear one. Through the NVD, swimmers and any other movement in the water are easy to spot from up to half a mile away.

It was a beautiful, calm, cloudless night, and with PL 1's engines shut down there was not a sound. I stepped out onto the bridge wing, took an NVD and scanned the surface of the water. At first I could see nothing of interest, but there was movement on the beach. Beams of light were scattered in the trees. Soldiers, likely a PLA patrol.

"Sir!" came a shout from the wheelhouse. "There are four or five small radar contacts to our port side, at about half a mile."

I went back inside and took a look for myself.

"There," said Kwan. He pointed at a small cluster of bright yellow dots on the dark screen. I took another look through the NVD. It took a few seconds for my eyes to readjust to the green glare but then I saw them, paddling steadily. I turned and nodded to the guys in the wheelhouse and we eased towards the swimmers. A loud thud broke the evening silence as the deck sergeant switched on one of our powerful searchlights.

The beam illuminated five swimmers keeping themselves afloat with inflated plastic pillows. Looking like terrified children, they shielded their eyes against the light, completely defeated.

A team of officers ran down to the lower deck, opened a hatchway and threw a line into the water. I leant over from the bridge wing and watched the swimmers being hauled up, one by one. They were a sad-looking bunch as they sat in their own puddles of water on the deck. Four young girls and one boy, teenagers dressed in blue and grey cotton Chinese pajama-style clothes. They looked tired and hungry, and were dripping wet. One girl looked around, trying to figure out where she was and what was going on. The others sat with their heads down, resigned to their fate.

Our cook appeared with a large saucepan of soup and some porcelain bowls. He ladled it out and handed it to the five kids who gulped it down. Kwan arrived with a clipboard and crouched down, asking them for their personal details and how long they had been traveling.

"They are farm workers," said Kwan after he had finished his questioning. "They come from a province called Fujian, which is eastern China. They have been traveling overland for about two weeks. They have no money and I don't think they have eaten in days. They also said that this is their first attempt to escape."

These were the first illegal immigrants I had seen, and my feeling of pity returned. Young people trying to break free from a life they didn't want. It felt odd. I'd left home too, and chosen to come to Hong Kong. Yet here I was stopping others doing the same thing.

On the beach, there were more torch beams. Whatever was happening was too far away to see or hear. The sound of our radio broke my thoughts so I went back up to the wheelhouse and we resumed our darken-ship routine. It didn't take long to spot more swimmers trying their luck. The drill for us was always the same. Upon spotting them on the radar, we moved in under darkness. The deck-sergeant illuminated them with a searchlight, then a team hauled them out. Over the next six hours we intercepted another eleven. All young, all terrified, and all in the same weakened state as the first group.

By 0400, things had gone very quiet in terms of activity. We hadn't seen any more swimmers and had decided not to bother Don with what had happened so far. It was, after all, routine stuff for North Sector and Kwan had handled everything very efficiently. Pointing at the radar screen he said, "I don't think any more will attempt to cross tonight, it's too late to begin swimming now. They would never make it across by sunrise."

I was sitting in Don's chair in front of the radar repeater. I rubbed my eyes, as I'd started to drop off to sleep.

"We are due a shift change in a few minutes," said Kwan holding up his watch and illuminating the dial. "I have just sent a situation report down to Mr Bishop. I am sure he will be up here soon to take over."

I looked at the radar screen one more time, it was blank. Nothing was moving. But as I turned away, a small yellow blip appeared in the center of the bay, just over a mile from our position. The contact was smaller than the ones I'd seen for the swimmers, so it probably wasn't a person. But it was definitely something.

"Mr Kwan," I said, "take a look at this."

"It's not moving," he said after staring at the screen for a minute. "Maybe just some rubbish floating in the bay?"

"We've got nothing else to do," I said. "Let's go and take a look."

The engines engaged and PL 1 eased silently across the calm dark waters of the bay towards the contact. As we closed in, I picked up the NVD and stepped outside. At first there was nothing. But then something moved. A man. I lowered the NVD and rubbed my eyes then took a second look. There he was, just a head above the surface, and now a raised arm.

"It's a swimmer!"

Kwan took a look through the NVD himself. He nodded. "Yes, let's go."

In under a minute we were hovering over the man, a searchlight was turned on and I could see that he was now face down in the water. But I had seen him move, he must still be alive.

I ran down to the lower deck where the crew were already at work. A side hatchway was open and a rope ladder had been lowered. One constable had managed to secure a boat hook onto the man's shirt and was dragging the limp body into the side of the launch. We needed to get this man out. I scrambled down the ladder myself and got a hold of the man under one arm and tried to lift the upper part of his body out of the water, but he was unconscious and too heavy to lift so I grabbed his hair and pulled his face out.

"Get a rope down here," I shouted.

The constable and I managed to secure a rope around the man's middle. Others came to help, while more gathered up on deck to form a hauling party. Slowly, with the rope now secured around the man's middle, we pulled him up. I steadied his head as best I could as he was still slumped forward. Sea water poured off him, drenching me and the constable. As he was hoisted up further, he began vomiting and coughing up water. He looked like he was near death. Up on deck, Kwan pushed his way in between the crew, grabbed the man and tried to revive him. As I climbed back on deck I noticed, for the first time, the state of his right leg.

"Jesus Christ, look at this," I said, pointing to the man's thigh.

The man was wearing long trousers and in the darkness we hadn't seen that his right trouser leg was split open. But now, under the passageway lights, we could see that he had lost a significant part of his leg. A chunk, the size of a football, was missing from the back of his thigh, with the calf and foot attached only by a tangle of sinews, tendons and broken bones. I'd never seen an injury so severe.

"We need to tie up the thigh somehow!" I shouted. "Get whatever we have in first aid, and cut up some sheets, we can wrap the leg with those."

One of the crew came forward unwrapping packets of bandages, gauze pads and a bottle of antiseptic fluid. He started to work on what was left of the man's leg. For a few seconds, all I could do was stare at the terrible wound. It was a mess of raw flesh.

"Propeller injury?" someone asked.

"That's a bite," said Kwan. "You can see the teeth marks, there, at the top, where the flesh has been ripped."

Kwan was pointing at a second bite, not as successful as the lower one, but the teeth marks were there in an arc shape around the top of the thigh.

"Shark?" I asked.

"Shark or barracuda. It's not uncommon at this time of year. I've seen this sort of thing before, but this is the first swimmer I've actually seen alive after an attack. They are usually chewed into small bits."

"We need to get him to hospital," I said.

Kwan stared at the man and shook his head. "I don't think he's going to make it. He's very pale and there's hardly any bleeding. He must have lost a lot of blood."

He turned and hurried off towards the radio room. I looked

again at the man. By now he had passed out. Someone tried to revive him. What was left of his leg had been slightly raised and was resting on a pile of pillows. The wound had been treated with red antiseptic fluid, which made the injury look even more horrific. Wrapped in blankets, the man was drifting in and out of consciousness.

"What's going on?" Don asked, appearing from behind me. He was rubbing his eyes and sipping from a coffee mug.

"We think it's a shark bite. We pulled him out about ten minutes ago, middle of the bay."

"Is he still alive?" Don bent down to take the man's pulse.

"Kwan has called for an ambulance to be at Sha Tau Kok pier, we have also informed the North Sector launches," I said.

"I'm afraid an ambulance will not be necessary," said Don, feeling for a pulse a second time. "He's a goner."

One of the sergeants tried too, but then shook his head and pulled the blanket completely over the dead man's head. Urgency turned to failure. The three of us stood there for a moment looking at the body on the deck.

"Better change that ambulance request to a coffin van. Poor fellow," said Don. He took another sip of his coffee and wandered off up to the wheelhouse.

Later that morning, Daniel invited us back on board his launch for a wash-up of last night's activities. We sat around the Mess table discussing the intercept positions marked on a chart. Joe came in and joined us. He looked a little better than the previous day. He smiled when he saw me and gave me the thumbs-up.

"Fifty-six illegals picked up in North Sector overnight," said Daniel reading from the morning's report. "That includes your sixteen, plus your shark attack. No landings reported on the Hong Kong side, so no dressing-down this morning. Well done, gentlemen."

I asked Daniel about the dead man, and if he had ever seen any like it before.

"Oh yes. Usually around this time of year, the currents bring in warmer waters from the Pacific. And with it come the bigger fish, sharks and barracuda. Looking at the bite marks on that man's leg, I'd say that was a shark."

"Before yesterday, I'd never heard anything about sharks or shark attacks in Hong Kong waters. Finding an illegal immigrant with most of his leg bitten off came as a surprise," I said.

"I'm sure it came as a surprise to the swimmer too," said Don as he bit into a bacon sandwich. I watched as tomato sauce oozed from between the slices of bread.

"We find lots of dead illegal immigrants in North Sector," Daniel said. "No one knows how many of those swimmers drown or die from other causes. But last summer, we were pulling at least one body out of the bay every night, and finding more washed up on the islands next morning. Many of these had been dead for some time and were in the advanced stages of decomposition. Hypothermia is usually the cause during winter. But some of those around this time of year could have been the result of shark attacks. Bodies decompose very quickly in the sea. Quite often, it's not possible for us to tell how they died. It's sad."

"What about autopsies?" asked Don, "What results come back from them? And fingerprints too?"

"You must understand that most of these illegals do not carry any ID, so a dead body in the sea around here is usually just that — an illegal immigrant who has died while attempting to cross the bay and decomposed in the water. End of story," said Daniel. "We file a report for each one, of course, and we sometimes include a possible cause of death, but usually we can't be sure, and so cause of death in our reports is listed as unknown. No ID, unknown cause of death. In many cases, I don't think an autopsy reveals much more. As for fingerprints, most dead illegals we pull out are already in an advanced state of decomposition. Prints are not possible. But if they are, then we do take them and pass them on. But the immigrants from China have no personal record in Hong Kong. Fingerprints always draw a blank. In my entire time up here on the border, I have never heard of a body being ID'd from fingerprints. The bodies we find are simply statistics."

In the hope of identifying the man we pulled out of the bay that September morning in 1977, we fingerprinted him. But Daniel was right. The reply from Marine HQ simply read, 'No record found'. The statistic I entered into our report was: 'Chinese male, ID unknown. Cause of death — shark attack.' And I never went swimming off PL 1 again.

11

BLACKBEARD THE PIRATE
黑鬍子海盜

SOMETHING WAS WRONG with Don. I stood in his office doorway at East Sector Base and peered in, trying to figure out what it was. Don was bent forward, over his desk, reading a report, his nose almost touching a pile of papers. I watched him for over a minute as he scanned the documents, never lifting his head once. Then I realized what was wrong with this picture. Don always read reports tilted back in his chair, holding his papers at arm's length above his head and, usually, with his size-13 boots propped up on the desk in front of him. I'd never seen him in this 'face down in a book' position. It just wasn't Don's way. I sensed something was amiss.

I'd arrived at the base that morning to begin a three-day patrol on PL 1. It was early November, it was cold and in recent weeks the seas had been very rough. Our last trip had been spent patrolling the eastern colony boundary. We called it 'patrolling' but actually, for those entire three days, we had just been hanging on, as PL 1 pitched and tossed her way over and through the giant rollers thundering in from the Pacific Ocean. For reasons unknown to me, I do not suffer from motion sickness, but some of the crew did, in particular the younger ones. During that last excursion, some junior constables hadn't surfaced from their bunks for the entire three days. I'd been down below decks several times to check on their condition, usually to find at least one with his head in a bucket, wrenching his guts up. Personally, I couldn't see the point in staying ten miles off-shore for three days. There was no other vessels out there, no one needed rescuing. No fisherman was stupid enough to go out that far and in those seas, they knew better. But Don thought otherwise, so that was that.

I took another look at Don from the office doorway as he sat at his desk, still with his head down. He realized someone was watching him and looked up.

"Ah, Leslie-boy, there you are. I'm just going to finish reading these reports and then I'll come down to PL 1. Pop off down the jetty would you, and see how the preparations are coming along."

I stared at Don, not believing what I was seeing. He was in full uniform, immaculately turned out, but for one thing. He hadn't shaved. And, by the looks of it, a razor hadn't touched his face for several days. Don was sporting a three-day growth of whiskers – the makings of a beard.

Facial hair, with the exception of a mustache (non-flamboyant) was not permitted in the Royal Hong Kong Police. It was written in black and white in the Police General Orders. And Don was a stickler for procedures, in particular those relating to an officer's on-duty appearance. I couldn't figure this one out, so I saluted, turned and went in search of Kwan. I found him in PL 1's armory.

"Mr Kwan, have you seen Mr Bishop this morning?" I asked.

Kwan was squinting into the firing mechanism of a Sterling submachine gun, checking to see if it had been oiled. He looked up. "Good morning, sir. Yes, I saw him in the office."

"And?" I asked, stroking my chin. "Notice anything?"

"Ah, you mean?" Kwan stroked his chin in response.

"Yes, he hasn't shaved, and he's in uniform. What's going on?" I asked.

"He's sick, sir. His skin is sick. He has a chit, from a doctor."

"His skin is sick? You mean a rash?"

"I don't know what it's called, sir, but he showed me a chit, from a doctor."

"Did he?" I turned around and went back along the jetty and into the office block. I needed to hear the story for myself.

"Sir," I said, standing at Don's office door, "PL 1 is ready for patrol."

"Ah, good, I'll just collect my things and be down in a minute. Oh, by the way, in case you are wondering, it's seborrheic dermatitis, a reaction from a new shaving soap. I can't shave until it clears up. Doctor's orders." He waved a piece of paper at me. "Letter from the doc. I went to see the DS yesterday, so it's been reported, it's all above board."

'Is it, indeed,' I thought to myself. I recalled that one of Don's drinking buddies was a doctor, an old Australian general practitioner, who'd lived in Hong Kong for decades. From some of the stories Don had told me, this doctor should have been struck-off years ago. I wondered if Don's drinking companion was the doctor who had signed the chit, coerced by Don into writing the letter, just so he would be granted permission to grow a beard? To me, this had all the makings of a 'Don Bishop plot.'

For the next couple of weeks our patrols continued to be uneventful in terms of policing. The eastern boundary remained rough, shipping remained scarce, young officers continued to throw up into buckets and Don's beard flourished, to the extent that the crew began referring to him as 'Blackbeard the Pirate.' On one occasion, whilst watching him eat his breakfast in PL 1's Mess, I thought that if a film crew suddenly appeared and said they were making a movie about sixteenth century England,

and were looking for a 'dead-ringer' to play Henry VIII, they need look no further. Other than a touch of ginger hair dye on his whiskers, Henry Tudor was sitting right there in front of me, scoffing sausages.

This beard-growing melodrama continued for a few more weeks until Don decided that an upgrade to his now-rugged nautical ensemble, was required. He took to wearing an off-white, chunky, Fair Isle, roll-neck sweater, under his uniform tunic. I christened this the 'Don Bishop U-Boat Commander' look, which was appropriate in more ways than one, as during our time battling those huge waves out on the eastern boundary, PL 1 spent more time underwater that it did above it.

In the south-eastern corner of Hong Kong's territorial waters, there is an island called Po Toi. In 1977, the population of Po Toi was no more than a couple of dozen. Most islanders had moved away some years before, either to the urban areas of Kowloon, or overseas. Now, only two families remained on the island, and both operated seafood restaurants overlooking the bay. These restaurants were very popular at weekends, when the restaurants would be packed with visitors from town and the bay would be full of pleasure craft. On weekdays, however, the island was deserted.

One morning, in early December, on day one of a three-day patrol, we steamed out of Aberdeen Harbor on PL 1 and headed east. I was up in the wheelhouse with Kwan when Don came stomping up. He pointed his beard at me.

"We are going to Po Toi," he announced. "Set a course," he ordered Kwan. "PL 1 needs a touch-up," he said, turning back towards me. "We will spend a couple of days there, in the bay. The crew can chip and paint the hull. There's nothing moving further out, so we might as well take advantage of the conditions."

I found this sudden change in deployment a little strange,

but the thought of not being thrown around all day was most welcome.

Upon arriving at Po Toi later that morning, we maneuvered into the calm waters of the bay and dropped the anchor. As the crew got to work on the hull, Don picked up the binoculars and trained them on the beach.

"There's movement in one of the restaurants," he said looking at me. "Let's go ashore for a spot of lunch. No point in hanging around here. I'm famished anyway."

With that he grabbed his beret and made for the stern quarter where PL 1's tender, the dory, was secured. Within minutes, the dory had been lowered and moored alongside PL 1 to take Don and me ashore. As Don got onto the ladder to climb down, a white pleasure craft about fifty feet in length slowly motored into the bay and came to a stop some distance away. Don, now on the ladder, looked over at the white boat with suspicion. A man, an expat, came out of the boat's cabin and started waving his arms above his head in our direction.

"That's the international distress signal," I said, looking down at Don.

"Yes, I know," he replied. "What the hell does this bozo want? He doesn't look in any distress to me. You wait here, I'll go over and sort him out."

With that, Don climbed down into the dory and set off with a coxswain towards the white pleasure craft. I, and the others on PL 1, watched them go.

Once alongside the pleasure craft, I could see Don talking to the man. Don began pointing at PL 1 and then out toward the open sea. In response, the man held his palms upwards, as though he was trying to explain something. After a minute, Don climbed up onto the deck of the pleasure craft, and the two men disappeared into the main cabin. Bored with this, I decided to check on how the guys were doing chipping PL 1's hull. From the upper deck, I could see things were progressing nicely. Everyone seemed happy at not being thrown about for a change.

After about fifteen minutes, Don emerged from the pleasure boat's cabin and climbed back down into the dory. I expected him to return to PL 1, to report what had happened, but instead he continued towards the island. Once there, he jumped ashore and struck out for the restaurant. The dory then came back to PL 1, collected me and we set off after him.

"What happened on board the pleasure craft?" I asked the coxswain of the dory.

"No idea, sir. Mr Bishop went on board himself. I heard some shouting from inside the cabin, but I didn't understand."

When I got to the restaurant, I found Don sitting alone at a table overlooking the beach.

"What happened on that boat?" I asked as I sat down.

Don didn't look up, he was studying the menu. "Mmm? Oh nothing. The man's a fucking imbecile. I think he's been drinking. I fixed his engine, no problems. He's okay now, forget it."

Don called the waiter over and began ordering lunch.

At the conclusion of that trip, I walked around the upper deck of PL 1, admiring the touch-up work. PL 1 looked like a new launch. As part of my end-of-patrol duties, I went into the wheelhouse to check and sign-off on all of PL 1's log books. When I looked in the Communications Log, I found that for the past three days the radio operator had been reporting our hourly positions as along the eastern boundary, and not at anchor in Po Toi Bay. I asked him why he had done this.

"It's Mr Bishop's order, sir," he replied. "He told me to send these positions, and not to report that we have been at Po Toi."

As Don had already left, there was nothing I could do about this now, so I decided I'd ask him about it when next I saw him.

I signed the book and pushed off home.

As I arrived at my flat, the phone was ringing. "Inspector Bird, this is the Marine Duty Controller, you are to report to the Deputy District Police Commander," said the voice. "Be at his office at Marine Headquarters at 1400 today. And be in full uniform." He hung up.

I looked at the phone in my hand, I was taken aback. Why did the DDPC want to see me? He didn't interview first-tour inspectors like me. He was too senior. I'd never met him before. I'd never seen him before. I didn't even know where his office was.

The DDPC was a Chief Superintendent Paddy Thursby. I'd once heard Don refer to him as 'The Hatchet Man,' but I couldn't recall why. He sounded like an awful character. And I knew Don hated him, which probably meant 'The Hatchet Man' didn't think very highly of Don. But why had I been summoned? And why so sudden? What did 'The Hatchet Man' want with me? I was worried to say the least.

At 1345, I arrived at MHQ and found Don sitting in the waiting room adjacent to the DDPC's office. He looked up. "Ah, Leslie, you too, eh? What have you been up to, then?"

"I haven't been up to anything. I have no idea what this is about. You?"

Don just stroked his beard in response, so I sat down next to him, and waited, in silence.

Shortly, a secretary appeared and told us we were to go in. The drill for entering the office of a senior officer was pretty standard. March in, in-step, with the senior one calling the time. Then, at a spot two paces in front of the senior officer's desk, halt. Then, together, salute, stand at attention and wait. This, Don and I managed to do without cocking it up. We stood there, at attention, in silence, staring at Chief Superintendent Thursby, The Hatchet Man, who was casually flicking through some papers on his desk. Eventually, he spoke.

"Good afternoon, gentlemen," he said, peering at us over the top of his gold-rimmed spectacles. He first eyeballed Don, then me.

"Sir," we replied in unison.

Thursby sat back in his chair and removed his glasses. "Gentlemen, you have, unless I am mistaken, just completed a three-day stint on PL 1 in East Sector, have you not?" He looked at Don.

"Yes, sir," fired back Don, emphatically. Don's voice was at Volume 10. It was almost a shout. I think I must have flinched at the ferocity. Obviously, Don was in no mood for silly games.

"Quite," continued Thursby, looking back at his papers. "During those three days, gentlemen, did you visit Po Toi Island, by any chance?"

Bloody hell, did we ever. We'd been there for three whole days. I glanced sideways at Don, who was thrusting his bearded jaw towards Thursby.

"Mmm," replied Don, giving the impression he had been so busy over the past three days that it was difficult to recall where we had been on patrol. There was silence, as both Thursby and I awaited Don's carefully thought-out answer.

"No, sir," replied Don definitively. I almost choked.

"No, Chief Inspector Bishop?" Thursby asked, his eyebrows slightly raised. "Are you sure? You have been nowhere near Po Toi this past trip?"

Don remained square-jawed, eyeballing Thursby. "That's correct, sir. We did not go anywhere near Po Toi."

Thursby rubbed his chin and stared at Don, "Oh, that's odd," he replied. "Because a close friend of mine was out on his yacht a couple of days ago around the Po Toi area. And after experiencing trouble with the vessel's engines, he anchored in Po Toi Bay to see if he could fix the problem."

Thursby looked directly at Don, who remained expressionless. I felt my palms begin to sweat. Thursby continued. "My friend tried to fix the engines himself but soon realized this was beyond his abilities, so he decided to radio for assistance. To his amazement, within minutes of sending the distress message, a Marine police vessel turned up." Thursby checked his notes, "The person in charge of this police vessel then went on board my friend's boat and offered to look at the engine. Ring any bells, Mr Bishop?"

There was silence for a second, then Don barked back, "No, sir."

Thursby stroked his chin once more and stared at Don. I was now seriously scared. Don had been caught out and The Hatchet Man was now going in for the kill.

"Naturally, my friend was very pleased to see the Marine police," he continued. "But unfortunately, things didn't turn out as he had hoped. You see, my friend claims that once on board his yacht, this Marine police officer asked if he could borrow the yacht's tool kit, so that he could try and fix the engines. My friend naturally obliged. He was happy that help had arrived. Once this Marine policeman had the toolkit, he then disappeared down through a hatchway. There then followed some hammering noises from down below, accompanied by quite a lot of colorful language. After a few minutes, the Marine police officer emerged from the compartment, clambered to his feet, swayed a little, then did something quite extraordinary." Thursby stared straight at Don, looking for a reaction. "Would you like to know what it was, Mr Bishop?"

Don didn't speak. He was staring defiantly at Thursby.

"Okay, Mr Bishop, I'll tell you. First, this Marine police officer took a small white towel out of his pocket and wiped the sweat from his forehead. Then he tossed my friend's toolbox and all his tools into the sea."

I could now feel sweat forming under the rim of my uniform cap. I snuck another glance at Don, who remained stone-faced, staring directly back at Thursby.

"There's more," continued the Hatchet Man, looking down at his notes. "After throwing the toolkit and all of the tools into the sea, this Marine police officer gave my friend some advice. He told my friend, and I quote, 'Your engine's fucked, sport.'" Thursby paused and looked up. Neither Don nor I spoke. Thursby was searching our faces for telltale signs. Both Don and I remained at attention staring straight ahead. My armpits had gone all clingy. I dared not look directly at Thursby or Don. I felt the room was about to explode.

"Doesn't ring any bells, then?" Thursby asked once more. I sensed that he was beginning to lose his temper. "Well, this might. My friend gave me a description of the Marine police officer, the one that tried to fix his engines but couldn't, the one that threw his tool box and all of his tools into the sea, the one that informed my friend that his engine was 'fucked'. Would you like to hear it?" Thursby didn't wait for a reply. "My friend described this Marine policeman as 'a brute of a man. Large bald head, thick set, wearing a white polo neck sweater under his uniform tunic.'" Thursby paused, looked up at Don, and added, "And he had a beard."

No one spoke. I snuck a sideways glance. To my amazement, Don was staring defiantly back at Thursby. Thursby then turned to me.

"Inspector Bird," he said. I almost shat myself at hearing my name. "You may leave now." He motioned me towards the door.

Without missing a beat, I turned and was out of there as fast as I could march. Outside, I placed my hand on the wall to steady myself, took a deep breath, straightened up, and headed for the Officers' Mess where I poured myself a stiff drink and slumped into a chair. My hands were shaking.

I sat in the Mess alone for about half an hour trying to imagine what was going on in The Hatchet Man's office. Don must be in deep trouble for sure. He'd thrown the Hatchet Man's friend's tools into the sea, told him his engine was fucked and just left him there. Shit!

I was still contemplating all of this when heavy footsteps sounded on the wooden floorboards approaching the Mess, interrupting my train of thought. The doors almost flew off their hinges as Don marched in. He looked like death itself had struck him. Without a word he made straight for the bar, where he snatched a bottle of scotch from a shelf and poured himself a large measure. He raised the glass in front of his face, gave his whiskey a nod of respect, and downed it in one. Don then shook his head, and made a sound similar to that of a horse after it had finished drinking from a trough. He then poured himself a second large one, turned, looked directly at me, raised one finger and said very slowly and deliberately, "Not a word, Leslie. Not, a, fucking, word. To anyone. Ever."

I never discovered how he managed to escape disciplinary action for throwing that toolkit in the sea. What I do recall, however, are the words of a fairly inebriated Dougie Kerr, the day before I joined the Marine Police: 'He's a law unto himself. He could get away wi' murder if he wanted, because the senior officers at headquarters are all terrified o' the man.'

Maybe Dougie was right.

12

A VERY LARGE COSSACK FUR HAT
哥薩克式皮草帽

It was a Friday evening in mid-December and, as usual when off duty, I popped into the Mariners Rest at Marine HQ for an early drink. Most of the younger officers in Marine gathered in the Mariners on Fridays, it was a good opportunity to catch up, to hear stories from other Marine sectors and get the inside info on any big cases that had been in the news. If Joe was in the Mess, we would always cluster around to listen to his North Sector escapades, in particular any dealings he'd had with the PLA. The sea border along the northern bays was also patrolled by Chinese gunboats, the *Gung On*. Like us, they were interested in apprehending anyone trying to sneak into Hong Kong. Sometimes, in their haste to pick up illegal immigrants, the Chinese patrols would stray over the boundary into Hong Kong territorial waters, leaving our patrol boats the job of pointing out their mistake. With everyone from Government House down treading on eggshells when it came to international incidents those night-time ops had to be handled with a high degree of diplomacy. Joe's stories were always popular. Also in demand were tales from the southern waters, in particular from those who had been involved with the interception of Vietnamese refugee vessels. It was fascinating to hear the refugees' stories about what they'd been subjected to by the new regime, tales of persecution that had convinced them to drop everything and risk their lives on ramshackle craft in the South China Sea.

The questions for me when in the Mess were predominantly about East Sector's rough seas and the various search-and-rescue cases we had been involved in. And, if there were any new inspectors present, I would be required to regale them with our Flying Dutchman case from start to finish. Of course, having Don as my boss was also one of my draw cards. Once talk of real frontline operations had been exhausted, the questions for me were the inevitable: 'What's Don been up to this week?' Or, 'Any new Diamond Don Bishop stories, Les?' Naturally, all queries such as these were asked when Don wasn't around.

As I was ordering a drink at the bar on this particular Friday, Inspector Danny Newmarch came in and pulled up the stool next to mine. I had met Danny several times before and I liked the man. He was in his early thirties and, prior to coming to Hong Kong, had spent several years in the British South African Police in what was then Rhodesia, today's Zimbabwe. He always had an interesting tale or two about his experiences in Africa. These days, Danny was the Sub Divisional Inspector at Mui Wo Police Station, which meant he was the police chief for the eastern half of Lantau Island. Because all outlying islands were sparsely populated and difficult to get to, they came under the control of the Marine Police. But it was rare to see an Islands officer in MHQ. They had their own headquarters on Lantau Island, which came with its own Officers' Mess. These guys only made the journey over to Marine HQ when directed to do so.

"Hello Danny," I said. "How's island life?"

Danny settled himself down and ordered a beer from Tony the barman. "All is well, Les, couldn't be better," he smiled. "It's been quiet in Mui Wo for some time now, which is how I like it."

He took a long swig of his beer.

"This afternoon I was called into MHQ for a meeting. That's all finished, so I thought I'd stop by and have a quick drink before catching the ferry back."

Danny and his wife Susan lived in the officers' quarter above Mui Wo police station. Even though Danny was required to spend almost all of his working hours on Lantau, I knew that even on his days off, he preferred to remain on the island and spend time with his family or go hill-walking rather than coming into town. He said the Lantau hills reminded him of his days in Africa where his police patrols comprised mostly of trekking long distances through the bush.

On this particular December evening, there was already a group of officers gathered at the far end of the bar. As Danny and I chatted away, a noticeable hush fell over the other group, and I turned to see Don Bishop walk into the Mess.

Don made straight for the far end of the bar and joined the others. Meanwhile, Danny was ordering more drinks and I couldn't help but feel that although he had earlier announced he was only staying for one drink, he was now getting a taste for it.

Sure enough, one drink led to several and before long, Danny, and everyone else in the Mess, was in a pretty lively mood. I could tell that Danny was getting a bit tipsy when he turned to me, drink in hand, and said, "Les, my good man. Susan and I have decided to invite one of the single officers for Christmas lunch at our house this year. After all, Christmas alone is no way to spend it. So what do you say?"

"Oh, that's very good of you, Danny," I replied, "but I already have plans for Christmas."

As I spoke, I hadn't realized that Don was standing right behind me.

"Danny, I'd be honored to come round," said Don. I turned

to see him raise his glass in salute. "I have nothing planned for Christmas Day. This is very decent of you. I'll catch the ferry over on Christmas morning."

I could see that Danny was taken aback a little by Don's statement and I think he surprised himself when he responded with, "Really, Don? That's great! Okay, you are very welcome. Susan will be pleased to see you."

I knew Danny was going to regret this in the morning but kept my mouth shut. Susan Newmarch was well aware of Don's off-duty drinking reputation and would be none too pleased with her husband's choice of Christmas lunch guest.

It must have been getting close to midnight that evening and the mood had changed several times in the Mess. A number of petty arguments had flared up and Don had upset everyone with a series of outbursts, but at least he hadn't resorted to violence.

"Oh, look at the time, I have to go," Danny suddenly announced. "I'm going to miss my last ferry back to Lantau." He looked at his watch.

"Bah, rubbish," Don said, slapping him on the back. "I'm going to buy you one for the road, Mr Newmarch."

"No, Don, I have to go. Last ferry and all that."

"No, you're not, Newmarch. No man refuses a drink from me," Don fired back.

Everyone in the Mess froze, looking first at Don and then Danny.

"You'll stay and have one more beer with your old chum Don."

"No, Don, really, thank you very much but I must run, Susan will be worried. We will be seeing you on Christmas Day though, eh?" said Danny, an anxious look plastered across his face as he edged towards the door.

Don stared into his beer. His hands gripped the bar either side of his glass. I could tell that the booze had got the better of him. He looked like he was going to smash his head on the countertop.

"All right!" Don shouted angrily. "Go back to Mui Wo. I always thought you were a lightweight, Newmarch. Go on, shove off."

Danny, although shocked, was thinking quickly. He spotted a lifeline to escape from his Christmas Day invitation. "So I guess that means you won't want to come to Christmas lunch then?"

"No, I won't!" shouted Don, angrily. "If you won't stay and drink with me, I most certainly will not be coming. You can stick your Christmas invitation where the sun doesn't shine, and as far as I am concerned you can shove your turkey up your arse."

"Okay," said Danny from the safety of the doorway. "I'll tell Susan then."

"Yes, you do that," replied Don, determined to have the last word. "And what's more, you can stick your turkey up her arse as well."

Danny hurried off before Don decided to chase after him. Don plonked himself down on a stool and the others gradually drank up and drifted home. I couldn't help but smile. Danny had managed to successfully un-invite Don for Christmas lunch.

In the weeks leading up to Christmas I did a couple more three-day patrols with Don on board PL 1 and he never uttered a word about the exchange in the Mess or what his plans were for Christmas Day. I assumed Don had either accepted the fact that he had uninvited himself to the Newmarches for Christmas or, more likely, he had forgotten about the whole thing, just as with Dougie Kerr's story of a drunken Don chasing his cook around the deck of PL 1 because his dinner was not to his liking. He hadn't gotten his own way on that occasion, so the whole thing was simply forgotten. Don's law was, 'If Don didn't win, it didn't happen.'

A few days before Christmas, I was in Marine HQ once more. I came in to collect some new kit and, as I was leaving the quadrangle to return back to East Sector Base, I bumped into Danny again.

"Ah," he smiled upon seeing me. "That's twice in two weeks. We must stop meeting like this."

I asked him about the heated exchange with Don.

"Haven't seen or heard anything from him since then," Danny said with a shrug. "I guess he's forgotten all about it, as he seems to do after his drunken rants. By the way," he added, lowering his voice, "I never mentioned the argument with Don to Susan, so if you see her sometime in the future please don't say anything. The last thing I need is an ear-bashing from her about drinking in the Mess with Don, and for inviting him over for Christmas. She would go ballistic if she found out."

Christmas Day came and went. I had a thoroughly good time spending most of it with my former training school squad mates in a restaurant in Central. It was good to see them all again and swap stories. On Boxing Day, I decided to call Danny to wish him Merry Christmas and to ask how his day had gone.

"The lunch itself went very well indeed," replied Danny over the phone. "We invited three young inspectors from West Sector, all single. It was their first Christmas in Hong Kong and they had nothing planned, so I think they really appreciated the gesture. Susan and I certainly enjoyed it and those three chaps were good company."

"Oh, that's sounds great," I replied. "I'm pleased everything worked out for you in the end."

"Well, it didn't completely go to plan, I am afraid," Danny said. "Something happened later on."

"What?"

"After our guests left, Susan and I settled down on the sofa with a glass of sherry to watch the Queen's Christmas speech on television. As we were watching, there was a knock at the door."

"Oh," I said, hoping it wasn't who I thought it was.

"It was Don," continued Danny emphatically.

"Oh dear. What did he want?"

"When I opened the door, he was holding onto the wall to steady himself, and he had a stupid grin on his face. 'Merry Christmas, Newmarch, frightfully sorry we are a little late, old boy.' He was slurring as he swayed back and forth on our porch.

"What did he want?"

"I couldn't believe what I was seeing," continued Danny. "He was wearing a very large Cossack fur hat which was quite dusty, as though it had been dragged across a field. And there was dried blood caked on the left side of his face. As he swayed from side to side in the doorway, it was quite obvious he was paralytic."

I knew that hat. After Don had a few drinks, he would wear it and claim he had Russian ancestry.

"And he wasn't alone," added Danny. "Standing behind him there was what appeared to be a tramp."

"A tramp?"

"Yes, a tramp, a shabbily dressed individual who was staring directly at me through wild, unblinking eyes with a strange little smile on his face. It was at this point that I noticed that Don was carrying a cat."

"A cat?"

"Yes, a damn cat! Listen to me, he had a filthy black cat tucked under one arm. But before I could say anything, Don turned, pointed at the tramp and announced, with a certain level of authority, 'This is Captain Jozef Gustav Miloslaw Zoldak, Polish Merchant Navy. Met him in a bar in Tsim Sha Tsui this afternoon.'"

"So he'd been down the bars all day. Who was the Polish

captain?" But Danny was now in full throw.

"I really couldn't figure out what was going on. All I could do was stare at these two odd characters and the cut on Don's head. But then Don nodded in the direction of the tramp, leant forward and whispered, 'Don't worry, Newmarch, he doesn't speak a word of English. He's Polish, you see.' Don then tapped the side of his nose with one finger and winked at me. I almost gagged from the booze stench on his breath."

"What on earth did they want?"

"Well, before I could gather my wits, Don straightened himself up, adjusted the cat under his arm, and marched in, pushing past me. And this Polish tramp character followed."

I could see it all clearly in my mind. This was going rapidly downhill.

Danny continued, "In the living room Susan jumped up from the sofa as Don strode in. 'Ah the Lady Susan,' he began before she could say anything, 'how delightful it is to see you once again, looking frightfully attractive as always if I may say so.' And with that Don removed his fur hat, took Susan's right hand, bowed, and kissed it."

I'd seen Don do this before with other women. It was a sure-fire sign that he was completely plastered.

"Susan, who of course was shocked to see Don, found herself staring at a deep cut on the top of his head and the dried blood on the side of his face," said Danny. "But her attention was then diverted towards the arrival of Captain Josef Gustav Miloslaw Zoldak of the Polish Merchant Navy, gamboling into the room behind Don."

"Jesus."

"Quite," said Danny. "And, of course, Susan was now looking at me for an explanation as to what was going on and who this drunken tramp character staggering around our living room was. But Susan being Susan, she was also concerned about Don's head. 'Oh dear, we have to get that cut seen to,' she said. But Don was too pissed to understand and began doing that thing drunks do when they try to hide the fact. Taking a deep breath and focusing through one eye, with one eyebrow raised, he waved his hat around in a circle, then held it to his chest, bowed, and said, 'At your service, my dear lady. Now, what was the question again?'"

I could just imagine what poor Susan Newmarch was thinking by now. Danny went on.

"So Don rubbed his head, smearing blood all over his big sweaty forehead, and then gave something of an explanation. 'Ah, that. An ashtray across the head. One of those heavy glass buggers, pardon my French. Hurt like hell at the time, but no matter. It will be fine. We are here, it's Christmas Day, and we are ready to celebrate. Oh, and this is my good chum, Jaffe.' And with that he proudly held the stunned cat aloft, which was also now half-caked in blood."

"Where did he get the cat from?" I asked.

"Wait, I'm coming to that. Susan was now giving me raised eyebrows while I was still trying to come up with a story that wouldn't land me deeper in the mire. But Don began hiccuping and belching, to the extent that I thought he was about to throw up. Captain Josef then fell onto the couch and went to sleep."

Although I felt sorry for the Newmarches, I was beginning to find this ridiculous tale entertaining. But Danny was deadly serious.

"So," he continued, "I thought I would calm matters a little by offering Don a drink, but all I got from Susan was one of those 'what the hell are you doing' stares."

"Really, I wonder why?"

"Well, that's what I thought. But Don agreed. 'Splendid idea,

Newmarch,' he said. 'Mine's a single malt, and give the Polish reprobate anything you like, he'll drink anything. Cooking oil will do.' So, without looking again at Susan, I shoved off to get some drinks."

"But what did this Polish sea captain do? And where was the cat?"

"Well, Captain Josef of the Polish Merchant Navy was sound asleep on our couch. And the filthy cat, now free from Don's grasp, seemed hell-bent on exploring its new surroundings. After, crawling all over Captain Josef's head, it climbed up our bookshelf and surveyed the scene from up on high."

I'd been in the Newmarches flat a few times. Their living room wasn't that big, with a sofa taking up center stage and a dining table to one side. With a drunken Don swaying around, plus the Newmarches, and the tramp and a cat, I imagined there wouldn't have been much room left over.

"Then this bloody cat decided it wanted to play with Susan's silk curtains. She only had them made last week by one of the top fabric companies in Hong Kong. They were not cheap. The damn cat leapt to the top of the bookcase and then launched itself onto the curtains, sinking its claws into the fabric and holding on about five feet off the ground. Susan shouted at Don to get the cat out of there, but all Don did was to gaze on with the look of a proud father watching his son score a goal in a school football match. He replied with, 'I call him Jaffe because that's where I found him this afternoon, in a gutter in Jaffe Road in Wanchai, just off Lockhart Road, near PHQ.' Don put emphasis on PHQ, as though mentioning the place justified the whole thing."

I tried to picture it. Complete chaos. Danny just kept going.

"Susan was now frantic and shouting for me to get that damn cat down as it was ruining her curtains. Don had dropped into my armchair and was chuckling away to himself, and if that wasn't bad enough, Captain Josef then got to his feet, staggered around a bit, and began fiddling with his trousers, looking for somewhere to relieve himself."

"So not an ideal ending to Christmas Day, then, Danny?"

"There's more," said Danny. "Once I caught the cat and threw the bloody thing out, I came back into the living room to find Susan in tears over the damage to her curtains. Captain Josef Gustav Miloslaw Zoldak of the Polish Merchant Navy was sitting on the floor and that drunkard Diamond Don Bishop was snoring his head off in my armchair. There was nothing left for me to do. I downed a stiff drink and went to bed."

"You just left them there?"

"Yes."

"Where's everyone this morning?"

"When I woke up, they'd gone and there was no sign of the cat."

"And Susan?"

"She was still there. But the only thing she has said to me all morning is that she is never going to speak to me again for the rest of her life."

13

TAI O
大澳

"IF YER CAN handle life with Don Bishop, yer can handle anything," Dougie Kerr held his beer glass up to the light.

It was just after 1700 and the Mariners Rest was empty apart from Dougie, myself, and Tony the barman. "How long have you been on PL 1?" asked Dougie.

"Fifteen months. I have been there since I left PTS. You know that, Dougie."

"Some would liken fifteen months on PL 1 to a prison sentence," he said after taking a swig of beer. "I served on the command launch with Bishop and found the man a bloody nutcase. It's remarkable how you have survived as his second-in-command fer so long."

"Funny you should say that. I've been thinking about applying for a transfer. Not just off PL 1 but out of East Sector altogether."

Dougie looked skeptical and shook his head. "You sure about that? You know as well as anyone that Bishop doesn't like traitors. 'Deceitful' is what he calls those who want out. He takes a transfer request out of his eastern empire personally." Dougie rubbed his chin in thought. "You know he has the capacity to make your life hell."

"That's probably true, but after fifteen months, I'm looking at my options. I'll probably put my request in as soon as I find something suitable. Anyway, how did you manage to escape PL 1 without being lynched?"

"Simple," said Dougie, flicking an imaginary speck of dust from his lapel. "I acted dumb and deliberately screwed things up." He smiled, raised his drink in triumph. "It drove Bishop mad. He just couldn't stomach my 'stupidity.' He actually kicked me off PL 1 himself. He is convinced I'm as thick as a brick."

"Yes," I said, chuckling at his recollection. "He's mentioned it, more than once."

It was my turn to raise a glass, this time to Dougie's cunning ways. "Here's to you, Dougie. I couldn't pull off a stunt like that. I don't have your thespian skills. I'll apply for a transfer in the conventional way and take my chances."

After all this time, the thought of working elsewhere appealed to me, and not just because of the notion of no longer working with Don. I also fancied taking on new challenges in a different environment. Other Marine sectors were busy dealing with illegal immigrants from China and refugees from Vietnam. This fascinated me. Joe Poon was full of stories from up in the border area. I'd had my fill of the rough seas out east, and life with Don had run its course. I needed a change. But as Dougie rightly pointed out, it wasn't going to be easy. To be granted a transfer I would need to apply, in writing, to the head of the Marine Police, and before he would agree to a move he would consult my sector commander, Don. How could I do this without being branded a traitor?

The following week, I was back at the East Sector Base reporting for a three-day patrol on PL 1. I found Dougie in the inspector's room.

"Here," he said thrusting a bundle of papers at me. "You'll

find this interesting."

"Vacancies?" I said, looking at the first page. I looked down further, to the Marine section. A sub divisional inspector posting at Tai O on Lantau Island would be available in August.

There were a few resident inspectorate positions for Marine officers at police stations on some of the larger islands such as Lantau and Cheung Chau. While I wouldn't be working on Marine launches for the duration, which was not ideal, this remote station posting could be the opportunity I had been waiting for. It was something different and I would be my own boss. And Tai O is at the opposite end of the colony from East Sector. I'd no longer be under Don's command; I'd be out of his clutches. This was my chance — and I decided to seize it. I read the vacancy announcement once more, grabbed a blank memo, inserted it into the typewriter and began to type.

Two weeks later, I received word that the job was mine. At the end of the month, I was going to be transferred from East Sector to Islands Division. But how could this be? The District Marine Commander would have consulted Don before sanctioning it, but Don hadn't said anything. I was suspicious. I was worried. Next day, I arrived at the East Sector Marine Base to sign on duty, get into uniform, and board PL 1.

"Mr Bishop is looking for you," said the duty sergeant as I walked into the report room.

"I thought he might be," I said, placing my kit down and making for his office at the end of the corridor. Since hearing my request had been approved, I'd been dreading facing Don. I felt sure he would be furious with me for wanting to desert his empire.

Don's door was open. He was at his desk reading a file.

"Ah, the new chief of police of Lantau is here. Come in, come in, take a seat," he said, with a worrying smirk on his face. "So, off to Tai O, then?"

"Yes, sir, I thought it would be good for my career development. Bit of variety, my own command, my own police station, even." I could feel the sweat forming in the middle of my back. In silence, Don continued to read his file. Then he looked up.

"Yes, of course, absolutely. It will do you the world of good. It did for me."

"You worked at Tai O?" I asked, surprised at his response.

"Oh yes. I was the SDI out there, in the late sixties, didn't you know? Good days. I was lord and master of Lantau then, took great pride in keeping those villagers in check. Had to let them know who was boss. It'll be good to go back and shake them up a bit."

"Go back?"

"Well, you will be lonely out there on your own, young Leslie. I will come and visit when I'm off duty, stay a night or two. There's plenty of room in the inspector's quarters above the station. We can go for a few beers in the village in the evenings. They will all be surprised to see me back there."

I just stared back at him in disbelief. I couldn't believe what I was hearing. Then it got worse.

"We can take a drive over the mountains to Tung Chung. That's the small fishing village on the north side of the island. It's part of your patch anyway and you will need to go there. It will be one of your duties, we can go in Short Arse, bah." He laughed.

"Short Arse?"

"Yes, Short Arse and Long Bottom, your two Land Rover police patrol cars. Tai O has two patrol vehicles. One is a big long-wheelbase one, which I always called Long Bottom. They use it for moving officers and kit around the island. And the other, your personal run-around, is a short-wheelbase jeep, which I used to call Short Arse, naturally. You can drive me over to Tung

Chung in Short Arse."

Don sat back and guffawed with laughter again. I felt as though a black cloud had formed above my head.

"What's so interesting about Tung Chung?" I asked.

"Grandfather Bennie lives there."

"You have family out there?"

"Not my family. Old Bennie Fung lives in Tung Chung village. He's about one hundred years old, or at least he looks it. He lived in London when he was a boy, speaks English with a cockney accent. Mad as a hatter. He walks around that little fishing village wearing a bowler hat and carries a furled umbrella under his arm. Spends most of the day swearing at the other villagers in English. They can't understand him, of course. He will love you."

"Why?"

"Because Bennie thinks of himself as cockney. He loves the company of white men, preferably British of course, and there aren't many of those around on Lantau. So, when he sees you, he will want to sit you down and ply you with grog," Don said, snorting with laughter. "He has the best collection of fine cognac. I used to spend days over there listening to Bennie babble away while polishing off his brandy. It'll be good to go back again."

I left Don's office with my dream of village policing in tatters. Now I understood why my transfer had gone through without a hitch. He obviously knew everything about Tai O and the characters who lived there and, by the sound of what I had just heard, he intended to use my new posting as an excuse to go back and run riot once again. I pictured those balmy summer evenings shattered by Don gamboling through my island utopia. But it was too late now. Everything had been approved. Would I ever escape the world of Diamond Don Bishop? I felt the dungeon doors closing behind me once more.

A couple of days after hearing Don's idea of how my time on Lantau would be spent, I received a phone call from Rob Naylor, the outgoing inspector at Tai O.

"Come over for the day. I'll show you around and you can meet the staff," he said. I headed over the very next morning.

Tai O was one of two police stations on Lantau Island, the largest island in Hong Kong. Mui Wo station on the eastern side and Tai O on the far western tip, straddling fifty square miles of mountainous terrain. Only a dirt track of a road joined one end of the island to the other. Rob Naylor met me off the ferry and we walked up to the station, a colonial chalk-white edifice sitting on a hill above the pier.

"Tai O police station was built by the British in 1902 as an anti-pirate outpost," explained Naylor as we walked. "Just look here, the walls of the police station here are two-feet thick." Naylor slapped the white stone walls of the police station, "built to withstand cannon fire."

"Cannon fire?"

"Yes, piracy was rife back then, so they were in need of robust defenses. In the mid-nineteenth century, a joint-British and American Navy took on a fleet of thirty-six pirate vessels and fifteen-hundred Chinese pirates in The Battle of Tai O Bay just around the point from here." He pointed out to sea. "About five hundred of the pirates were killed in action, drowned or were wounded, with a thousand more taken as prisoners. Fourteen of the pirate ships sank in the battle. Years later, just after the construction of the police station here, three police constables were killed in another exchange with pirates on the nearby island of Cheung Chau."

As we reached the station gates I could see that the windows were encased in heavy metal shutters. "Those shutters are also a leftover from those anti-piracy days," he explained. "You can see they are fitted with vertical slits so when under attack the officers inside could return fire." He pointed up. "The station also comes with a watchtower and a searchlight, and there are four cannons overlooking the perimeter fence."

I looked out across the Pearl River. Scattered further out to sea, were several small deserted islands. The sunlight reflected off the green-blue ocean. "This is a wonderful position," I said. "And this place is more like a castle than a police station."

As I spoke, a large black mongrel came running down the pathway, its tail wagging furiously. "Ah, you will be inheriting the station dog here, by the way. Come on, Ratbag," said Naylor patting the dog's head. "He's getting old now, poor thing. He's been here over ten years. He barks too much, but he excels at his job, which is primarily keeping snakes out of the police station." The dog ran around Naylor's legs excitedly. "The island is crawling with them and Ratbag here loves nothing more than to patrol the long grass, kill snakes, and then leave them in a bloodied mess at the foot of the station steps, as a warning to others. Rumor is that he inherited this tactic from his first owner, Diamond Don Bishop, who I think you know."

"Yes, I do, thanks for reminding me."

Naylor knew Don well, as did everyone in the Marine Police. Bishop's rabble-rousing reputation seemed to come up in most conversations I had with other officers.

We spent the remainder of the morning walking around the station and meeting the staff, which included the person who was to be my amah, or housekeeper.

"This is Ah Sam," said Naylor. The old woman looked to be in her sixties and was well under five feet tall. She was dressed in a black, formal Chinese pajama style suit, with the baggy trousers that stopped a few inches above the ankles. Her greying hair was pulled tightly back in a bun. Naylor made the introductions and she graciously bowed her head in response. I smiled and told her in my best Cantonese that I was pleased to meet her and that I was very happy she was going to be looking after me.

"Ah Sam has worked at the station since the Japanese left in 1945, so thirty-three years," said Naylor. "She will cook your breakfast, lunch, and dinner; clean your quarters; do your washing; iron all your clothes; and prepare your uniforms each morning with effortless efficiency." Ah Sam smiled, bowed and scurried off towards the kitchens. "Let's go up the Officers' Mess and I will tell you a bit more about the station."

"Officers' Mess?" I queried. "But I thought the SDI was the only officer posted out here?"

"He is, or rather you will be," replied Naylor leading the way. "Nevertheless you have the entire top floor of the station as your quarters. That's three bedrooms, a dining room and an Officers' Mess, which doubles as your living room. And, of course, a view to die for."

We climbed up a flight of sturdy wooden stairs. At the top, there was a heavy metal grill door.

"I'll explain why that's here after we have finished our tour," he said, noticing my puzzled look at the door's sturdy padlock.

Naylor led the way along the corridor that ran the entire length of the upper floor. Through the wide arched windows, there were clear views of the South China Sea and a cluster of small islands. The last room at the end of the corridor was the Officers' Mess, or my living room which formed the upper westernmost corner of the building. Through the white-framed, louvered windows I looked again at the South China Sea. The sky was a cloudless blue and the sea was flat calm. A three-masted Chinese junk, under sail, was making its way south out of the Pearl River. It hardly seemed to be moving in the gentle breeze. There was an overwhelming silence.

"This is incredible!" I exclaimed. "It's as though we have been trapped in time. And this room is how I imagine a suite at the Raffles or the Peninsula Hotel."

"It's better than that, Les," said Naylor sitting down at the bar and pulling a cold drink from the fridge. "We are so cut-off out here that hardly anyone from HQ visits. It takes half a day to get out here from Marine Headquarters, and so half a day to get back. Senior officers can't be bothered to make the trip out."

"*Saan goh, wong daai yuen.* The mountains are high, the king is far away," I said.

"Exactly. You are going to become one of the very privileged few to be posted to Tai O. As you observed earlier, living out here is like stepping back in time, by about one hundred years, I'd say." He smiled.

"I must admit, we appear cut off from the outside world," I said looking out to sea once more. "What do you do for company, if you don't mind me asking?"

"You mean female company, I assume?" Naylor smiled. "The first thing to understand is that you have no private life in Tai O." He pointed out of the window, back towards the village proper. "Everyone out here knows everything about everyone else, especially about the foreigner that lives in the big white police station on the hill. As you have seen, to get to the station you must walk through the center of the village and then along the coastal path. Anyone visiting is followed by a thousand pairs of inquisitive eyes, every step of the way."

"A bit daunting for a girl, I suppose?"

Naylor pulled a bit of a face. "Especially a local Hong Kong girl. They understand the gossip, and occasional offhand remark. Oh, and don't even think of trying it on with any of the local village girls. They all have hundreds of relatives living around here, all of whom will follow her up the station if she is brave enough to visit. That is a complication you really don't need."

I looked out again across the sparkling blue waters of the South China Sea. With hardly a breath of wind, the junk had barely moved. The silence was captivating. Seductive, even. I felt good about being here. It was a unique place with a unique history. I felt lucky to have secured the post. I was convinced I'd made the right decision to take on this job. I also had a feeling that working at Tai O was not going to be the sleepy outpost that many would have me believe.

"You were going to explain about that heavy metal door?" I asked.

"Ah, yes, the cage door," said Naylor leading the way back into the Mess. "Locals will have you believe there are supernatural companions for you here in the station." He laughed at the expression on my face. "In the form of two ghosts."

"Ghosts?"

"One ghost is that of a former Indian constable by the name of Teja Singh. Singh was posted out here over sixty years ago. He died in the corridor, just there, on 17 July 1918." Naylor pointed towards the open door to the corridor. "The commanding officer at Tai O at the time was Crown Police Sergeant Thomas Cecil Glendinning who, several days before, had detained Singh for the theft of cash and a wrist watch from the junior officers' barracks. The following day, after being charged with larceny at the Hong Kong Magistracy, Singh was allowed out on bail and returned to Tai O to collect his personal possessions. While in the barracks downstairs, Singh found a loaded gun belonging to one of the other off-duty constables, so he took it and went in search of Glendinning and revenge. He found his commanding officer sitting at the report room desk," said Naylor, pointing towards the stairs. "As Glendinning looked up from his work Singh shot him once in the chest. As the SDI Tai O slumped forward onto the report ledger, Singh shot him a second time, this time in the forehead, killing Glendinning instantly."

"Bloody hell. Murder."

Rob nodded. "So, everyone else in the station, upon hearing the gunfire, dived for cover, including Glendinning's wife, who had been in the report room talking to her husband at the time."

"The wife was there too?"

"It must have been awful for Mrs Glendinning to see her husband shot and killed," said Naylor, "but she had no time to think as Singh turned the gun on her and fired several more shots."

I sat, open mouthed, hooked on the story.

"She ran for the stairs and up here to the officers' quarters where her baby son was sleeping. Singh followed up that staircase firing more shots as he went. Once up here, Mrs Glendinning managed to barricade herself and her baby son in one of the bedrooms, out there." Naylor flicked a thumb towards the adjacent room. "This kept Singh at bay for long enough until an armed shore patrol from a Marine Police launch turned up. Realizing he was now outnumbered, Singh, in one last gesture of defiance, started a fire up here on the top floor."

"He set fire to the station?"

Naylor nodded. "A large portion of the upper floor here was gutted as a result, but Mrs Glendinning managed to lower the baby out of a back window into the arms of one of the station staff, then she jumped down herself. They were both saved."

"What happened to Singh?"

"The Marine patrol tried to talk him down, told him the game was up. But he refused to listen and eventually turned the gun on himself. He died just there, as I said before, in the corridor. We still have a news clipping from the day." Naylor pushed a file across the bar. Inside was a faded sixty-year-old copy of the

China Mail:

The SDI Tai O, Crown Police Sergeant Thomas Cecil Glendinning, who was only thirty-six, was buried today with full Police Force honors at the Hong Kong Cemetery in Happy Valley. At the funeral the pastor of the Union Church read the eulogy. He said: 'Crown Sergeant Glendinning held his post at a remote and backward spot, the only European in a large population reputed by those who know it to contain many evil elements. Few of us perhaps give much thought to the position of a man in such circumstances as these — solely responsible from hour to hour for British law and order in a part which pirates and other ill-doers haunt, with only Asiatic subordinates to assist him.'

"I wonder what *evil elements* await me at this *remote and backward spot* once I become *solely responsible from hour to hour for British law and order*," I said.

"*Pirates and ill-doers* no doubt," replied Naylor smiling. "And remember, you've *only Asiatic subordinates to assist you.*"

I tried to imagine the scene here on that day sixty years ago. Poor Glendinning, murdered at his desk by one of his own men.

"So, returning to the matter of the cage door at the top of the stairs," said Naylor. "After Glendinning's murder, two things happened here. Firstly, a telephone was installed at the station. I am sure it was the same machine that is in place today. As you saw in my office, it is that enormous contraption that takes up half the space on my desk. The receiver weighs a ton by the way, and in order to be heard by the person on the other end you will need to shout your half of the conversation down the trumpet-shaped mouthpiece. And if it's raining, the damn thing packs up altogether."

"And the cage door?"

"That was the second addition. After the murder, that grill

door was installed across the top of the stairs leading into the quarters, so the resident inspector could lock himself in if he felt he was about to be murdered."

Naylor looked for a reaction.

"Have you ever locked it?" I asked.

"Honestly, no. But I actually like that unsightly door because it makes me feel there is something of a divide between work and my upstairs living quarters." He took a drink. "And, of course, I know that if I was about to be shot by one of my own men, I could lock it." He smiled again.

"And the two ghosts are?" I asked.

"Glendinning and Singh, of course. It's believed they both walk the corridors of the station at night. Glendinning between the report room and your office, and Singh is up here in your quarters. Do you believe in ghosts?"

I don't, but I humored him. "Have they been seen?"

"The night shift claim to have seen them many times, usually on a dark and stormy night."

"Have you ever seen them?"

"No, but I have been woken by Glendinning's bagpipes." Naylor practically fell off his stool laughing at the look on my face.

Despite the tales of the police station's paranormal activity, and Rob Naylor's attempt at humor, Tai O's colorful past made the place even more appealing to me. Notwithstanding Don's threat to come and stay, I was looking forward to working there. While the skylines of Hong Kong and Kowloon reached further towards the clouds as rampant construction continued and the streets became ever-more congested with cars, smog, and swelling populace, life on Lantau meandered along at a pace of its own, detached from the worries of 1970s city life. In the weeks that followed, I said my goodbyes to everyone at East

Sector. Kwan reminded me that Marine is one big family and that he and I would surely work together again in the future. As a parting gift, Dougie presented me with his personal collection of girlie magazines. "There's no women out there, you know," he said handing over a stack wrapped in brown paper. Finally, there was an unexpected convivial farewell from Don Bishop. "Be seeing you soon, young Leslie," he said shaking my hand.

Had I really escaped the Bishop Empire without consequences? I figured only time would tell. At least he hadn't crushed my hand this time.

14

AM I UNDER ARREST, INSPECTOR?
幫辦，係唔係拉咗我

THERE WAS NO road between Tai O police station and the village, only a mile-long narrow coastal path, so in my first few days there I found myself walking a lot. The indigenous villagers of Tai O are Tankas, or sea gypsies, who traditionally live on junks. Over the years, most built their homes on solid ground, although some still preferred living in stilt structures dotted along the edges of the narrow creek that ran through the center of the village.

My daily sunrise patrol became a highlight, just as the village came to life. I passed by the modest homes as cinnamon-skinned men with cigarettes hanging from their mouths chatted and prepared their nets and boats for the day's work at sea. Women dressed in sarongs sat on the stoop cradling their young while others milled around inside cooking breakfast. The only sounds at that time of the day were the clinking of pots and the sizzle of stoves, offset by the gentle splash of waves as they kissed the shore and the cacophony of children's laughter as they skipped to school. I would pass this scene and these people each day, as a foreigner and an outsider but also as their protector. It was an odd state of affairs, one which drew affection from some and rejection from others. My morning patrols were a steady mix of smiles and suspicious stares.

There was one other white man living on my half of Lantau, the priest of Tai O, Father Don Giovanni Vigano. Rob briefed me about him before he left.

"The old priest has led quite an amazing life, and is a bit of a character," he said, "I think you and the father will get along very well. Your challenge will be language. Unfortunately he can only speak a lick of English, but he can get by in Cantonese, and is fluent in Mandarin. He spent his early years as a priest in northern China and, like many other Catholic missionaries working in China in the late 1940s, was imprisoned as the country turned to communism. After being incarcerated for four years, he was freed and he made his way to Hong Kong. Father Giovanni has been the priest of Tai O ever since."

After a few days in the job, I decided to pay the father a visit. The chapel was a modest structure, located on the outskirts of the village. I walked up the tree-lined track to the front of the church, pushed open the main door and peered into the darkness. The air inside was cool. Sunlight streamed in as I ventured a little further, the rays falling across the first line of pews and a small wooden table stacked with bibles.

"Les! Les. Is it Les?" came a lively, accented voice from the shadows.

"Yes," I said immediately, trying to make out the owner of the voice.

"Come, come," said the voice again. "I am here."

As my eyes became accustomed to the change in light I took a couple of cautious steps into the church, doing my best not to trip over anything, but only succeeding in walking directly into the advancing figure of Father Don Giovanni Vigano as he emerged out of the darkness. I looked down at a small, slender man. He had a bright smile and twinkling green eyes that reflected the sunlight as it washed across his face. He grabbed my right hand between both his and shook it enthusiastically.

"Come, come, Les. Please, this way," he said, guiding me through the church and into a back office. "Si, si, a-Rob he tell me, Les will come. He say Les will come, si," he muttered as he fussed around putting away papers and straightening cushions. "Please, sit," he said, pointing to a vacant armchair. "Tea," he announced with a broad smile.

I nodded and he rushed out, returning after a minute with a tray of small porcelain cups and a plate of delicate pastries.

In a mixture of broken English, elementary Cantonese, and some Italian, the latter of which I understood little, I ascertained that Father Giovanni loved three things: God, altar wine, and football. 'Inter Milano eez-a-much-a-betta than-a Leev-a-pool.' He also knew Don well and they had formed an oddball friendship when he had served in Tai O some ten years before. The father had a gaggle of stories about him and acted them out for me, which made me chuckle, watching a sixty-year-old wiry streak of a man pretending to be an overweight oaf. He stuck out his belly, hunched his shoulders, scowled, and staggered around, kicking things and shouting obscenities in broken English. 'Out-a-my-way. Bah!'

Over the next few months our friendship grew, while our methods of communication remained basic. I discovered that the father's Cantonese was actually very good so the villagers found it highly comical that their only two foreign residents often communicated in their own tongue. When the father and I dined together in one of the village restaurants, the locals would pull up their chairs so they could eavesdrop. When I got a little muddled with my Cantonese, there was always advice shouted from the crowd that had gathered at the rear. When one of us got a sentence or phrase spot on, it would be accompanied by laughter and applause. Dinner was never dull in Tai O.

It was a Saturday morning and I left the station to walk through the village to where I parked my patrol jeep. As it was a weekend, I planned to drive over to Tung Chung to visit our police post there. I had a team of four officers stationed at the post. They were four of my most trusted men and, while they were mostly self-sufficient, it was my duty to visit them regularly and see how they were getting on. Being a Saturday the center of Tai O village had been set up as an open-air bazaar. As I walked down the track, I could tell by the noise from the main square that the market was already in full throw. From the outskirts, I could hear the shouts and screams of the stall-holders doing their best to out-do each other and sell their produce. Bargain offers, two for the price of one, three for the price of two. The sellers' voices ricocheted off the warm stone walls of the village shops and through the branches of the leafy trees that surrounded the market.

The first row of stalls I came to were crammed with every kind of seafood imaginable, most of it still alive. Crowds of people clustered around to see large fish, lobster, crab, and eel splashing for their lives, desperate for a way out of the enormous, solid, open-topped glass tanks. Villagers and visitors alike argued and discussed the merits of the thrashing sea creatures on show. I made my way across the square to where a row of trestle tables piled high with garments had been set up. The women vendors screeched the merits of their goods. Just as was the custom in mainland China, the older villagers of Tai O didn't trust banks with their hard-earned cash, preferring to keep their life's savings in gold, close by, where they could taste it — in their teeth. This was certainly apparent today by the number of gold molars on display, as the old women made their marketing pitch, with each set of teeth an indication of how good business had been.

I passed a line of rickety stalls piled high with loose shirts and trousers, all of different colors and textures. Women buyers jostled for position, keen to capture the best bargain. I noticed a girl at one of the stalls. She had her back to me as I approached. She was examining a light blue shirt, which she held up for a better look. The girl was young and pretty, her raven black hair pulled tightly back into a ponytail that hung down to just below her waist. She glanced in my direction, but quickly turned away, tossing her head to one side so that her long ponytail flew across her back.

"This is nice, I like this one," the girl said in English, holding up the shirt for her friend to see. The girl examined the stitching and felt the quality of the cloth. "I think I'll buy this for my boyfriend," she said turning and looking directly at me. "What do you think?" She held up the shirt up in front of my face.

I stopped, taken by surprise and found myself looking at a light-blue denim shirt, behind which, I felt sure was the prettiest girl I'd ever seen.

"Would you wear this?" said the voice from behind the shirt, she peered out, blinking. She smiled. For a moment, I was speechless.

"You buy shirt for police inspector," crowed the old woman from behind the stall, "I give you special price." She cackled, showing a neat row of gold teeth.

I stepped forward and felt the material. My attention was focused entirely on the girl. "I think your boyfriend is very lucky," I replied. "If you buy him this shirt, I mean."

The girl turned her back on me and threw the shirt back on the stall. Her girlfriend held her hand up to stifle a laugh. I couldn't take my eyes off this girl. She was stunning.

"Am I under arrest, inspector?" she said, still rummaging through the garments. I detected a smile.

"That can be arranged," I said, joining in her game.

"This shirt won't fit you," she said, prodding the blue shirt. "It's Chinese size, not *gwailo* size." She turned and looked directly at me. Her eyes were eager, expressive. She had an olive tint to her complexion. I noticed that she wore little make-up. Her skin glowed, completely flawless.

Realizing that every other pair of eyes in the market were now taking more than a passing interest in my conversation with this girl, I asked, "Are you visiting, or do you live on Lantau?"

"Just visiting," she said, pulling at her pony tail. "We came here early this morning on the ferry from Central.

Maria was a little taller than the other women at the stall even though she was wearing flat shoes. She wore a simple white dress. A narrow belt accentuated her slender waist. She explained that this was her first visit to Tai O. "My friend here, and I came for something different to do, to see a place not many Hong Kong people have seen."

During the next half an hour, we walked through the village to the road proper, where the two girls planned to take a bus across the island to Mui Wo in the east. As we walked, Maria Tan Wing-kei told me about her family. She was eighteen years old. Her father owned a garment business in North Kowloon and she, as the eldest of six children, was expected to eventually take over the business. She had an infectious personality. She spoke with excitement about her plans to carry on her father's company. She asked me about myself and was surprised when I told her that I actually lived above Tai O police station. "You live out here?" she said hesitantly, pointing at the station perched amongst the trees on a distant hill.

"Yes, this is where I work. But they do let me out occasionally, for good behavior."

She smiled. "You really live up there?" she asked again.

"Alone?"

"Yes, I am afraid I do live up there, but I'm not exactly alone. There's a whole posse of policemen, plus a dog, and some snakes. It can be quite crowded at times. Oh, and two ghosts."

She gave me a look, searching, truth or humor? I decided to clarify things.

"I've never seen the ghosts."

She began to laugh, quickly covering her mouth with a hand. It was at that moment I that I decided I had to see this girl again, and I told her so. She feigned surprise.

"Me? How? I hardly know you. You live out here. I don't know. It's so far."

As her bus pulled away, Maria turned and looked back and smiled, and I glanced down at a piece of paper she had given me, upon which was written a telephone number. I carefully folded it, put it in my pocket, climbed into the Land Rover and headed for Tung Chung.

In the week that followed, my thoughts were often of Maria, but with so much still to learn about the job and the surrounding area, I had to try and put her to the back of my mind, at least for now.

Lantau's villages are dotted over the mountainous terrain and along the craggy coastline of the island, which meant my patrols, both on foot and by jeep, consumed a large chunk of my day. Aside from the occasional dispute over a rogue animal or promiscuous wife, there wasn't that much policing needed on the island. I imagined that law enforcement on Lantau hadn't changed much in sixty years and that my routine day was much the same as Glendinning's back in 1918.

Before he left, I asked Rob Naylor which village I should visit first.

"Sha Lo Wan on the northern coast. I haven't been there for

some time, so they are due a visit." He pointed to the large map that covered one of the report room walls. "You should follow the coastal path and skirt around the base of the island's mountain slopes. The villages in this area rarely have visitors so you should send word beforehand as the elders like to prepare."

At 0530 one morning, during those first weeks, our foot patrol set off from the station. It was an early start but I wanted to avoid the worst of the day's oppressive heat. In addition to myself, there was one NCO and three constables. Dressed in bush gear, we trekked slowly in single file along the coastal trail with my sergeant leading the way towards the village at Sha Lo Wan. We all carried long walking poles, primarily to thrash through the undergrowth, but also to tackle snakes should the need arise. From high points, as the sun came up, we could see clearly across the Pearl River to the Chinese coast. The only sounds that accompanied us on these long hikes were our boots on the track, the occasional curse after becoming snagged by a thorn bush, and the wind off the sea. It was hard to believe that this was part of one of the world's busiest cities.

Three hours later, we arrived at the outskirts of Sha Lo Wan. News of our visit had been received and a group of elders were waiting to greet us. There were handshakes all round, after which our party was led towards the village proper. As we walked a bevy of laughing children joined in, and by the time we arrived at the main hall the entire population seemed to have tagged onto our group. I felt like the ringmaster of a traveling circus as it trooped into town.

Outside the main hall an aged gentleman, introduced as the village representative, awaited us.

"This is the VR, Mr Chan." My sergeant took on the job of performing the introductions. "And this," the sergeant pointed towards me, "is the new police inspector at Tai O, Inspector Bird."

There were nods and smiles all round as we shook hands. I noticed lots of curious faces in the ever-growing throng. Children risked coming a little closer, pushing between the legs of their parents so as to get a better look at the action.

Rob Naylor had been vague when explaining what exactly happens during one of these visits. "Oh, it's mostly posturing and bluster from the village elders," he had said. "They like to use our visits to impress upon the other villagers that they are the ones in charge."

Armed with no other information than this, I was ushered into the main hall and to a single chair positioned on a raised platform facing row upon row of seats, which were quickly filling up with noisy villagers. Chatter resonated around the hall, while many of the women covered their mouths as they conversed with their neighbors. The whole gathering was a hotchpotch of shuffling chairs and excited laughter, mostly from the children, who were being seated to the rear.

As I sat in my elevated position, I began to feel uneasy. I was very conscious that all eyes were now on me and that I was going to be the focal point of some kind of official event. What the hell was going on? I looked around for my team. They were seated off to one side, and were now huddled in conversation, preoccupied with something else and paying no attention to what was going on out front. Under my breath, I began to curse Naylor. He would have known about this, but hadn't said a word. I was beginning to suspect that I had been set up and, at this very minute, Naylor was sitting in the Mariners Rest back in Marine HQ having a good old chuckle to himself. But I had no time to reflect on that now as the elders were filing in, each one bowing to me, as though I was a visiting emperor. I was obviously the star attraction and, prepared or not, it was now show time.

As the hall fell silent, all eyes turned towards the main door as Mr Chan walked in and took up a position at the center of the hall between myself, on my podium, and the elders and the villagers. An older man followed Mr Chan. This old chap looked crestfallen. He had the appearance of someone whose whole world had collapsed around him. Intrigued by this, and suspecting it was the commencement of affairs, I sat up and looked as formal as I could.

"Mr Wong's pig has died," announced Mr Chan in a loud and commanding voice, the force of which took me a little by surprise. Mr Chan pointed towards the old man. "Pig farming has been Mr Wong's livelihood for his entire life."

There was silence from the audience, although some were nodding in agreement.

"But now he has no means to support either himself or his sick wife. What can be done?" The VR waved his hand to indicate a conclusion of his summary of Mr Wong's plight. Everyone in the hall looked to me.

"It's your turn to speak, sir," whispered my sergeant from the side. For a second I was taken aback. My turn to speak? What was I supposed to say? Rob Naylor had said nothing about me being required to provide on-the-spot resolution to the villagers' dilemmas, and from an elevated position in front of the entire population. But it was too late now. Alright, I thought, stop looking stunned. I straightened up and coughed.

"Thank you, Mr Chan, for explaining Mr Wong's, err, predicament," I began in a voice I hoped would carry to the back of the hall. "These are tough times. I offer Mr Wong my condolences."

I looked to Mr Chan for a response, perhaps a nod of approval, but my initial effort was met with blank stares from both the VR and the audience. I needed to say more.

"Would it be feasible for Mr Wong to acquire another pig?" I asked hopefully.

Mr Chan scratched his head, looked down at his shoes, and let out a sigh. The hall remained silent. Then I had an idea, I took out my notebook.

"I will make a record of Mr Wong's case and pass the information to the Social Services Department of the Hong Kong government. I will ask what assistance can be offered."

I looked up at Mr Chan as I wrote, but the silence continued. He shifted uneasily from one foot to the other. My offer wasn't enough. "I will also follow up this case myself, and will send word once I receive the government's response."

This time Mr Chan looked directly at me and gave a satisfied nod. The entire hall let out a combined sigh of relief and everyone began to chatter at once. My solution, as improvised as it was, had been accepted. As Mr Wong was led away by an elder-escort, I looked over to my sergeant who smiled and gave me the thumbs-up. I had passed the test. Then, an old woman was led out to the center of the hall. Bloody hell, the pig farmer was just the first case. There was going to be more. How long had they been saving up their problems, waiting for our visit?

"Old Woman Ho's cabbage patch has been mysteriously damaged," announced Mr Chan in the same authoritative tone as in the first case. He pointed to the old woman who was now standing where Mr Wong had stood before her. Old Woman Ho nodded in agreement with the VR's opening statement and looked to me with a hopeful expression on her face.

"She suspects foul play," continued the head man. I began to take out my notebook, but before I could write anything, Mr Chan offered circumstantial evidence. "But, on the other hand, the damage could have been caused by a recent heavy rainstorm. What can be done?" he concluded looking to me once more.

It was becoming clear that the older generation on Lantau

Island looked upon the police as the ultimate authority on just about everything. Not only criminal matters but anything, such as deceased farm animals and swamped vegetable patches. I was also beginning to realize that there was a belief that if the chief of police so wished, he could wave a magic wand and all would be well once more. But I wasn't sure what the VR was getting at in Old Woman Ho's case. Rain damage?

I looked over at my sergeant and motioned him to come over. He shuffled across the hall in a contorted, bent-double bow, as though he'd been summoned by royalty. I assumed his deformed, kowtow-hobble was his idea of respect for the occasion.

"What do you think the VR is asking?" I whispered to Quasimodo once he'd perched himself next to me.

"It's about a cabbage patch, sir," he said, craning his neck to look up.

"Yes, I know that, sergeant. But is he giving us a clue? Is there a hidden meaning, something I've missed?" The sergeant looked blank. "About the heavy rain?" I said in the hope it would trigger something.

"Rain, sir? I am not sure, sir. What do you think, sir?"

"That's what I am asking you. What's he getting at?"

All eyes in the hall were upon us as the sergeant and I discussed this woman's vegetables. The sergeant looked confused, "I don't know, sir."

"All right, it doesn't matter, go back to your seat. And whatever you do, don't curtsy." He shuffled backwards, head still bowed, royally dismissed.

I nodded at Mr Chan, trying to look as though I knew what was going on while scribbling some nonsense or other in my notebook for effect. I then began what I hoped would be an acceptable solution to this second serious case.

"After the conclusion of this meeting," I announced, "I will conduct a thorough investigation. No leaf unturned." There was more nodding and whispers among the elders. "I, together with my police patrol officers…" I pointed to my clueless sergeant and his team, seated to one side "…will visit the cabbage patch in question and get to the bottom of the matter."

Mr Chan nodded once more and Old Woman Ho was led away seemingly happy that her dire predicament would not only be the subject of a formal police investigation but also that it had been broadcast to the entire village population.

Next case was Mr Chan himself. He took up position at the center of the hall and put his hands on his hips.

"The village school is not receiving enough help from the District Office," he said pointing outside. "The roof leaks when it rains and some of the windows are broken. It is in need of repair. Our request for funding has been met with no response."

He looked directly at me and folded his arms. This was something I could help with. I made a couple of notes.

"I am visiting the Islands District Office tomorrow morning," I said. "I will personally bring this matter up with the district officer. It is unreasonable to expect the children to study in such conditions. I will send word of the response."

The head man nodded, seemingly satisfied with my solution. He then signaled for the next case to be brought forward. All in all, there were nine cases heard that morning, all of which ended with me promising to either deal with them personally or to be in contact with the appropriate government department for action. Everyone seemed happy with the outcome, in particular my sergeant who, I later discovered, had won a considerable amount of money from his three constables by betting that I would be able to maneuver my way through the Sha Lo Wan theatricals. No thanks to him, I might add.

Afterwards, as tea was served, I took a walk around the

hall and chatted with some of the elders. On a wall at the rear, I spotted a black-and-white framed photograph of a group of villagers. Right in the middle, at the front, and twice the size of everyone else, was Don Bishop, in full police uniform and looking like his hemorrhoids were playing up. At Don's feet was a huge dead boar.

"Mr Bishop," explained the VR appearing at my shoulder. "He liked to hunt with us."

The VR smiled and looked for a reaction. Hunting was illegal, but obviously Don, as chief of police, had not only condoned it, but had also taken part himself. This was typical Don Bishop.

"Do you have a gun now?" I asked.

"Oh, no," replied the VR quickly. "After Mr Bishop left, I sold my rifle." He looked admiringly at the photograph once more. "Mr Bishop was a good shot," he added, looking pleased with himself.

Despite his unorthodox ways, I found many of the locals on Lantau were actually fond of Don Bishop. Possibly because he would allow them to carry guns, and then join them in the hunt. Or possibly it was because he was a better shot than any of them. Or maybe he actually did a good job?

The village of Tai O is divided into two halves by Tai O Creek. This fifty-foot-wide stretch of water flows from an estuary in the north, to Tai O Bay in the south. The existence of this creek means that the western half of Tai O, the half on which the police station stands, is an island. This made living in Tai O in 1978 interesting, because there was no bridge across the creek. The only way for pedestrians to cross from the 'mainland-proper' side to the half on which the police station stands, was via a contraption, known locally as the Tai O rope ferry. This ferry was more of a rickety wooden platform than any kind of boat. It was oblong in shape, had no bow, no stern, no sides to hold onto and no engine.

Propulsion was provided by two old Tanka women, who pulled their floating platform from one side of the creek to the other, via a rope that was stretched across the creek. One end of this rope was attached to a concrete post positioned outside the Tai O branch of the Hong Kong and Shanghai Bank, whilst the other end was secured to a metal ring, fixed to the wall on the side of the dried-salt-fish shop.

This 'ferry' had a varying maximum passenger capacity, depending on how the Tanka women felt at the time. Villagers, and police officers, wishing to cross the creek would line up on the stone steps and wait for the wooden platform to meander from the opposite side. The fee for one crossing was twenty cents per person, ten cents per pig - if traveling in a metal cage, whilst ducks and chickens in wicker baskets crossed free of charge. In the event of a fishing vessel wishing to pass down the creek the whole operation would stop, temporarily, whilst the old Tanka women tied rocks to the rope so that it sank to the bottom.

As far as I knew, the old Tanka women were not in possession of a license to operate this business. With no license, there were no rules or regulations, there was no maximum passenger capacity (for people or animals) and no certificate of seaworthiness. In fact, if you had asked me, as the senior police officer at Tai O, what the health and safety regulations were in respect of local rope-ferry operations, you would have received a shrug of the shoulders in return.

This creek-crossing system worked extremely well, unless someone wanted to cross after 2200. That wasn't possible, because the two old Tanka women would have gone home to bed, taking their rope with them.

One Sunday evening, I was out on a mobile patrol of Lantau Island in my police Land Rover. Apart from Ratbag, the station dog, I was alone. After that first Sha Lo Wan visit, I'd gotten into the habit of driving around the island alone. I preferred to arrive at remote villages without prior warning. That way, there was no special ceremony arranged for me and I got to see the island for real, rather than the one the villagers, or my men, wanted me to see. Ratbag too preferred it this way as he was free to sit in the front with his head stuck out of the side window. I think he saw himself as Patrol Dog Ratbag of the Royal Hong Kong Police Force.

That evening, I had been up to the monastery at Po Lin on the Ngong Ping Plateau. I went there from time to time to visit the Buddhist monks and see what was on offer in their vegetarian kitchen. On the drive back down to Tai O, I glanced at my watch, it was 2130, so there was plenty of time to catch the last ferry before the old Tanka women packed up for the night. As I parked my Land Rover on the outskirts of the village, I could see that all was quiet in Tai O. The shops were closed, the streets were deserted and the stilt houses were in darkness. The people of Tai O were very much an 'early to bed, early to rise' community. I walked in silence towards the creek. Occasionally, Ratbag would shoot down a side alley in pursuit of some creature or other. More often than not, he would come flying back out again with his tail between his legs. The rats in Tai O were bigger than him.

As I turned into Market Street, I stopped. Damn, there was no rope across the creek, and the ferry was tied up. Those bloody old women had gone home early. Cursing, I walked toward the stone steps and looked down at the decrepit wooden ferry tied to a post below me. The rope, that was usually suspended across the creek, was nowhere to be seen.

I considered my options. I could walk back through the village and wake up old Mr Wong, the salt fish man, who had a telephone. From his shop I could call the station, and summon help. But the Wong family house was in darkness, and I didn't wish to disturb them. I could go back to my Land Rover and use the radio to call Marine Police Headquarters, and ask them to telephone Tai O Police Station. But I immediately ruled that option out, as I knew some smart-aleck staff officer would see my message in tomorrow's morning report. Then I would be inundated with crank calls suggesting clever ways for me to find my own police station. I looked down at Ratbag.

"What shall we do?" I asked him. But he just looked back at me and wagged his tail.

Then I had a thought. Lashed to the side of the ferry was a long bamboo pole. The Tanka women sometimes used it to push themselves free if they got stuck. I could untie both the ferry and the pole, then use the pole, gondola-like, to punt my way across the creek to the opposite side. Once there, I would secure the ferry and walk home. Tomorrow morning, when the old Tanka women found their livelihood on the wrong side of the creek, they would simply call for help from one of the many fishing boats around at that time, and get it towed back. Easy.

"Come on, Ratbag," I said, walking down the steps.

I had never punted before. But I had seen pictures of undergraduates at Cambridge University punting their punts along the River Cam. The Tai O rope ferry resembled a punt. A bit heavier maybe, and a bit wider too, but more or less the same. I climbed onboard and began untying the pole whilst Ratbag sat at the top of the steps and watched me. He didn't look so sure.

"Come on, Ratbag," I said. "We'll be across in no time."

He (somewhat reluctantly, I thought) padded down the steps and flopped down on the ferry. I detected an element of doubt in Patrol Dog Ratbag.

Once I had untied the pole, I waved it around a bit, just to get the feel for the punting action. It was heavier than it looked, which I thought a good thing. The heavier the pole, the more power I could apply. Next, I undid the knots at either end of the ferry, and we were free.

I figured that the first thing to do was get away from the steps, so I rammed one end of the pole into the brickwork and gave it a shove. We made about five feet. I then climbed onto the back end of the ferry and angled the pole back towards the steps once more. With a second shove, we moved another five feet, and were now almost a quarter of the way across the creek.

I took stock of my position. Here I was, the chief of police for the western half of Lantau Island, in uniform, in this remote village, in the dead of night, punting a delapidated old raft (which, arguably, could now be classified as 'stolen') across a creek, in order to return to the police station. If my father could see me now, I wondered, what he would make of it?

With Ratbag and I now out of pole-range of the steps, I prepared to make my first proper vertical punt. Balancing on the rim of the ferry I carefully placed one end of the pole into the water and searched for the bottom. I knew the creek wasn't that deep, only about six feet, so with a pole of ten feet in length, it should prove perfect for the job in hand. I bent forward a little more, prodding at the creek bed. It seemed a bit soft, so I poked around until I hit something solid. It felt like rock, so I put my full weight into it, and the ferry began to move further toward the middle of the creek.

'It works!' I thought, looking over my shoulder at Ratbag, who was watching me out of one eye. "See," I said, "I told you this was a good idea."

But as I spoke, my elation with that first punt was cut short. As I tried to retrieve the pole from the creek I found that it was stuck on something on the bottom. I attempted to yank the pole upwards, but it refused to budge, it had become snagged on something very heavy, and the ferry was still moving. Now, bent double, I struggled to hang onto the end of the pole. But it was no use, as the ferry continued to drift towards the middle of the creek, I gradually ran out of pole. I let go.

As we drifted a little further, I stood on the rim of the ferry and looked back at the pole, sticking up, vertically, in the middle of the creek, like a digit. 'Same to you,' I thought to myself.

The result of my first overenthusiastic punt, and subsequent loss of the pole, was that Ratbag and I were now 'cast adrift' on the Tai O rope ferry. As we came to a stop, I scratched my head. We were about six feet from the snagged vertical pole and twenty feet from the opposite steps.

"This is not good," I said to Ratbag. I am not sure if dogs can raise their eyebrows, but he seemed to be making a good job of it now. And, for some reason, Oliver Hardy's words, 'Well, here's another nice mess you have gotten me into', came to mind.

I looked up and down the creek. There was no one around, the village was in darkness. I considered dropping over the side and swimming to the steps. But then I saw a massive rat, the size of a cat, slide into the water from under one of the stilt-houses. It swam around a bit before ducking under the ferry. I looked back at the pole, then at the steps. It was at this point that I realized something was happening. We had begun to move. We had begun to move, because the fucking tide was going out - and now, we were drifting, silently, down the creek and out to sea.

Tidal movement in Hong Kong is slight. At least it was on that particular night off Tai O. As Ratbag and I meandered across Tai O Bay, adrift on the 'stolen' rope-less, rope-ferry, I looked around. In the shadows, the Tai O fishing fleet was at anchor for the night, the boats moored in-line, the fisherman, no doubt, in their stilt-houses, asleep. To my right, in the distance, high on the hill, I could easily make out the bright lights of my police station.

'I hope no one sees us,' I thought. Then, 'No, I hope someone does see us.'

I sat down on the edge of the ferry and looked ahead across the Pearl River Estuary. As I stared out to sea, I began to realize the ridiculousness of the situation we were now in. But before there was time for me to start feeling sorry for myself, lights appeared, way out at sea. Three lights, one single green, one single white and a red. A boat, and it was coming our way. I stood up to get a better view. As it drew closer, I could make out the sound of the boat's engines. It was a fishing trawler. A Tai O fisherman, returning late to his mooring. This could be the lifeline that Ratbag and I needed.

While the late arrival of a fisherman was good news, it occurred to me that this fisherman would not be expecting the Tai O rope-ferry to be drifting across Tai O Bay in the dead of night. It was dark, and we had no lights, the skipper might not see us. He might miss us, or worse, there was a chance of a collision. I began waving my arms above my head, I shouted out, in the hope that he would hear me above the noise of his engines. At first, the fishing vessel just kept coming, but then the engines died and the vessel began to slow. He had seen us.

As the fishing vessel came close, a cry came from the darkness of the vessel's wheelhouse, *"Wei, jo mat yeh?"* "Hey, what are you doing?"

The shout was angry, the fisherman obviously didn't approve of boats drifting around in the bay at night, and with no lights. As the fishing vessel stopped next to us, a grizzled face appeared over the side, squinting, trying to make out who we were. The fisherman began to shout at us. I couldn't quite make out what he was saying, but I am sure it was something about my parentage. The fisherman pulled out a torch and shone it in our direction. As his eyes became accustomed to the change in light, he froze. He had seen me, in uniform. His eyes widened and his mouth slowly opened, his jaw was working but no words were forthcoming. For a second, we stared at each other, until a woman appeared at his side, his wife. Her look of anger slowly changing to one of alarm, then fear. "*Aiya!*" she screamed and disappeared. Three more faces popped up, children, in a line next to their father. They hung over the side, open-mouthed, staring down at me and Ratbag on the Tai O rope-ferry.

"Throw me a line," I called, breaking up their obvious bewildered state, "Back to the creek," I pointed in the direction of Tai O Village. Upon hearing me speak, the fisherman family burst into life, all shouting and pointing at once. The fisherman and his wife collided into each other as they bolted in opposite directions. I looked at Ratbag, who decided these theatricals were of no interest to him. He slumped down and closed his eyes.

After a few seconds the fisherman reappeared with a length of rope, I could hear him muttering to himself, '*Bomban, gwailo, ma fan...*' 'Inspector, foreigner, trouble...' He threw one end of the rope down to me and scurried off towards the stern of the vessel.

Eventually, and after much faffing around, the Tai O rope-ferry, with Ratbag and me on board, was secured to the stern of the fishing vessel, via a single length of rope. And so, the procession back to Tai O creek began. I sat down on the rim of the ferry and watched the fishing vessel do its work. Three little faces looked back at me from the stern.

'What stories will this family have by morning?' I thought. 'What are these kids going to tell their friends? Will anyone believe them?'

Naturally, I chose not to officially report the fact that Ratbag and I had liberated the Tai O rope-ferry that night, and that we had, involuntary, circumnavigated Tai O Bay. I didn't think it would be in my own interests if the whole of Marine Police

District got to hear about it. Of course, being a village community, the news circulated around Tai O like wild-fire. Next morning, the sly grins and muffled conversations in the police station told me that my staff were already well up-to-date with every detail of my little escapade. I wondered how much exaggeration had already been applied to the tale by the fisherman and his family. Not that our adventure required any.

The two old Tanka women certainly knew about it, too. The next time I took the rope-ferry across the creek, one of them untied the bamboo pole and, accompanied by cackles of laughter, handed it to me, suggesting I take command. Joining in with their game, I took the pole, weighed it in my hands for a few seconds, shook my head and handed it back.

15

PORT OF FIRST ASYLUM
第一收容港

THE DUTY SERGEANT arrived at my office doorway after having run the length of the corridor from the report room. He had a look of panic plastered across his face.

"Sir, sir!" he gasped. "The Marine duty controller is on the phone." The sergeant's mouth remained open, gawping in anticipation. He pointed at the phone on my desk. "He's on the line now, sir. And he wants to speak to you."

It was rare for the duty controller to call Tai O Station himself. He was the operational head of the Marine Command and Control Centre. His job was to oversee all maritime operations, colony-wide. If he called you personally, you knew there was something important going on. You knew it would be urgent. And you knew you were about to become involved. I picked up the phone.

"Bird here, sir."

"Inspector Bird, the Marine district superintendent is holding a highly confidential briefing tomorrow morning on the Vietnamese situation, which has become dire. The government is about to announce new measures in dealing with refugees. The DS will therefore brief all sector commanders and other key staff, including you, on these measures and Marine's involvement. Be in the operations room at Marine HQ at 0900. I have arranged a launch to pick you up at 0600 from Tai O pier. Be in full uniform."

He was gone.

Not only was it rare for me to be called personally by the duty controller, it was also a first for me to be called into Marine HQ for a briefing. I was a small potato in the scheme of things and usually received my orders via dispatches, not by phone. New measures in dealing with refugees, originating from the higher echelons of government? Full uniform? This sounded big.

The following morning, I arrived at Marine HQ well before 0900 so I headed upstairs to the Mess to grab a cup of coffee. As I walked in, a group of chief inspectors, including Don Bishop, were finishing breakfast.

"Ah, the SDI Tai O will be joining us for this morning's fun and games," Don announced upon seeing me. He put down his knife and fork. "Come and sit next to your Uncle Don," he said patting an empty seat at the breakfast table.

"Good morning, sirs," I said to the assembled brass around the table as I sat down next to Don.

"In with the big boys today, Leslie?"

"I received a call from the duty controller yesterday. He told me to be here for the briefing. Any ideas?"

"How much do you know about what's been going on with Vietnamese refugees, Hong Kong's position, and what's been happening out at sea?" asked Don.

"Well, I've been reading the occasional report that gets sent to Tai O, and I see the newspapers, of course."

Don dabbed his mouth with a napkin and looked at me. "As I thought. You know nothing. Come with me," he said pushing his chair away from the table. Don stood up and headed for the door. I grabbed my cup and chased after him.

"In here," he said opening the doors to the Mess annex, a small room with a few easy chairs and low tables where officers could get away from the hubbub of the dining room. "Grab a seat," he said, closing the doors behind him. "There's half an hour before the briefing begins so I have just enough time to bring you up to date. You can't go into the DS's meeting without knowing what's been going on. Most of the others…" Don jerked a thumb in the direction of the main Mess "… will have some idea already."

I sat down and placed my coffee on a side table. Don didn't waste any time. "I am going to assume you know nothing, which is probably an accurate assumption."

"Well I do know a…"

He held up a hand. "Now we only have twenty-nine minutes before the start of the DS's briefing so just shut up and listen."

I took a sip of coffee and sat back. It was the beginning of a Don Bishop lecture.

"Since the fall of Saigon in 1975, Viet Cong forces have been trying to reunite the northern and southern halves of their country. But many people from the south, in fear of the new communist regime, and probable retribution for siding with the Americans, decided that this new arrangement was not for them. They have been fleeing the country in their thousands, in all directions. To begin with, many crossed the land border into Thailand, but that option was soon closed down. So, for the past year or so, they have been taking to the sea in whatever boats they can find, heading for Singapore, Malaysia, the Philippines, Indonesia, and here. But you know this bit already."

This was common knowledge, but I knew better than to interrupt. I nodded.

"Initially, Western governments shirked responsibility for resettling any of these refugees. But just last year, with the beginning of the Viet Cong's oppressive treatment of the Hoa – they're the ethnic Chinese in the south – the Hong Kong government decided to make a stand. They elected, via the United Nations High Commissioner for Refugees, the UNHCR, for port of first asylum status. To accept all refugees." Don paused and looked at me. I nodded again that I was following.

"So, the first bit of big news for you and the others, that you will learn in the briefing today, is that subsequent to Hong Kong's port of first asylum stance, the UNHCR is to establish their main Vietnamese refugee handling operations here in Hong Kong."

"Wow."

"Yes, wow. This means the UN and their highly-funded circus will be setting themselves up in Hong Kong in order to facilitate all resettlement cases. And we, as the maritime representatives of the Hong Kong government, are going to be welcoming the refugees. In fact, the whole shebang has already started. Did you hear about that first group of Vietnamese to arrive on a ship called the *Clara Mærsk*?"

I nodded. I did remember reading about it in the newspapers.

"Well, they were resettled in Europe, which has set a precedent. This new Hong Kong-based UNHCR resettlement process will continue where that case left off. What do you think of that?"

"Port of first asylum, plus the UNHCR?" I asked. "Isn't that going to encourage the Vietnamese to come here, knowing they have a chance of resettlement in the West?"

"Yes. It's both a brave and risky move by the Hong Kong government. We are a small colony, and we may end up dealing with the bulk of the Vietnamese exodus. But it's the right thing to do. It's a humanitarian gesture by Hong Kong that comes in the nick of time. Do you know that other Southeast Asian nations are getting so annoyed with all these refugees arriving on their shores that some are now pushing the boats back out to sea? In my book, that is tantamount to murder."

"So we are going to get tens of thousands of Vietnamese refugees coming to Hong Kong, aren't we? Much more than have already arrived?"

"Correct. It's going to be a busy time, but that's our job, isn't it? Anyway, with the UNHCR facilitating resettlement programs with Western nations, Hong Kong is not going to be the final destination for these refugees. We are merely acting as the port of first asylum, a stepping stone to a new life for these people."

"That's a pretty big deal for Hong Kong. But just one thing, sir, how do you happen to know this?"

"Ah, well, good question, you see I have been here in MHQ for the past few days helping the DS draft his briefing notes. The top brass has known about this for some time."

Don stood up and walked over to the window, checking his watch. He was silent for a moment. "But there's more," he said sitting down in an armchair opposite.

"More?"

"Yes, much more, I am afraid. In Vietnam, the mass exodus triggered a slew of corrupt officials to exploit this situation and make money from the refugees' plight. These officials work for the *Cong An*, or PSB, the Public Security Bureau, a wing of the Interior Ministry in Ho Chi Minh City. The ruse is a simple one. Hundreds, sometimes thousands, of willing Hoa refugees are loaded onto cargo ships for a fee taken by middlemen, with the corrupt officials acting as puppet masters. The fare for this 'passage to the free world' ranges from eight to ten taels of gold per adult. These escapees are also required to sign a declaration with the PSB waiving any future claim against the state and donating all their belongings and assets to the government. These bastards are bleeding their own people of all they have to secure a passage out of Vietnam." Don shook his head in disgust.

I'd read of a couple of recent cases, in which thousands of

refugees arrived in Hong Kong crammed into large ships. "So the Vietnamese government are behind that 'big ship' racket?" I asked.

Don nodded. "They are indeed. A pseudo-captain and crew are hired by the PSB for each rust-bucket freighter to ship the human cargo to whatever Southeast Asian port can be convinced to allow them to land. We have dealt with two of these ships here in Hong Kong already."

"You mean the *Huey Fong* and the *Skyluck*?"

"That's them. You will recall that in the final days of last year, the Marine Department here in Hong Kong received a message from a Taiwanese national claiming to be master of a 4,187-ton Panamanian-registered freighter, the *Huey Fong*. This captain claimed his ship had rescued more than two thousand Vietnamese refugees from sinking boats at sea and requested permission to dock in Hong Kong. But a swift investigation into the movements of the ship concluded the story was phoney. And, as the *Huey Fong's* next scheduled port of call was Kaohsiung in Taiwan, the Marine Department's response was to point out the international maritime agreement stating that shipwrecked survivors rescued by ocean-going vessels should land at the ship's next scheduled port of call, and that he should continue onto Kaohsiung and not enter Hong Kong territorial waters."

"But he still came in?" I said.

Don held up a hand. "The master of this ship didn't reply to that message, while a second message was also met with radio silence. We, together with the Royal Navy, were alerted, and four days later the *Huey Fong* was intercepted by a flotilla of our launches and a navy patrol craft just outside Hong Kong waters, where she was forced to stop and drop anchor."

I'd read in the press how some international aid agencies at the time began accusing the Hong Kong government of being inhumane by initially keeping a large shipload of refugees out at sea. It had developed into a difficult situation for everyone involved.

"This left Hong Kong in the crossfire of an international backlash for not allowing the refugees to land," continued Don. "We were accused of causing prolonged suffering, even though Hong Kong has shown leniency to refugees since 1975, while certain other Southeast Asian countries have flatly refused passage, with some adopting the protocol of simply guiding ramshackle refugee vessels back out to sea."

Don stood up and checked his watch. "In the first few days, while our government deliberated over what to do with the *Huey Fong's* crew of traffickers and her 2,703 refugee passengers, more information emerged. We discovered that she had left Bangkok weeks before with only one registered passenger and had sailed to a location south of Vung Tau in Vietnam. Sources reported the ship had then been met by a Vietnamese government vessel and escorted to an anchorage in the Mekong Delta. After paying for their passage in gold, the refugees were allowed to board. Most of the gold went to the Vietnamese officials, while the remainder was divided between the crew."

"So it was organized right from the top?"

"Yes it was. But here in Hong Kong, the ramifications of allowing the *Huey Fong* to dock and refugees to disembark was that it set a precedent for the traffickers. With other Southeast Asian countries refusing entry, the colony would be seen as a soft touch, the go-to destination for the people-smugglers to off-load their cargos. It was a tough situation for everyone."

"Why didn't we just refuel the ship and escort her towards Kaohsiung?"

"Too dangerous. The refugees were packed-in like sardines. They were in poor condition; they wouldn't have survived another sea journey. So after further deliberation, the government felt they had no other option but to allow the refugees to land. We went on board and arrested the crew. A search found gold to the value of US$1.4 million hidden in the ship's engine room. This was either the crew's payment for the trip or what they had stolen from the refugees en route to Hong Kong. As for the refugees themselves, they were taken ashore and, after a processing period, were accepted for settlement by the US, Canada, Australia, Britain, and other European nations."

"What was the final outcome of the trial of the skipper and crew? And what happened to the gold?"

"After being found guilty of several conspiracy charges, trafficking in human cargo, endangering life at sea, and a number of other international maritime offenses, the Taiwanese captain and his crew of nine were sent to prison for a total of fifty years. The captain himself got seven years. At the end of the trial, the judge referred to the whole saga as 'a voyage of deceit from beginning to end.' The gold seized on board was presented in court as evidence and, as far as I am aware, it's now with the Treasury Department awaiting disposal claims. But, with the successful legal conclusion of this case, we all thought at the time that this was going to act as a deterrent to any further such illegal and immoral big-ship people-smuggling activity. But, as you are aware, it did not have the desired effect."

"You mean the *Skyluck*?"

Don nodded, "Just a few weeks later, the *Skyluck* arrived in Hong Kong. Its captain, possibly knowing the outcome of the *Huey Fong* case, sent no message requesting entry into port and tried to sail the ship, under cover of darkness, directly into Victoria Harbor."

"Jesus, if over two thousand refugees from that second ship had landed in Central District, that would certainly have set the cat amongst the pigeons."

"Indeed, if our patrol launches hadn't stopped the *Skyluck* from entering the inner harbor, we would have had refugees wandering around Central business district and the ship's criminal crew making a run for it. Very embarrassing for us. So now it's back to square one for the Hong Kong government with what to do with this *Skyluck*, her crew, and her 2,651 refugee passengers. This is a very sensitive ongoing situation."

"Where is the *Skyluck* now?"

"Under guard in a sheltered bay off Lamma Island and so far no landing has been permitted. As with the *Huey Fong* conspiracy, the Hong Kong government does not intend to be held to ransom by people smugglers and in any case, there are already thirty-thousand refugees housed in temporary camps around the colony. These camps are at full capacity."

"Is there any information available in respect of further ships like these coming here?"

"While I understand there are representations being made at government level, we must assume, in the short term, that this state-organized people-smuggling will continue."

"One last thing, sir, before we go," I asked. "Why am I here?"

"Because you are in charge of Tai O, the most westerly point of land in the whole of Hong Kong. You and that bloody great white castle of yours stick out like a sore thumb from the South China Sea. So refugee vessels coming in from Vietnam from the west could well head for the first bit of *terra firma* they see. That's Tai O, and that's why you are here."

16

WE ARE GOING TO NEED REINFORCEMENTS
極待增援

BACK AT Tai O a few weeks later, I received a telephone call from Don. "Good morning, Leslie, how is the back of beyond?"

"Way back, thank you, sir," I replied. Since the *Skyluck* had arrived in Hong Kong, Don had taken quite a bit of unjustifiable flack from certain elements of the local media. As the senior on-scene policeman, they were holding him responsible for 'holding the refugees hostage.'

"As the DS said, this is just the beginning," he sighed. "Mark my words, there are thousands, hundreds of thousands, more to come." There was silence for a moment while we both contemplated this. "Anyway, good news," he continued, "I managed to wangle a few days off, so I'm finally ready to accept your invitation and come for a visit. I'll take the midday ferry to Mui Wo tomorrow. Pick me up at the pier, there's a good chap."

It had been over a year since Don had threatened to visit me at Tai O and empty my fridge. In that time, I'd prepared a host of excuses for this moment, but I surprised myself by replying, "Okay, that suits me, sir. It's my day-off tomorrow. I'll pick you up in Short Arse."

Then my thoughts turned to Maria. She would be

disappointed. I had arranged to go into town the following day to see her. Despite the logistics of having to travel for half a day between Tai O and Hong Kong Island, I had been seeing her most weekends. If I had a leave day, I would take the early ferry into town, then return to the island on the last ferry of the day. If I had to work over a weekend, Maria would travel out to Tai O, usually on the Saturday. She would then stay over and take a late ferry back into town Sunday night. It was hardly ideal, but we made the best of it. We had planned to go and see Woody Allen's new release, 'Annie Hall,' at the cinema in Causeway Bay the following day, but this was now not to be. I picked up the phone, making my excuses.

"I'm sorry, I can't leave the island tomorrow. I have to work." She asked if she could come over to Tai O instead. "No, I am afraid not. There's a senior Marine commander coming over to visit the station. He may stay overnight. I'll call you next week."

It wasn't a lie as such. Looking after an off-duty Diamond Don Bishop was work. But I knew Don needed a break from all he had been doing recently in dealing with these big refugee ships out on the front line. He'd been working long hours and the morale of his launch crews — those who had become de facto aid workers — was rock-bottom.

The next day, I bundled Ratbag into the Land Rover and made it to the pier on the other side of the island by 1300 with time to spare. As it was my official leave day, I was in civilian clothes. I rested on the bonnet of Short Arse and closed my eyes. As I leant my head back, the sun washed over my face. It was a wonderfully clear sunny day and the dock was buzzing with activity as Don's ferry idled up to the pier.

He was soaked in sweat as he marched down the dock towards us, a white handkerchief in hand, which he used to mop his bald head. Ratbag jumped all over him, wild-eyed with his tongue flapping around.

"I hope that pile of junk has a good air conditioner," he said, pointing at my Land Rover.

"Good to see you too, sir," I said as we shook hands.

"Let's get going if that's okay with you," said Don. "Never did care for this end of the island. Too many expats. Let's get over to Tai O."

He climbed into the passenger side, dragging the dog with him. We set off along the South Lantau Road, heading west.

"I had a great time when I served out here," Don said staring out of the window at the rice paddies as we went. "Just me and Ratbag." He glanced over. "I was wondering if you were going to turn up in uniform today. I see you decided on the casual look."

"Well, it is my day-off."

"You know, in the old days, before there were roads out here, officers hardly ever left the island. Even on their days off. It took almost a whole day to get from Tai O station to the Mui Wo ferry pier. Not worth it, really. Some officers posted out here actually went a bit troppo," said Don, chuckling. "I was half-expecting to find you wearing a grass skirt and your face painted with woad as part of your island ensemble." He grinned to himself.

"Tai O is still pretty laid-back, but not quite that laid-back," I said. "Now, tell me about the current *Skyluck* situation. How come you were involved again? And so soon after the *Huey Fong*?"

"You know, stopping the *Skyluck* before she entered Victoria Harbor was just a piece of good fortune." Don shifted in his seat again, huffing and puffing until he finally settled down.

"Sounds like good police work rather than good luck to me," I said, glancing to my left at Don, who appeared to be dozing off.

"Just imagine it!" he said, sitting up. "If that ship had made it to the inner harbour, and put all 2,651 refugees ashore, right

at the doors of City Hall! Can you imagine the hullabaloo?" He
laughed at the thought. "But, you know, if they had succeeded,
every people-smuggling racket would be eyeing Hong Kong at
this very minute. It really was a close-run thing."

Just then, my Land Rover radio crackled to life. 'Tai O Jeep,
Tai O Jeep, come in. Over.'

I snatched the handset. "This is Tai O Jeep, go ahead. Over."

'Tai O Jeep, this is Tai O Station, sir, there is information from
Marine Control. Something is happening at Lo Kei Wan. Over.'

"Lo Kei Wan, that's the small bay over those hills to our left,"
I said, looking at Don.

"It's between here and Fan Lau Point," he said, pointing to
the ridge.

"Tai O Station, what is the problem, over?"

'Tai O Jeep, sir, no further information but the duty controller
just telephoned the station looking for you. He said there's a big
problem, it's urgent.'

"Damn it, on my day off," I muttered. "Someone's reported
their cabbages have been trampled on."

"If it's come from Marine Control, then it's more than crushed
vegetables," said Don. "If we drive further along here, we can
leave the Land Rover at the foot of those hills and hike over.
There's no path up there and the undergrowth looks quite thick,
but we could hack our way through."

He looked at me for agreement. I nodded.

"Tai O Station, this is Tai O Jeep, this is CIP Bishop on set," he
said, taking over. "The SDI and I are proceeding to Lo Kei Wan,
ETA 1500, over."

"I thought you said nothing ever happened here, Leslie? I
came over here for a rest, not a bloody day's police work." Don
folded his arms and closed his eyes. Ratbag lay across his feet
again and slept.

I pushed the Land Rover as hard as it would go. The road funneled into a dirt track. Rocks and boulders made for a bumpy ride as we ascended the side of the steep hill. Don and Ratbag slept on. Then the track ended, and within a few minutes our wheels became entangled in the scrub. I cut the engine, which stirred Don who cursed and flung open the door as Ratbag bounded out, happily darting up the hill, leaping around the shrubs and dense foliage.

"Bit Sherlock Holmes and Doctor Watson, isn't it? With our trusty bloodhound, bah," said Don.

In the lee of a vertical slope, there was not a breath of wind. The heat was incessant. I picked up a sturdy-looking stick and thrashed at the long grass as we started our ascent.

"Better the snakes know we are coming."

We were soon drenched in sweat and covered in cuts and scrapes as we plowed on upwards through the heavy thicket.

"What do you think we will find on the other side?" I asked as I scrambled over a cluster of large rocks.

"Hopefully an air-conditioned bar," grunted Don. He pulled the sleeve of his shirt free from a thorn bush, ripping a hole near the elbow. He swore under his breath.

After half an hour, we made it to the top of the hill where we were hit by the sea breeze and a panoramic view of Lo Kei Wan beach below. The narrow stretch of sand was just a few hundred yards in length, surrounded on three sides by cliffs and thick jungle.

"Holy Mother of God," Don broke the silence. "We are going to need reinforcements. A lot."

"Jesus Christ," was all I could muster.

A large ship, a freighter of about 3,000 tons, had sliced the beach in two and was perched with its bows almost touching the undergrowth below us. The ship was well and truly high and dry and appeared to have plowed into Lantau Island at full-speed. From our high position on the hillside, we could see down into the open cargo hold, which was packed full of people.

"Refugees," muttered Don. "Vietnamese. There's more than a thousand people crammed in there. Its another damn people-smuggling ship." He shook his head.

As we looked down, we could see that some of the refugees were already climbing up the inside bulkhead walls. Some, towards the stern section, had succeeded in reaching the top and were jumping into the sea and swimming ashore.

"Come on," said Don, "we have work to do."

We scrambled, tumbled, slipped, and scrambled some more until we burst out of the bushes onto the beach. Ratbag, naturally, had beaten us down and was now turning circles on the sand chasing his own tail in excitement.

About fifty men had already made it ashore and were advancing from the ship up the beach towards us. We brushed ourselves down and took stock of the situation. The group of young men looked a desperate lot, their clothes dirty and torn. More poured over the side of the ship into the sea. They waded ashore and headed for us.

"Right, let's sort this lot out," Don said, setting off down the beach towards the men.

As we went it occurred to me that neither Don nor I were in uniform. I was dressed in shorts and an old t-shirt while Don, also in shorts, had a piece torn from the sleeve of his shirt.

As we approached, the group stopped. Don stood in front of them, then, at the top of his voice, he announced in English, "We are the Royal Hong Kong Police, and you lot are all under arrest. That's all of you."

For a second there was total silence while the ever-growing group stared at the two of us. Then a gaunt elderly man wearing only a sarong pushed his way to the front. He held out his hands, palms up, pleading.

"You are police?" he asked in English with an American twang.

"Correct," replied Don.

"Oh, thank you, thank you. At last we are safe. They left us to drive the ship. They ran away, we didn't know how to drive. They left us and took our gold. They took our money. They robbed us."

"You are all safe now, we are the Hong Kong Police. I want you all to sit down right here. Translate that," he said to the spokesman.

The elderly man turned and shouted what sounded like orders. Some of the men began to sit. Others were hesitant.

I walked among the group, motioning them to sit down. I smiled in the hope of offering reassurance. More men and women clambered along the beach, many women were carrying their young. All looked exhausted, dirty and close to starvation.

On the stern of the ship the words Sen On were crudely painted in white. It was obvious the ship's name had been hand-painted, as the letter S was facing the wrong way.

The story the refugees told us was one similar to those who had arrived on board the *Huey Fong* and the *Skyluck*. The difference with this ship being that shortly before arriving in Hong Kong waters, the captain and crew had opened the cargo hold and shouted instructions to the refugees on how to drive the ship. They said Hong Kong was east and to head there. The captain and crew then boarded a small boat and left, in the direction of Macau. The refugees had no idea how to stop or slow the ship, and so they steered the out-of-control freighter towards the first land they saw. Here. The bow had gouged a thirty-foot deep groove into the beach. The front section of the ship was completely buried, and it looked ridiculous.

Don and I managed to get those already on the beach to sit down in one group. There were about three hundred, mostly young men. Others were jumping from the side of the ship into the sea and were swimming ashore. I motioned for them to join the seated group. "We need to make sure none of these wander off," said Don. "You take up a position to the rear, over by the tree line. I'll deal with those wading up from the ship."

Under a cloudless, pale-blue sky I looked around at what Don and I had stumbled into. Hundreds of terrified refugees were huddled together on the pristine white-sand beach. The beach was deserted but for the enormous freighter whose rusty-black bow towered above us. On the shore, dressed in a pair of dark blue shorts and a white baggy shirt that flapped in the breeze, and with no police insignia in sight, Don Bishop strode through the surf barking instructions at the ever-growing group. Don Bishop, the man in-charge, keeping control.

Thirty minutes later, a foot-patrol from Tai O police station broke out of the undergrowth at the western end of the beach and came jogging towards us. I recognized one of my sergeants leading the way. "Get your guys to form a cordon around this lot, Leslie," ordered Don, pointing at the seated group. "At least we now have some uniforms on the scene."

"What about the refugees still on the ship?" I asked Don.

"There's nothing we can do until we get more support from a patrol launch. There's no way anyone can climb up the side of the ship from down here. For now, we wait."

Within an hour, a fleet of Marine Police vessels were moored just off the stern of the freighter. An army of officers scrambled up the side of the *Sen On* onto the deck, with Don and myself leading the search. On the deck of the ship, we found a further five hundred refugees, while in the bowels of the hold, we found five hundred more, the ones too sick or too weak to climb out on their own. Many were women, and most had small children and babies clinging to them. The smell was overpowering. With no water or sanitation these people had been through hell. We began the job of helping them out of the hold and onto the Marine launches. It was a long afternoon's work.

Just before nightfall, the last of the refugees had been transferred to our Marine craft and were on their way to the medical and immigration reception areas that had recently been set up at the western harbor entrance. Don and I stood in the shadow of the empty wreck of the Sen On and watched them go. Ratbag lay snoozing in the shade.

"I recall you once called me a *hak jai*, bad luck, sir," I said looking at Don. "Maybe you have assumed ownership of that title?"

"Bah," he muttered, choosing to ignore my attempt at humor. He turned and headed back towards the hills. "Come on, young Leslie, I think we deserve a drink."

17

LOSING THE 'ROYAL' TITLE
皇家不再

On 24 September 1982, the prime minister of the United Kingdom walked down the steps of the Great Hall of the People in Beijing having just concluded her first meeting with China's paramount leader, Deng Xiaoping. The subject of the talks was the coming expiry of the ninety-nine-year lease on Hong Kong's New Territories, and the future of the British colony itself. Either side of Margaret Thatcher, as she descended the steps, were a number of her aides and a delegation of Chinese officials. In the weeks prior to her visit, there had been intense speculation in local and international media as to how the prime minister's talks with the Chinese would go. The British, the press reported, were pushing for an extension to the lease, which was due to expire in 1997. Everyone in Hong Kong was eager for news.

As Mrs Thatcher neared the foot of the steps, she tripped and fell forward onto the pavement. She went down as though she had been hit by a sniper's bullet, ending up on her hands and knees on the large white flagstones. Officials rushed to help her to her feet and into a waiting car. Mrs Thatcher was obviously a little shaken by her fall, but otherwise unhurt. Next day, a photograph of the British prime minister sprawled in front of the Chinese delegation hit the front pages of newspapers around the world.

"That's it," announced Don Bishop, crumpling his copy of the *South China Morning Post* on his lap. He was sitting in a leather-bound armchair in the Mariners Rest having just finished breakfast. Everyone in the Mess looked up from what they were doing. "It's all over," continued Don, tossing the newspaper on the floor and folding his arms in disgust. "We are all well and truly stuffed. That's S, T, U, double F, E, D, stuffed."

"What on earth are you talking about?" asked Dougie Kerr, who was sitting at the main table.

Don glared. "What I am talking about?" He snatched up the newspaper and rattled it at the whole room. "What I am talking about is this bloody picture. That's what I am talking about." He was flushed in the face. The veins on the top of his head were bulging.

"Ach, so what, she's just tripped," replied Kerr.

Don shook his head. "You don't get it, do you? How long have you been in Asia? How long have you been in Hong Kong? Have you been living with your head up your backside since you got off the boat?" He glared at Dougie. "This is a sign." He rattled the newspaper again. "Our prime minister is on her knees, in front of the Great Hall of the People." Don threw the newspaper back on the floor and kicked it. "Right in front of the Chinese delegation."

"There's been no announcement. We still have'na any idea how the talks went," offered Dougie.

"She fell on the steps of the Great Hall of the People, immediately after discussing the future of our last significant colony." Don was exasperated. "Here!" He stabbed a finger in the direction of the floor, just in case anyone was in any doubt as to where he was referring. "What do you think the future holds for us now?"

I recalled a newspaper editorial from a couple of years earlier after the governor of Hong Kong, Sir Murray MacLehose, returned from an official visit to Beijing. The governor stated that in a meeting with Deng Xiaoping, the Chinese leader, had 'made him aware of China's aspirations to resume sovereignty over Hong Kong.' The editorial called for clarification as to what this meant, and asked if Deng's statement was linked to the expiry of the ninety-nine-year lease on the New Territories in 1997. Maybe there really was something in what Don was saying.

There was a large group of us in the Mess that morning. We had been called into Marine HQ for the monthly operations conference. It was still very early and we had an hour to spare before going in. But now Don Bishop had a bee in his bonnet, and everyone had to know. There was silence for moment while the tension in the room subsided a little. But Don hadn't finished. He turned to Joe Poon, who was focused on the task of picking up a fried egg from the top of a bowl of congee with his chopsticks.

"What do you say to this?" asked Don, holding up the newspaper once more.

Joe looked up and shook his head. "It's not good, is it?"

"Ah, see, listen to him," declared Don, he pointed at Joe. "Even he agrees with me. The Chinese know. This is an omen, bad *fung shui*. Her fall signifies the outcome of the talks. It doesn't matter what she says now. Everyone in Hong Kong already believes the worst. China will take back Hong Kong."

"We are going to lose the Royal title, aren't we?" said Joe, who surprised me by agreeing with Don.

Don went quiet for a moment, deep in thought. "Yes," he whispered finally. "The Royal title, yes, you are right." He pointed at Joe again. "Beijing won't be having that, will they? The Royal title, I mean. The Royal Hong Kong Police will be no more. And, that's just fifteen years from now, 1997. I will still be a serving officer," he said as though just remembering he had been sentenced to death.

"You mean you *think* you will still be serving then," said Dougie. "If you are correct, and China does regain sovereignty, our terms of employment may change well before 1997. You might get the chop before then."

"That's a point," exclaimed Don, his eyes now wide as he considered the possibilities. "They are going to come in here and turf all us *gwailos* out."

Don caught a slight smile from Joe and rounded on him. "As for you locals..." he pointed at Joe "...you have nothing to laugh about. You lot are up shit creek without a proverbial paddle, for sure. Yellow running dogs — that's how Beijing refers to Hong Kong Chinese. Your new masters will be coming down on you lot like a ton of bricks. All of us white skin pigs will be thrown out, but you lot have got nowhere to go. And you have taken the Queen's shilling, remember."

Joe looked up from his breakfast. "The ownership, or sovereignty, of Hong Kong has been debated in China since the British took possession 141 years ago. Anyone who knows the Chinese well has suspected that it's been their intention to eventually take back Hong Kong. I don't think China has ever seen the colony as anything but a loan, a borrowed place."

"Well, that certainly appears to be the case," said Don, standing up and pacing the room. "If China decides to take back Hong Kong, the first thing we need to be concerned about is what will happen between now and 1997. As you say, the changes will begin before then. Promotions, for example. They will be a thing of the past for us older officers. Our shelf-life will be redefined. What's the point in promoting expat or local officers whose employment will end before the change of sovereignty?"

"You mean old dinosaurs like you and me, Don," said Daniel

Holden-Foster who, up until that moment, had been preoccupied with the SCMP crossword. "It will not affect me because I'm not bothered about further promotion, so I am all right. But if Hong Kong does revert to Chinese rule in 1997, I am sure there will be significant changes in the force, both before and afterwards." He went back to his crossword.

Don stared at Uncle Daniel. "It's all very well for you to say that, Daniel. You will be retired before 1997, but what about him, and him, and him? And me? I am not as ancient as you." Don wasn't happy. "Most of us are contracted to serve past 1997. We have served the good people of Hong Kong for ten, twenty years. What guarantees will we have before and after a change in sovereignty?"

On this particular morning in 1982, after the initial talks on the post-1997 future of Hong Kong had been concluded, there were conversations like this going on in police messes and canteens across the territory. The word was uncertainty. Uncertainty about what was going to happen if the British left and the Chinese took over. More specifically, the uncertainty as to what would happen to the men and women of the Royal Hong Kong Police Force. We found out two years later.

In December 1984, during a second visit to the Chinese capital, Margaret Thatcher and Premier Zhao Ziyang signed the Sino-British Joint Declaration on behalf of their respective governments. China would take back Hong Kong on July 1, 1997. The change of sovereignty was ratified. Some would say that Prime Minister Thatcher fell for a second time.

Some days after the announcement, I went in search of Don at his office in MHQ. The report outlining the agreement had been published in the morning's newspaper and I wanted to hear his thoughts on this.

"Listen to this, Don," I said walking in. He looked up from the pile of papers on his desk and I read aloud from the newspaper. This is what it outlined:

In the Joint Declaration, the PRC Government stated that it had decided to resume the exercise of sovereignty over Hong Kong. This transfer of sovereignty (referred to as the "unification" by the Chinese press, and the "handover" by the British press) would see an end to more than 156 years of British involvement since the preliminary cession by China of Hong Kong Island on January 20, 1841. In the Joint Declaration, the PRC Government listed its basic policies regarding Hong Kong after the "unification." In accordance with the "one country, two systems" principle, the socialist system of the PRC would not be practised in Hong Kong, and Hong Kong's previous capitalist system, and its way of life, would remain unchanged for a period of fifty years until 2047. Also included in the Joint Declaration, military forces would be sent by the Central People's Government and stationed in Hong Kong, but would not interfere in the internal affairs. Responsibility for public order would remain with the Hong Kong Police.

"It will be different for us in Hong Kong," said Don, sitting back in his chair and gazing out of the window across Victoria Harbor.

I put the newspaper down. "In what way?"

"When the British have previously given up their colonies, places such as the West Indies, Kenya, Fiji," Don said and pointed out of the window, "they did so to independence. Those countries became their own masters. Before their handovers took place, everyone knew exactly who was going to take charge. They knew which of the senior local officers, those already serving, would head the government. Here, it will be different. We will be relinquishing possession to another sovereign power. The locals here in Hong Kong will not be their own masters. That's different, isn't it?"

"Yes, I see what you are getting at. But in the Joint Declaration, it says that Hong Kong's way of life will remain unchanged for fifty years. So why should we worry?"

"No, you are missing my point. If you think China is going to allow the people of Hong Kong to run Hong Kong the way they want, after the handover, then you are very much mistaken. This place will be controlled by the powers that be in the north."

"It's going to be difficult for the likes of us then, isn't it? Us foreign officers," I said.

"If we stay on, we will be required to switch allegiance, from the Crown to China. Switch loyalty. You realize that, don't you? In Fiji, Kenya, and whatever, they had an idea of how things would be afterwards. Here, we have no idea as to what communist China will do. So what do we do, switch allegiance and hope for the best? And how are we going fit in, if at all? Will we have a role to play? What will that role be? Will we simply be put out to pasture until it's our time to retire? The Joint Declaration specifies that all senior government positions will be held by Chinese so, to me, that spells reduced promotion opportunities for the likes of us." Don pointed at me with his file. "You mark my words, we are going to feel the heat from the changing of the guard. You just wait and see."

"It is thirteen years from now. A lot can happen in that time. I am sure it will become clearer in the years ahead."

Don shook his head. He didn't seem convinced. "The whole situation doesn't bode well." He sat down at his desk with a huff and looked at some papers, seemingly exasperated by the subject.

Don had several good points. But I had been doing some research on what had happened to the expats serving in government in former British colonies. I tried again.

"I read somewhere that it is standard procedure for the British government, when leaving one of their colonies, to offer expatriates who have been recruited to serve solely in that colony the option of an early pension and, in some cases, a loss-of-earnings sum if they agree to leave before independence."

"An early retirement package for expatriate officers. You mean a please-take-the-money-and-bugger-off package. An incentive to quit the force and leave."

"I read that officers in some of these former colonies were offered quite attractive early retirement packages."

"Well, firstly there are no guarantees here in that respect, but it's not just the money, is it? It's the job, it's the place. Here. We came out to Hong Kong for a career, didn't we? A career we are already well into. And that career may well be cut short. How old will you be in 1997? Your career will be sliced in half. Cut off in your prime, so to speak. It's disappointing, that's all. Anyway, come 1997 I don't think I will be ready to retire. You know what happens when old coppers retire, don't you?"

"What?"

"They go back to Blighty, do a spot of gardening, and then keel over and die. With a last gasp they fall into their rose bushes and peg it, right on the spot. Dig their own grave, no less." Don slammed his file shut and stood up. "That's not for me." He walked out leaving me to contemplate the whole thing.

For me, this was more than a just a career decision. Come 1997, I would have far more than my personal situation to consider. Maria and I had decided to get married for one thing, which probably would mean children, maybe a house, a mortgage even? In 1997, I would be in my mid-forties, too young to be put out to pasture. What would I do if offered a take-it-or-leave-it scenario? What would 'it' be? Ten more years in the job, with no front-line operational roles, stuck in a back office, crossing off

LES BIRD

the days on the desk calendar, waiting for retirement, waiting for old age? I wouldn't be free to just walk away from the job if things didn't suit me. Not a way to be settling down and starting a family.

Later, I caught up with Joe Poon. He was sitting alone in the Officers' Mess drinking coffee. I was keen to hear how the news had been received by the local guys.

"What's your take on the big news?" I picked up his Chinese-language newspapers from his table and held up the front page. "The signing of the Joint Declaration?"

"The junior officers, the constables, and sergeants are talking of nothing else, of course," he said. "Everyone is worried about their futures, their careers after 1997. But even at this early stage, with things unclear, most seem resigned to the fact that they have no other choice but to continue to work as they always have done and just hope for the best come the handover. Hong Kong is their home, and they are Chinese after all."

"They are not worried about any retribution, for being in the service of the dreaded imperialists, then?"

"There is some concern, but as I said everyone is very matter-of-fact about it. Whatever will be, will be." Joe took a drink, pulled a face, then spooned more sugar into his cup.

"What about you, Joe? How do you feel about all this?"

"You know, some senior locals are already preparing to emigrate overseas. Those who have the funds are looking to acquire Canadian or British citizenship, obtaining passports for themselves and their families. Some say they will definitely go. I guess some just want the security of holding a foreign passport, so that they have an option to leave if they wish."

Joe shook his head. I could tell that he didn't approve of all this 'sinking ship' mentality.

"And you? What do you think about your future in the

force?" I asked.

"Well, for a start, I agree with what some are saying in that we are no longer our own masters in this historic process. We are caught in a difficult position but we must continue to do our job. That's why we joined up, to serve the people of Hong Kong no matter who is pulling the strings. But I already sense that some believe that they must not be seen as being confrontational to our future masters."

"I don't for a second think duty, performance and loyalty to the job will change in the slightest," I said. "But morale for local officers must be affected, just as with some of the expats."

"I think most local officers feel something of a strain, of being torn between two masters. I also think that most feel that China is going to test our loyalty and allegiance towards the new sovereignty. How this will happen, I don't know. But it will happen."

"I was discussing things with Don earlier. He is forecasting a 'please-take-the-money-and-bugger-off' offer for expat officers and the implementation of a localization policy, a policy that fast-tracks locals for promotion and deploys them into plum frontline jobs."

"Possibly. But one thing I must tell you is that local officers don't feel sorry for you guys," Joe said. "We think expat officers will be the privileged group in this. Bishop is probably correct, you are going to be given a choice. Unlike us."

Joe was right. We expats were worried about our futures, but the local guys had plenty to contemplate, too. I wondered if this predicament was going to cause a split, a division between local and expat officers, and would this division gradually intensify in the run-up to 1997? It was just the uncertainty of it all.

18

HARBOR AIR CRASH
港內墜機

FOLLOWING THE announcement of the coming shift of sovereignty, and despite everyone's concerns, in the years that followed nothing seemed to change, certainly not at the grassroots level. For most of us, it was a case of getting on with the job in hand and leaving future issues to be dealt with when the time came. The RHKP continued to recruit officers from overseas and relationships between local and expat officers remained very good. It was as though everyone in the police force had pushed the whole issue to the backs of their minds for now. Promotion, too, for both locals and expats continued throughout the force. The level playing field remained level, and there was no obvious evidence of a localization policy, as I discovered in 1987 when I was promoted to chief inspector.

Naturally, I was very pleased by this, but the first time I put on my new uniform and stood in front of the mirror I felt very odd indeed. I was now the same rank as Don Bishop. I looked at the three silver pips on each shoulder. It just didn't seem right. I thought back to those early days on PL 1, when Don was 'The' chief inspector and everyone, myself included, looked upon him as God Almighty. That large bull head flanked on either side by the three silver pips. Looking at myself now, with the same rank on my shoulders, I felt like a fraud. Like a minion trying on a king's crown when no one is looking.

When the news came through that I had been promoted, it was Don who was the first to congratulate me. With the crushing handshake and the sly smile, I could see that he was genuinely pleased by the news, although I was suspicious that this joy was partly due to the fact that he envisaged lots of celebratory drinks coming his way. Don had always seen me as his 'prodigy,' and now in the role of proud father, I could hear him boast that he had 'taught him all he knows.'

A few months later, early one Saturday morning, Maria and I were married. We fronted up at the registry office in City Hall in Central and were duly declared man and wife. There was very little pomp, and even less circumstance. It was all very matter-of-fact, with the service lasting just twenty-five minutes. It was the way we both wanted it, a minimum of fuss. In attendance at the service were Maria's mother and father, two of her close friends, and three of my own, one of which was Joe Poon, who was my best man. After the service we walked across Gloucester Road to the Mandarin Hotel where we had breakfast.

For the next twelve months, life was good. Maria and I were happy and I had been given my own command in Marine South, where our police fleet had been enhanced with new, state-of-the-art, patrol launches. These vessels greatly improved our search-and-rescue capability and significantly helped in dealing with the Vietnamese arrivals. Things were generally more manageable. But for me, all this changed in July 1988 with one phone call, from the office of the head of the Marine Police, Regional Commander Jack Devereux.

"Why does the old man want to see me?" I asked the staff officer on the other end of the line.

"I have no idea. I am just relaying an order from the top." He hung up.

Devereux was a short, heavy set, individual with thirty-plus years of top-level policing under his belt. He was known as a hard man. If there was bad news, he told it like it was, always straight to the point and always the truth. His press conferences frequently sent Police Headquarters into a tailspin. It was no secret that the commissioner of police didn't care for Devereux's direct manner one bit. Personally, I liked him, as did most in Marine. He was well-respected for his no-nonsense manner, plus his unfailing support of those under his command. But being called in to see Devereux without knowing the reason made even the toughest policemen sweat a little. It certainly did me.

I arrived at Marine HQ in uniform at the time specified. After finding my way to the waiting area outside his office I sat and worried until Devereux's secretary called me in. Devereux was pacing the room behind his desk.

"Police Headquarters has agreed to upgrade the rank of the officer commanding SBU to that of chief inspector," he began as I came to attention on the carpet in the middle of the room. "I want you to take over command of the unit."

There was no messing around, no pleasantries, no 'how are you?' Straight to the point. I hadn't even had time to salute.

The SBU was a small, elite, maritime unit of one hundred men and a dozen small fast pursuit craft, or rigid hull inflatable boats (RHIBs). The primary role of the unit was marine counter-terrorism. The men were a highly-trained specialist group. I'd been an observer at one of their training sessions some months before when they executed an assault on a huge Maersk Line container ship as it was entering Hong Kong waters. The unit arrived in their high-speed interceptors and put a team of heavily-armed officers up the side of the ship and onto the deck in a matter of seconds. It was very impressive. I knew that, when not under training, the unit also served as a multi-purpose task force for use against serious waterborne criminal activity. If a smuggling syndicate was getting the better of divisional resources, SBU would be deployed to eradicate it. I knew that Jack Devereux was proud of his boys.

"May I ask a question, sir?"

"Yes, go ahead." Devereux sat down at his desk and turned his attention to an open file.

"All members of the unit are volunteers, is that correct, sir?"

"Yes, that's correct, Bird, all officers in the unit are volunteers." He looked up at me. "We call for volunteers when we need to, then handpick the ones we want after a selection exercise. But yes, they are all volunteers."

"But, you are ordering me to take command, sir?" I asked.

Devereux didn't hesitate. "No, Mr Bird, I am not ordering you to take command. You are volunteering. Now, that will be all." He waved me away. I saluted, turned and marched out of his office.

I already knew many of the guys in the unit. Joe Poon for one. Joe had applied to join six months before. He'd gone through a selection process and was now one of the two team leaders in the unit. I felt good about him being there. Also Sergeant Kwan had been the unit's senior NCO for over two years. He, too, had been promoted upon transfer and was now in the rank of station sergeant, which is a position similar to that of sergeant major in the army. I was pleased to be working with these two very professional officers once more. But when I told Maria the news, she didn't react well. She had heard of this specialist Marine unit and had met some of the officers and their wives at social gatherings. She knew they were a task force that worked irregular hours and were known for their non-conventional tactics. Recently, the newspapers had reported on the injuries of three members of 'a marine fast pursuit unit' whose vessel had collided with a smuggler's speedboat during a high-speed chase.

"That means you will no longer be working on the big launches?" she asked.

I nodded.

"The unit has those speedboats. I have seen them before. You took me to that display last year. They were crashing through the waves." She looked at me.

"Yes, that's them. They are called RHIBs. The men are very highly-trained," I offered in the hope this would reassure her.

"I spoke to some of the junior ones from the unit that day. They told me about the unpredictable hours they work and all the dangerous things they get up to. Will you be doing that? How will I know what's happening while you are on duty, and if you are safe?"

I got questions such as these for quite some time.

Unpredictable hours and danger were certainly two of the conditions that came with being a member of Devereux's Boys. But despite being an elite unit, certain senior officers in Marine didn't care for SBU. Because some of the work was of a covert nature the unit frequently operated in divisional waters without first informing the Marine commander of that area. This upset a number of senior officers. Commanders liked to know what was going on in their division, and when they found out that the SBU had taken action and made arrests without informing them first, they were none too pleased. Don in particular was no great fan of SBU. I'd once heard him refer to the unit as 'a bunch of bloody cowboys,' but only when he was sure he was well out of Jack Devereux's hearing.

SBU had no land-based headquarters building or set of offices *per se*. The unit operated from a variety of structures — collectively known as forward operating bases, or FOBs — that were located in key strategic areas around Hong Kong. Each overlooked the waterways and channels favored by smuggling syndicates and the gangs engaged in the running of illegal immigrants out of China. If a particular inlet or cluster of remote islands became the hangout of a criminal gang we could move the whole unit into the nearest FOB and be up and running within a matter of hours. It was a smart tactic, and one that SBU used frequently to great effect. But not all of the unit's work took place in remote areas.

Victoria Harbor is the narrow body of water that separates Hong Kong Island from the Kowloon peninsula. The harbor's deep, sheltered waters and strategic location were instrumental in Hong Kong's establishment as a British colony and its subsequent development as a trading center. Today, Hong Kong is one of the world's busiest ports with more than 200,000 ships navigating its waters each year. Think Hong Kong and you will inevitably think of the harbor teeming with a never-ending procession of small coastal traders and ferries zigzagging to and from the outlying islands, jostling for position at the narrowest point where the Star Ferry crosses every few minutes. By day and night, the harbor is a hive of activity.

On the morning of August 31, 1988, just four weeks after I had taken over command of SBU, it was raining heavily, and had been all night. We had been deployed inside Victoria Harbor to help the Marine patrol launches stop and check Chinese junks that had recently been entering the harbor without clearance from the Immigration Department. Our job that night was simple and mundane, to stop these vessels and check their documents. It was boring work and the guys hated it. But recently Jack Devereux had been getting flak from Police Headquarters about SBU's lack of productivity and 'his elite unit' doing "nothing but training."

"Do a couple of patrols in the harbor," he ordered. "Check lots of vessel licenses, arrest someone for something, anything, not displaying the correct navigation lights or something like that. Record everything you do. Give me something tangible, no matter how insignificant. Keep the commissioner and the finance people off my back."

At that time Hong Kong's international airport was at Kai Tak on the Kowloon peninsula. The airport's runway jutted out like a pointing finger into Victoria Harbour. Kai Tak Airport was known for its dramatic landings. When flights were directed from the west, the approach was low and towards a range of mountains. Upon reaching a small hill marked with a huge orange and white checkerboard as a visual reference point, pilots were required to make a forty-seven-degree right turn to line up with the runway and complete the final leg of the landing. Typically, aircraft would enter this final right turn at a height of about 650 feet as they flew over and almost between the buildings of the densely populated Kowloon City. From a spectator's point of view, watching large passenger aircraft banking at low altitudes and taking big crab angles during their final approaches was quite thrilling. This final maneuver became widely known in the piloting community as the 'Hong Kong Turn' or 'Checkerboard Turn.' As for the passengers, as they looked out of the aircraft windows directly into the buildings they were flying past, it is not surprising that this phase of the landing became known as the 'Kai Tak Heart Attack.'

Because of the wind direction and the poor visibility on that particular August morning, air traffic control were directing flights to land from the east. All aircraft were making their final approach over the sea, directly towards Kowloon City.

By first light, we were tired and bored with checking licenses, and soaked to the skin. Like most of the guys in the unit, I was looking forward to the end of the patrol, drying out, and grabbing something to eat. I looked at my watch, 0800, end of the shift and time for the unit to stand down, so I gave the order and we began to ease across the harbor towards the Marine Police base on Hong Kong Island, where we could refuel the RHIBs and carry out routine maintenance. There was a canteen at the Marine base, so the thought of a hot cup of tea or coffee was high on everyone's agenda.

Joe Poon, who I had appointed as the unit's second-in-command, was driving one of the RHIBs. As we crossed the harbor, he came close and called across. "I'll take care of the boats," he shouted, pointing at my RHIB. "I'll get them refueled and hosed-down. This one's engines need looking at anyway." He pointed towards the stern of his RHIB. I waved back at Joe and headed for the base.

As always in the mornings, the canteen was crammed with officers either going off duty or just clocking on. Most were Marine Harbor patrol officers, but I noticed a couple of my lads had beaten me to it and were busy pouring huge amounts of sugar into their hot milky tea. As I was about to order coffee, the double doors flew open with a resounding clatter.

"Air crash! Air crash in the harbor!" shouted a young constable, who then immediately turned and ran out as fast he had come in.

The room exploded into life. Chairs went flying, cups and saucers crashed and clattered, everyone was up and running for the doors. I was out and taking the stairs three at a time down to the moorings. I could hear our boats' powerful engines already revving below. All around people were shouting, running, and throwing equipment. I jumped into the first RHIB. A sergeant engaged the dead man's switch and turned a key. Blue-grey smoke spewed from the large outboards.

One of our RHIBs went hurtling past. I saw Joe at the console. We took off after it in the direction of Kai Tak, just a mile away on the opposite side of the harbor.

Rain continued to pelt down as we hurtled across the dark green waters at sixty knots. Joe's RHIB was just ahead throwing up great plumes of spray as it hit the bow wave of a passing ferry. I took a quick look behind. Through a break in the storm, I caught a glimpse of Hong Kong Island's iconic skyline. Neon struggled to penetrate low-hanging cloud. There was an almighty bang as a RHIB to our right hit a wave and took off, clearing some twenty feet through the air before slamming back into the harbor waters, engines screaming at their limit. Visibility was down to two hundred feet as we careered into a curtain of driving rain. My sergeant pulled his goggles down just in time as a wave of filthy water slapped us full in the face. I cursed and spat out a mixture of seawater and engine oil.

As we flew across the harbor, questions raced through my head about search, rescue and injuries. All we knew at this time was that a passenger aircraft had crashed into the harbor.

A blue flashing light directly ahead came into view, then another. There was activity on the Kowloon Bay side of the runway, but we still couldn't see what was going on. I pulled back on the telegraphs, slowing us to a crawl as we closed in on the lights.

"Wah!" exclaimed my sergeant as the scene opened up in front of us. There, still floating on the surface of the harbor waters, was a large commercial aircraft.

The plane, a white CAAC Trident, had broken its back immediately behind the cockpit position. The nose section had snapped forward, leaving a gaping hole on top of the fuselage. The only thing that appeared to be keeping the main body of the aircraft afloat was the tail section, which clung precariously to the sea wall. The cockpit itself, broken and pointing downwards, was partially submerged in the murky waters. It looked like it could go under any minute. To compound matters, the central tail engine of the aircraft was on fire.

There were survivors. On the grass bank just off the runway, we could see clusters of bedraggled-looking people, passengers and crew, sitting or lying down. A few more were crawling along a wing towards the runway wall where Ambulance and Fire Service staff were helping them to safety. Other rescue personnel, dressed in high-visibility jackets, ran around carrying stretchers and oxygen tanks, attending to those who had made it. Two airport fire engines arrived, sirens blasting across the water. Firefighters leapt out and began dragging hoses and equipment towards the burning engine.

Our RHIBs were circling around the crash site looking for the best place to get in close. It was then that I saw Joe's RHIB edging alongside the aircraft's starboard-side wing. But I couldn't see Joe. Where the hell was he?

As we moved closer in, I could see clearly the interior of the broken section. It was a tangle of jagged, twisted metal and dangling wires dripping with oil and water. Cabin debris was strewn everywhere while large pools of aviation fuel spilled out onto the surface of the harbour. Some of my guys were hauling themselves up from their boats and into the gaping hole in the fuselage.

"Where is Inspector Poon?" I shouted to the sergeant at the console of Joe's RHIB.

"He was first inside the aircraft." The sergeant pointed at the huge crack in the plane's side. "Billy is in there with him."

I could now see that the cockpit was rapidly filling with water. The nose section looked ready to snap away from the main body. If it did, it would certainly go under, taking anyone inside with it. "Come on, Joe."

We inched our way along, bumping and sliding against the

underside of the aircraft to where Joe's RHIB was moored. As we
did so, someone began scrambling out of the crack in the plane's
fuselage, then Joe's face came into view. He clambered out.
Billy Lee, Joe's radio man, followed, the antenna of his portable
waving around above his head. Joe dropped into his RHIB. He
looked around, gasping for air, and saw me looking directly at
him.

"Is there anyone in there?" I pointed at the nose of the plane.

"Passenger section is clear, looks like they're all evacuated.
But we can't gain access to the cockpit." He was shouting above
the noise of the fire engine sirens. Joe wiped the water from his
face. "The cockpit door is under the surface and locked from the
inside. There's debris blocking our way in. The pilots must still
be in there." He was struggling to catch his breath. His hair was
matted over his forehead. He looked distraught. "I can't breach
the cockpit. I can't get them out."

We needed help fast. We needed cutting equipment.

An airport rescue boat arrived with two divers on board. Joe
called out to them as they hurriedly prepared their gear, telling
them what he had seen inside the broken aircraft.

The first diver went in. The second followed. I kept the RHIBs
in close. If the aircraft's nose section came away from the main
body while the divers were inside, we would have a whole new
disaster on our hands. Minutes went by. I just hoped there was
sufficient air inside the cockpit – an air pocket, something to help
keep the pilots alive. One of the divers came scrambling back out
of the wreckage.

"We need lights," he shouted into his radio. "The visibility is
poor!" Then, "No, no! We need to cut our way through the debris
to reach the door, and then cut through that."

The diver was angry and frustrated by the difficulty they were
facing. A second airport rescue boat arrived, this one carrying

cutting equipment and large spotlights. We went alongside so the rescue crew could transfer their gear to the fragile aircraft, which continued to totter off the edge of the runway.

The divers working on the plane now had all the equipment they needed to cut through the debris and prize open the sealed cockpit door. But it took time.

After ten minutes one of the divers reappeared from inside the aircraft. I went in close to find out what was happening.

"Six," he muttered, removing the breathing apparatus as he scrambled out. "All inside the cockpit." He dropped into our RHIB and sat down, exhausted. "They are all dead."

The flight that crashed that morning was CAAC flight 301 from Guangzhou. On board the Hawker Siddeley Trident were seventy-eight passengers and eleven crew. All passengers and cabin crew were evacuated to safety. All six in the cockpit died. The pilots never stood a chance inside the locked and submerged nose section.

The official investigation into the accident later blamed adverse weather conditions combined with pilot error. The report went on to say:

> "While attempting to land in heavy rain and restricted visibility, the right wing clipped runway approach lights causing the right main landing gear to be ripped from the wing. The aircraft then became airborne once more before hitting the runway six hundred meters further down. The lopsided aircraft then veered sideways off the runway and crossed onto the grass verge. As it slid, the nose and left main landing gear collapsed and the whole aircraft skidded across a parallel taxiway and into Kowloon Bay."

The rescue service divers were commended for their brave efforts to save the cockpit crew that morning, and in the weeks that followed, Joe Poon and Billy Lee were also commended by Jack Devereux for their brave attempts to gain access into the cockpit and for their support of the divers. They were both praised for courage, professionalism, and devotion to duty of a very high order.

This had been quite an introduction to the post of commander of the SBU. It was only by chance that we had been in the inner harbor at the time of the accident. Even then, despite some very brave efforts by the rescue services, we had failed to save the lives of the flight cockpit crew. The incident did, however, give me a chance to see what the members of the unit were capable of, and how they conducted themselves during a major incident. I was particularly impressed with how everyone remained calm, with the NCOs directing and communicating throughout. It was also reassuring to see how everyone had immediately switched on in an emergency, as I knew the unit was frequently called upon to operate in dangerous circumstances.

19

FORGOTTEN ISLAND
被遺忘的小島

A<small>FTER THE HARBOR</small> air crash, SBU were redeployed back along the northern sea border with China on anti-crime patrols. For the next ten months, with Joe as my second-in-command, we pushed the unit to its limits in our attempts to stop one of Hong Kong's major crime problems: smuggling by speedboat. High-value goods, such as stolen luxury cars, were being smuggled from Hong Kong into China where they were being sold in exchange for arms and ammunition. The weapons were then smuggled by speedboat in the opposite direction, where they were put to use in armed robberies. We were under pressure to stop this racket. It was dangerous work for all involved, and it was at this time that I became concerned about Joe.

Joe Poon always led from the front. He led by example. In my opinion, he was the complete professional. But recently he had become frustrated with our inability to eradicate the blatant cross-border crime. The smugglers' superior speed in their purpose-built boats, together with their ruthless avoidance tactics, formed a combination that proved difficult to stop. We knew the identities of the criminals crewing these speedboats which, in a way, made things worse for Joe. He began to take things personally. During high-speed chases, Joe began to take unnecessary risks. I felt that his obsession with catching certain gang members was clouding his better judgment. He was putting himself and his team in danger. I had to confront him about it. I caught up with him at the unit's forward operating base in Mirs Bay. He had once more returned from an eventful but fruitless overnight patrol. Joe flopped, tired and distraught, into a chair and kicked off his boots.

"No result from last night, then?" I asked, already knowing the answer.

"They are too quick for our RHIBs. We need better kit, faster boats." He picked up the morning's report and pointed to the first page. "Twelve speedboats spotted overnight." He looked up. "We gave chase with all of them, but they got away in the darkness. It's that syndicate operating out of Daya Wan again. We should be allowed to open fire. It's the only way."

Some of Joe's team came in carrying their gear. They also looked worn out, dejected. Joe's disappointment was weighing heavily on his men. He closed his eyes and put his head back. I took another look at the confidential file on my desk, and pulled out a pack of photographs from the inside sleeve. During one of our night-time operations the week before, two smugglers' speedboats, in their attempts to avoid Joe's RHIB, collided in the darkness of Tolo Channel. The four smugglers involved were all killed in the crash. The case, and our unit, once more made headline news. The photographs, taken for evidence purposes, were pretty gruesome. I looked up at Joe.

"Joe, you awake?"

He raised a hand without opening his eyes.

"How's things at home, Joe? How's Kitty taking all this stuff in the press about our intercept tactics?"

"Last week's collision didn't help matters. Kitty doesn't know I was involved. But she is not stupid." He half-opened his eyes and stared at the ceiling fan that continued to gently move warm air around the room. "She nags me all the time about taking care and hanging back. She wants me to request a transfer out of the unit. There's always tension at home. She is worried about my safety. Our safety."

The tactics we employed against these smugglers were the only ones available to us — chase, intercept, and arrest. As the law stood, we needed to make the arrest while the act of smuggling was in progress, while the speedboat and its cargo were underway. It was the only way the case would stand up in court. "You need to catch them red-handed," advised Jack Devereux when we were first deployed along the border, "or their highly-paid legal teams will tear your evidence to shreds and they will get off with some petty theft case."

Those employed to drive these speedboats were ruthless, and would go to any lengths to avoid being stopped. They operated only at night, without lights and at high speeds. A chase was inevitable, which made it a very dangerous game indeed.

"It's the same for us all, Joe," I offered. "Maria is trying to get me to commit to a finish date with the unit, which I just can't do. Anyway, I hear there is a move by PHQ. They are requesting changes in legislation that will give us the power to seize these purpose-built speedboats in circumstances other than during high-speed chases. Seize them in the shipyards, if we can prove they have been used for smuggling."

Joe nodded, but still pulled a face. "Well, if that happens, all well and good. But until it does, we do what we do." He laced his boots and headed off down the jetty to supervise some engine repairs.

I obviously needed to do something, either about our current tactics or about Joe's one-man crusade. I was troubled, until I received a phone call from Assistant Commissioner Jack

Devereux, who took the issue out of my hands.

"I am taking SBU off anti-crime work. You are to get your whole unit, including all your boats, your RHIBs and support craft, out of Mirs Bay and down south to help out with the escalating situation at Tai Ah Chau," he ordered.

"Sir," I began, taken aback a little. "I know we haven't been getting great results along the border of late, but I am working on some changes. I am sure we will get on top of this if you give us more time."

"Mr Bird, it's nothing to do with what's happening in Mirs Bay, this is about priorities. Yesterday Marine Police were handed a humanitarian crisis, so now it's all hands to the pumps. I need you and your whole unit down at Tai Ah Chau tomorrow."

The order came as both a blow and a relief. I was annoyed at not being given the time to tackle the smuggling, but relieved to get Joe out of his dilemma, at least for now.

In some ways, I wasn't surprised at being redeployed to Tai Ah Chau. I had been following the news for months about how the Vietnamese boatpeople situation had been deteriorating. Recently, criminal gangs in Vietnam had begun spreading false rumors that amnesty would be granted simply by landing on Hong Kong soil. Lured by the promise of a better life in the developed world, tens of thousands believed what they were being told and paid for a passage out of Vietnam. This in some ways mirrored the 'big ships' racket, only this time small wooden craft were the vessels of choice.

As this new scam became apparent, the United States, Australia and the European nations that had initially agreed to offer permanent residency to the Vietnamese, started to become more selective about who they accepted. They began imposing stricter entry requirements to their own countries. They preferred to accept only genuine refugees and not those now classified as economic migrants.

This left Hong Kong with a problem: what to do with the continuing influx of Vietnamese, those no longer considered refugees. A small territory such as Hong Kong couldn't absorb them, so the Hong Kong government felt it had to act, and it did. In accordance with the 1951 UNHCR Refugee Convention, Hong Kong announced the implementation of a Comprehensive Plan of Action (CPA) separating political refugees from economic migrants. From here on, all economic migrants arriving in Hong Kong would be classified as illegal immigrants and be detained in closed detention centers. At the same time, the UNHCR, together with the authorities in Hong Kong, opened talks with the Vietnamese government with a view to initiating a program that would see those classified as economic migrants repatriated to Vietnam.

Despite these measures, Hong Kong insisted on retaining its port-of-first-asylum policy, allowing all new arrivals to land. Unlike certain other Southeast Asian nations, it would not turn the boatpeople away. But the consequences for Hong Kong were costly. There were now ten closed detention centers and three transit camps housing sixty thousand people. Some of these centers were former prisons. Others had been military camps. The Argyle Street Camp was built to house refugees back in the late 1930s. It was later used as a prisoner-of-war camp by the Japanese during their occupation of Hong Kong in World War II. Another holding center was the former government explosives and military ammunition facility on Green Island, at the western entrance to Victoria Harbor. Because of its strategic position, this facility became the center for screening and segregating new arrivals. Hong Kong was doing the best it could, but conditions were far from great.

In early May 1989, some of the more hostile Vietnamese,

those already classified as illegal immigrants, earmarked for repatriation and housed in closed camps, began to take matters into their own hands. Fights broke out between different ethnic groups. Northerners attacked southerners. Hunger strikes began, fires were started as inmates burned their bedding and anything else they could get their hands on. Anarchy prevailed.

Then, just the day before Devereux's call, things really came to a head. At the Whitehead Camp, the largest closed camp in Hong Kong, a full-scale riot broke out. Upon discovering they were going to be repatriated, the inmates there turned on staff, who fled to safety. Whitehead became a war zone. One large group of young men tore down one of the camp boundary fences and escaped into the rural areas of the New Territories. Those left inside continued to destroy anything they could. Some climbed onto the rooftops and began a protest. They made 'Long Live Freedom' banners, photographs of which were plastered all over the front pages of the world's newspapers.

The rioting spread throughout other camps, and it was at this point that the Marine Police were drawn into the fray when the commissioner of police called Jack Devereux and gave him an order he didn't like one bit. Knowing Devereux as I did, his response came as no surprise. One of Devereux's staff officers later related the conversation to me:

"With due respect, sir, you must be joking!" said Devereux.

The commissioner wasn't joking.

"It's only a temporary arrangement, Jack, for just a few days, until they can free up some space at the reception center on Green Island. With the rioting, especially at Whitehead, and the situation as fragile as it is, the government has decided to cease all movement between camps, until Monday at least. The government needs more time, and you are going to help them get it."

"Are you seriously telling me that you want us to hold all new arrivals out at sea, on their ramshackle boats, on the open ocean, indefinitely?" asked Devereux.

"The government needs more time to sort this rioting situation out. They suggest you escort all new arrivals to a bay, off a small island called Tai Ah Chau, on the southwest territory boundary. Do you know it? I am told it's sheltered there. You can hold them in the bay for a few days. Don't allow them ashore as there's no intention of using this island to actually house these people. You will need to hold them at sea, on their boats, until a decision is made as to where you will be taking them."

"Sir, many of these boats are barely seaworthy when they arrive. Some actually sink within hours of being intercepted, and Tai Ah Chau is a deserted island. It is probably the remotest point from anywhere in Hong Kong. There is no food, no fresh water, no electricity, no medical facilities, no communications, no control, no nothing. It's a barren island."

"You must hold onto them, Jack, at least for a couple of days. And do not let them ashore. We will be moving them to the Green Island center in a day or two. They are to remain on their boats, that's an order."

Devereux scratched his head. "Sir, if you are ordering me to hold an unknown number of sinking boats full of people, many of whom are malnourished and in need of medical assistance, out at sea for an indefinite period, you are, quite frankly, mad. . . sir."

But there was no point in arguing, Devereux was outnumbered and outranked. He cursed as he hung up the phone.

Within twelve hours of the instruction being given, Marine Police intercepted sixteen boatloads carrying over one thousand Vietnamese. They were all now at anchor in the bay to the west of Tai Ah Chau. As everyone in Hong Kong waited to find out what would happen next, I gave the order for SBU to pack up and move south to Tai Ah Chau.

Earlier that day, Marine Police Superintendent Michael Aitken had been appointed to oversee and execute the commissioner's new directive. Aitken thought this duty would last one, maybe two days, at the most. He was expecting word later that day that he could begin moving the boatpeople to the Green Island Reception Center. Some of the Vietnamese boats had already sunk and refugees were squatting on the open decks of the police launches waiting to be told what to do. But when the message came, it was not the one Aitken expected. He was told there was still no room at the center, that no movements would take place and, due to the poor condition of the Vietnamese boats, he should allow the one thousand Vietnamese asylum seekers to go ashore on the tiny island of Tai Ah Chau. Jack Devereux was not surprised by Aitken's reply to this order.

"Sir, as you know Tai Ah Chau is a small deserted island. It's about one square mile in size. There are three or four dilapidated village houses. They are ruins actually, but most of the island is just rocks, scrub, and a few clusters of trees. There's no proper shelter, there's no fresh water. As of right now, we are holding thirteen hundred Vietnamese down there, many of whom are women and children. There's no electricity, no toilets, so there are already sanitary issues. And there are more on the way. What am I going to do with all these people, sir?"

"You will need to put a team of officers ashore to help sort them out. Try and keep the Vietnamese on their beached boats where possible. Marine Department is towing down a large flat barge that they will secure in the deeper waters, just offshore in the bay. We can use it as an operations platform. I am also redeploying SBU from Mirs Bay, they will be with you tomorrow morning. Their shallow water capability will prove useful."

It was now Aitken's turn to scratch his head. He knew the situation was not sustainable. And there was another pressing issue that bothered him. "Sir, there are both North and South Vietnamese arriving on these boats. Some of these people are probably genuine refugees, while others are not. We are starting to discover former Viet Cong soldiers mixed in with the families. Look what has just happened at the Whitehead Detention Centre. What will this other group do when they discover they are going to be screened out and sent back to Vietnam? Tai Ah Chau is a barren island, there's no way to properly manage this."

Devereux was as concerned as Aitken, but the order had come from a higher place than Police Headquarters.

The next morning the sun was searing with not a cloud in sight and the humidity was stifling. I arrived at Marine South Headquarters with Joe Poon. At least there was one person who seemed pleased we had been redeployed. "Good day to populate a deserted island," said Joe with a smile.

"Careful, Joe. There's going to be some pretty discontented Marine policemen around here this morning. Best keep the humor down to a minimum for now."

We found one discontented policeman very quickly.

"Good morning, sir," I said standing at the open doorway of Michael Aitken's office.

He looked up from his papers and scowled.

"Oh, great, the cavalry is here. Come in and have a seat." He also looked as though he hadn't slept in days. "All right, tell me what you've got. And it had better be good."

"A hundred men, divided into two shifts, twenty-four hours on, twenty-four hours off, no sleep required by the on-duty officers, so you get fifty officers at any one time. Six RHIBs and two logistical support craft. Each boat is licensed to convey up to eighteen passengers but we have had thirty on them when no one is looking." I paused.

Aitken smiled for the first time.

"The unit will be here at 0900, sir. We will need to refuel, which will take half an hour, so we can be down at Tai Ah Chau by 1030 this morning."

"Good." Aitken looked out of his window at the busy Aberdeen Harbour. The huge red-and-gold floating restaurants, the Jumbo and Tai Pak, took center stage while small sampans zig-zagged between fishing junks returning with the morning's catch. "You have both worked in this division before, so you know Tai Ah Chau, right?"

Joe and I nodded.

Aitken walked over to the large chart spread out across a table. "There is a small jetty on the western side of the island. Adjacent to the jetty there's a derelict village house. That's where we have set up the island's police operational post. We are putting in radio communications and a generator this morning," Aitken pointed out the positions. "There are just over thirteen hundred Vietnamese and a total of eighteen boats currently in the bay on the west side. I was told an hour ago that about eight hundred are currently sitting along the shore while five hundred remain on the sturdier of the beached craft."

I took a quick glance at Joe. He was no longer looking as cheerful as when we arrived.

"Now, the next phase of this new arrangement is where you can help. We need to escort the Vietnamese boats from the interception point on the international boundary to Tai Ah Chau." Aitken pointed once more to the chart. "This is possibly where some of your small craft can help out." He looked at Joe and me.

"Accommodation on the island?" I asked.

"Oh God, where do I start," muttered Aitken. "There are the

existing structures. These include about four derelict houses with varying degrees of roofing. There are also a few crumbling foundations where houses once stood. Some of these have broken bits of wall still upright. They can be used to help form the beginnings of somewhere to take shelter. We have been promised tents from the military, but how big and how many, I do not know at this time. Then there are the Vietnamese boats themselves. These can be used as accommodation on the beach."

"There are both North and South Vietnamese on the boats that are currently arriving aren't there?" asked Joe. "And I heard that some of the North Vietnamese men are former military."

"Yes, both North and South Vietnamese on the same small island without any physical segregation. That problem speaks for itself. The Vietnamese army is currently being demobilized, so some of the new arrivals are army veterans, and remember the new repatriation policy is common knowledge, so they will find out pretty soon that they could eventually be segregated out and sent back to Vietnam." Aitken paused. "So, we are expecting resistance and disruption from them. Then we have the families, and the children. There are going to be lots of medical concerns. There's no sanitation, no toilets." Aitken looked up from his papers. "There will be young women too, and a lot of single men. Frankly gentlemen, we have a recipe for disaster."

"One last question, sir," I asked. "Who is in charge on the island?"

"Well, that would be your old chum Chief Inspector Donald Bishop," Aitken said, a wry smile across his face.

After leaving Aitken's office, Joe and I headed down to the pier where our unit was busy refueling. "This is going to be a tough job, Joe," I said.

"I know. And it will be worse with a bad-tempered Diamond Don Bishop in charge, that's for sure."

"We will take all RHIBs and the support vessels down to Tai Ah Chau," Joe said once the whole unit had gathered round. "Leaving in thirty minutes from now. This is day-one of a major operation. There is no written operational order and no one really knows just how this camp is going to work. Remember, the majority of the Vietnamese will be in poor physical condition. There will be women and children, they will be afraid of what is happening. But also, remain alert to anything untoward. Remember, there will be troublemakers. Help where you can, but remain firm."

Joe turned to me. "Anything else?" he asked.

I shook my head. "No, let's go."

It was a hot, cloudless morning. The sea was flat, not a wave, which made perfect conditions for our small craft to make good time. After leaving the Marine base, we travelled north of Lamma Island and straight across the West Lamma Channel, averaging fifty knots, passing the island of Cheung Chau to our left before transiting south of Lantau Island. Six RHIBs and two Sharkcat support craft, all in single file, cut through the crystal-clear waters. The white foam bow waves from each vessel shot out on both sides of the formation. I turned and looked back from the console of the lead RHIB. It wasn't often I saw the whole unit at full speed in daylight. We often joked about how we could ski off the back of these RHIBs. Today's conditions would be perfect.

Just forty-five minutes after leaving the base, we approached the remote rocky coast of the Soko Islands. As we slowed and cruised near the barren northern rocks of Tai Ah Chau, I pulled alongside Joe's RHIB.

"After we round the point, I will go and look for Don Bishop, see what we can do first, to help," I shouted over the sound of our idling outboard engines. "You go and have a look around, do a recce, see what's what. I'll meet you in about half an hour."

Joe nodded as we motored into the bay. "Wow!" he shouted. "It's Armageddon."

20

IT WAS AN ARSE OF A DAY
狼狽的一天

THE SIGHT that greeted us was staggering. The western side of the tiny island had been transformed from a deserted bay into a scene resembling the D-Day landings. Refugee boats of every shape, size, and condition were littered across the beaches and inlets. Some were still afloat, some half-submerged, with others broken and aground. At the center of it all, the wreck of a large wooden vessel was on fire. The boat was listing heavily as flames made quick work of its dry beams. Black smoke billowed upwards. It was the smell of the burning oil, mixed with the all-too-familiar stench of rotting wood that greeted us. In other areas, police launches were nudging their way through the clutter. Loud hailers directed more incoming Vietnamese boats. A Royal Navy landing craft was attempting to get alongside the tiny jetty. One of the sailors was shouting something at the people on the pier head. An assortment of other small government craft were darting here and there. I kept getting whiffs of gasoline from the dozens of outboard engines. The smell lingered in the sweltering air. The whole bay was a barrage of noise and activity. It was difficult to know where to begin. I waved at Joe, and pointed to a pontoon anchored to one side of the bay. There looked to be about five hundred refugees squatting on the pontoon's flat surface. Small groups of men, women, and children huddled together. Marine policemen clambered amongst them. The entire bay was buzzing.

Ashore, next to the whitewashed walls of the derelict house, I could see a jetty crowded with hundreds more Vietnamese. The refugees sat in the heat, waiting to be told what to do. A couple of police officers with clipboards moved amongst them making notes as they went. There were nods and shakes of the head from the refugees as they were spoken to. I took off my beret and wiped the sweat from my face. The sun's rays burnt the skin.

"Where is Chief Inspector Bishop?" I shouted across to a Marine police sergeant on the pontoon who was trying to organize a group of women and children into a covered area that provided some shade. He shook his head and raised his hand to his ear, suggesting I should use my radio to locate him.

I turned my RHIB around and made for the packed pier head. Everyone's attention seemed to be on whatever was going on there, so I maneuvered closer. I heard him before I saw him.

"Get that generator inside the house, and tell that lazy lot sitting under the tree that if they don't lift a finger to help, I'll throw them all in the sea."

There are few people I have met that I could truly say have a commanding presence. But for sure, I was looking at one now. This was a situation where you need a Don Bishop to take charge. No precedent, no nonsense, don't mess with me.

The first thing I noticed about Don that morning, apart from the fact that he was dressed in full uniform, was that he had what appeared to be a white tea towel tied around his head. But this was not any ordinary tea towel. This one was fashioned in a Cleopatra-style arrangement. It was tight around the top, and came with a French Foreign Legionnaire's curtain affair that hung down the back and around both sides, which covered his ears. I assumed the whole thing was fashioned to protect his bull head from the burning sun. In uniform, with his big round face protruding from the front of his striking, self-made, pharaoh-style headgear, the figure of Don Bishop resembled a cross between Field Marshal Erwin Rommel and Genghis Khan. Not a man to argue with.

"You there. Yes, you!" Don bellowed at a young fit-looking Vietnamese man. "Move those boxes inside."

Don pointed a long wooden stick at the boxes of what looked like rations and to the door of the house. The Vietnamese man jumped at Don's command and started dragging the boxes.

"Excuse me!" I called, looking up from my RHIB which was now just below where Don was standing on the jetty. "Could you tell me who's in charge here?"

Don slowly turned and looked down. "Bah, young Leslie, it's about bloody time you got here. I hope you've brought that rabble of a unit with you. We received word you were coming. Quite frankly, I am surprised you lot could tear yourself away from all that sunbathing." It was the usual Don Bishop welcome. I tied up the RHIB and climbed up the steps to where he was standing. We shook hands.

"So, you seem to have everything well under control here," I said looking around at the mayhem.

"Organized bloody chaos." Don waved his stick at the large group of people sitting in front of where we were standing and shook his head.

"There are more coming." I pointed out to sea where a police launch was escorting three more wooden boats towards the island.

"Ah, yes," said Don glancing down at a clipboard. "Another two hundred and thirty-eight guests for the Hotel Tai Ah Chau. Intercepted an hour ago off Fan Lau Point. That makes our score

1,724 as of right now, plus at least two more boatloads that have been spotted on the way. My guess is we will exceed two thousand by nightfall."

"Don, how can we help?"

Bishop tucked his clipboard under his arm and straightened his headgear.

"The first shipment of rations has been delivered. It's on that pontoon in the bay. If your small boats can transfer that first load here, onto the island, I can arrange for it to be distributed."

"What about fresh water?" I asked.

"It's arriving now, on that landing craft." Don pointed over towards the beach next to the jetty.

"Is it not possible to provide any segregation on the island, Don? North from South, families from single men, former soldiers from the others?"

"Not enough men. No equipment, and at night no lights. Basically, no."

With over one thousand Vietnamese arriving on a daily basis at the international sea boundary, interest in our tiny island began to increase. The following morning, a government spokesman announced, "Tai Ah Chau is a temporary emergency holding center for Vietnamese boatpeople before they are screened at the Green Island Reception Center."

Don Bishop's response when he heard this was predictable. "Bah!" he scoffed as he rocked back on the wooden crate he was sitting on inside the command post on the jetty. He turned down the volume on the portable radio that looked like it was a remnant from World War II.

"I think Security Branch knows full well that with almost three thousand Vietnamese on this island already, and many more on the way, this situation is no longer temporary. Where are they going to relocate three thousand people on a permanent basis? Government is stalling, playing for time while they think about what to do next. That's all well and good but this camp, for that is what it has become, is not a temporary arrangement."

As the heat of the day began to melt everyone on Tai Ah Chau, Don began looking for someone to take out his frustrations on. He started with me.

"Leslie," he grumbled after reading a message from Jack Devereux. "Make yourself useful. Go and do a reconnaissance of the island. Assess the situation as a whole. Priorities, where do we need to focus our resources? Where is everyone located? What's their condition? What shelter do they have? Plus where are the ex-military located? Are they in groups or are they fragmented, potential flash points? Report back."

I found Joe outside talking with Billy Lee. Billy reminded me of the character Radar in the TV show M.A.S.H. He was young and fresh-faced with a pair of wire-rimmed glasses perched on the end of his nose. If ever I needed to send a radio message, I would turn to look for Billy only to find him standing next to me with his pad and pen at the ready. When I needed to lay a hand on a particular piece of kit, Billy would be there handing it to me before I asked for it. It was as if he had a second sense for what I was going to do next. Joe Poon thought the world of Billy Lee. He'd adopted him as his own personal assistant.

"Come on, you two, we are going for a hike," I said grabbing a walking stick. We set off, with me happy to be out of Don's way. At the first beach, we found a dozen or more grounded wooden Vietnamese boats. Groups of people, families, sat huddled on the open decks, while others were inside the tiny cabins. Stretched above some of the boats were tarpaulin covers, strung up to offer some protection from the sun's burning rays. Women sat cradling their young. Men just sat there doing nothing in particular. They stared back at us as we passed. Some men, dressed in just their underwear, were taking a bath in the sea. In the center of the bay there was a partially-submerged boat, which looked like it had been stripped of everything, including its cabin roof.

"I can't understand how some of these wooden boats have made it here from Vietnam," said Joe, pointing out to sea. "It must be five hundred, six hundred miles that way."

"I don't think they have, Joe," I said. "Most have come the long way round, hugging the Chinese coast, past Hainan Island and Macau. Many of them have stopped off in China before striking out for Hong Kong. It's not difficult to figure out, really. As you say, many of the boats are simple river craft with a flat keel, with hardly any draft. They are not sea boats."

We marched on, into the next bay.

"The only thing these people have been given since they arrived yesterday is a drink of water from the launch that intercepted them," said Joe referring to the notes on his clipboard. "It says here that they have been self-sufficient since then." He looked up. "Self-sufficient, on what? There's nothing here."

Further along the beach, we could see more makeshift shelters erected inside the tree line. Wooden masts from sunken boats formed the framework for these structures. Some had rusty corrugated iron sheets for roofs, some had torn and ragged sails rigged up between the trees, and there were even small one-person huts built entirely of flattened cardboard ration boxes.

As we walked, the Vietnamese watched us, expressionless. Billy Lee made extensive notes so that he could file a report once we returned to the post.

It was a similar scene at the next bay. More fragile structures erected along a grass verge parallel to the beach. In one, there was a group of fit-looking young men. I guessed they were in their late twenties or early thirties, all with cropped hair. We stopped to take a closer look. Their structure was more of a bivouac, much sturdier than the others we had seen. These guys had found rope and had secured the roof with tight knots. They had dug into the hill to give their hut, for that's what it was, support and protection from the elements. The young men stared back at us, chiseled features, hard faces.

"Some of these guys are wearing military clothing," said Joe. "Soldiers, North Vietnamese for sure. I wonder what they, and others like them, will be getting up to after dark when they get bored."

Joe walked up to the group and spoke to them in Cantonese, asking how they were. There was no response, they just stared back in silence.

"Yeah, from the North, military," he said. "South Vietnamese can usually speak some Cantonese, or at least understand. These boys haven't a clue what I was saying."

"What's more disturbing is they didn't look as if they cared what you were saying." I pulled out my water bottle and took a swig. "These guys are recently demobilized from the North Vietnamese army for sure. I am not surprised former soldiers have decided to try their luck as refugees. There can't be much going for them back home."

Joe went down to the water's edge and washed some gunge off his boots. "This open camp condition..." he pointed back up at the island "...without proper control, it's asking for trouble. I hope this is going to be resolved very soon."

We moved on up a grassy hill towards a small structure that many years ago had been a village house. There must have been over fifty people inside, mostly families. As we walked past, we had to take care not to step in any of the human faeces that were scattered all around.

Joe shook his head. "There is going to be a huge problem in the very near future, if there are no sanitation arrangements established here. Without a permanent fresh water supply, and with no washing or toilet facilities, in this heat and humidity, we are going to have infection and disease pretty soon."

On a hill overlooking the southern side of the island, we could see two of our RHIBs motoring slowly around the closed-area perimeter. Beyond was the South China Sea. Billy Lee tried his portable radio without any luck. He fiddled with the switches, then checked the aerial. "Nothing, sir. The radio is fine, the batteries are fine. Seems to me that the whole island is a black spot, no reception."

"Our radio communications with Marine Control and our patrol launches are practically non-existent," Don confirmed, after we had returned. "It's a bit like World War I. If I need to pass information to a patrol launch, I have to send a runner with a written message in that rubber dinghy to the police launch in the bay. The runner then returns half an hour later with the reply." He shook his head. "What are we going to do in an emergency? Start banging dustbin lids together? Whichever genius selected this island deserves a clip around the ear."

I was watching the Royal Navy landing craft approach the beach as Don continued to complain. On board I could see Dougie Kerr, so I climbed down from the jetty and walked along the shore towards where they were about to beach. I was sure Dougie would have some choice words on the whole situation. About fifty of the more helpful Vietnamese men came forward to greet the landing craft.

"Are these our volunteers?" shouted Dougie when he saw me, pointing towards the group on the beach.

"They will carry the kit from the landing craft up to the command post," I said. "What have you got here?"

Dougie jumped over the side of the landing craft, landing in a few inches of water, he took a kick at a small wave before holding up his list. "Sleeping mats, disinfectant, plastic rubbish bins, plastic sheets, mosquito repellent, eating utensils, blankets, more dry rations, barrels of fresh water," he replied, reading from his clipboard. "Plus anything else I could scrounge." He looked up and smiled. "I managed to procure a second generator from the barrack sergeant at Marine HQ. And — wait for it—" he bowed, tipping his cap " —an old wooden desk that we can put to use at the command post."

"That's great, Dougie, well done. That water is like gold dust around here. And Don will be pleased with the generator and that desk."

"Aye, I thought he'd need somewhere ta rest those massive feet of his. How is the King of Tai Ah Chau by the way?"

"Like a bear with a sore head. He's up there, in the post, if you want to talk to him."

"Nah, think I'll pass. I'll leave His Lordship be fer now."

As the landing craft ramp slowly came to rest on the sand, Dougie's crew began to arrange the Vietnamese men into a line.

"Have you heard the weather forecast, Les?" said Dougie.

"No, we have been here all day with no radio comms."

"There's a typhoon crossing the Philippines heading east-northeast. The Royal Observatory is speculating that it may turn north once it's over the South China Sea. It could be heading here."

A typhoon. I looked around and tried to imagine what a severe storm would do to this island. The flimsy-built structures, some made entirely of cardboard, wouldn't survive the first decent gust. Same for the rickety wooden boats that cluttered the bay. Beached or afloat they would either be completely destroyed or upturned and sunk. I felt sure that if this place was hit by a typhoon, it would be obliterated. With more than three thousand refugees on the island, and with more on the way, something had to be done, and fast. And Michael Aitken was on to it.

"The conditions on the island are appalling," he said during a live radio interview later that day. "This is no way to house or detain such a large group of people, and we still have no news on how long we will need to keep them here on the island. Now, with news of an approaching typhoon, we may be forced to evacuate the island."

"If the typhoon hits Hong Kong, where will you put three thousand people?" asked the reporter. "They are on an island miles from civilization."

"I have no idea. I really have no idea," Aitken replied.

Aitken was inviting trouble from Police Headquarters with his negative comments. He believed that, outside of those who had actually visited the island, no one fully appreciated the dangers involved in trying to move thousands of people in storm conditions. He was exhausted and he had decided to try and shake the government into action with a few choice phrases. It seemed to work. Later that day, as Typhoon Dot swept northwards across the South China Sea towards Hong Kong, the government announced that Tai Ah Chu would be evacuated. But that posed more questions. Where were we going to put these people? How were we going to get them there? And, what would happen to the camp during the storm?

"There's that sturdy concrete-block drug rehabilitation center on the island of Hei Ling Chau," said Jack Devereux. "I've been told that the center has quite a few buildings currently underutilized. Security Branch estimate we can put about two and a half thousand Vietnamese there."

"How do we move them?" asked Aitken.

"If we move them today, we can make use of two Royal Navy landing craft," Devereux said. "By tomorrow the navy feels it will be too dangerous to try this with the approaching storm, so we are going to begin the transfer as soon as possible. Today. There's a lot to do."

"Okay, that accounts for two thousand five hundred. But the head count on Tai Ah Chau as of right now is just over three thousand seven hundred."

"The government is relocating six hundred out of the Green Island Reception Center to one of the larger camps, so I am told we can move some of ours in there. Again, this can be done today."

"And the remainder. That leaves another six hundred."

"I don't know yet. I am working on it. I'll get back to you."

The order from Aitken to Don Bishop and his fifty officers on Tai Ah Chau was a simple one. "Everyone on the island is going to be evacuated and moved to a safer location today. Sea transportation is being arranged. Your job is to prepare all three thousand seven hundred Vietnamese for the move. They can take all their belongings with them, provided they can carry them themselves. Anything that can't be carried must be left behind."

As the winds picked up, flimsy huts, bits of boat, corrugated sheets, and assorted paraphernalia blew across the island. Then came the rain, a deluge, turning the island into a swamp. Don Bishop fittingly summed it up. "It was an arse of a day."

But, slowly and remarkably, everyone was evacuated off Tai Ah Chau. As the final landing craft left the island, Bishop found the radio link he had been searching for and called Marine Control. "Where am I taking this last batch of six hundred Vietnamese, over?"

"Word from the refugee coordination center is that all camps and holding centers are now full," came the reply. "We have been told to make our own arrangements for the six hundred you are currently evacuating, over."

Don Bishop looked at the Vietnamese squatting and huddled

together on the open deck of the flat-bottomed landing craft as it pitched and rolled in the seas south of Lantau Island. He stared at the radio receiver and scratched his head. "Fat lot of use you are," he muttered.

But Michael Aitken had a solution. "Bring that last lot back to our base in Aberdeen. We will look after them ourselves. We have the workshops, storerooms, and the covered car park. We can pull down the storm shutters and house them in there until the typhoon passes."

As Hong Kong's Royal Observatory hoisted the Number Eight Tropical Cyclone Warning Signal, all schools and offices closed. The public were warned to stay indoors and the Marine Police and Royal Navy took six hundred Vietnamese in a landing craft to the operations base on the south side of Hong Kong Island. Later that day, as the typhoon reached an intensity of sustained winds of 185 kilometers per hour, Hong Kong came to a standstill; everyone battened down the hatches and waited. But Typhoon Dot gradually turned westward, passing to the south, heading towards the Chinese Island of Hainan. Hong Kong had escaped, but Tai Ah Chau hadn't.

Once the worst of the storm had passed, Don and I took one of the larger Marine Police patrol craft out of Aberdeen to assess the condition of whatever was left on the island. It was a pretty arduous trip, but once there we could see from one mile out that most of the Vietnamese boats that had been left behind had been destroyed. The bay was full of wreckage. Through binoculars I could see the house on the jetty, but all of the makeshift structures had been blow away. It was as though no one had ever been on the island.

"Take a look at this," said Don handing me a radio message. On Hainan Island, just to the west of Hong Kong, fourteen hundred homes had been flattened, with over sixty-thousand more damaged. "If there had been a direct hit on Hong Kong," said Don, "anyone left on Tai Ah Chau would not have survived."

In 1989, the year we evacuated Tai Ah Chau, more than 34,000 Vietnamese arrived in Hong Kong, the highest number in ten years. This huge influx came as a surprise to the Hong Kong authorities who had banked on the impact of the Comprehensive Plan of Action, including the segregation and repatriation policy, taking effect quickly. With this continued influx, the government was left with little choice but to rethink its immediate short-term plan for Tai Ah Chau. The result being that the camp continued to be used as a temporary holding center for two more years until 1991, when a new purpose-built center was constructed on the island. Once completed, the Tai Ah Chau Detention Centre thus became the fourteenth permanent Vietnamese center in Hong Kong. It was able to accommodate ten thousand people.

21

OPERATION SEAGULL
海鷗行動

AT THE CONCLUSION of the Tai Ah Chau duties, Joe and I returned to the unit on the Chinese border and resumed the work we had been involved in prior to the redeployment. But no sooner had I arrived back than I found myself dragged away once more. In just a matter of days, I received confidential orders from Jack Devereux to report to the Director of the Narcotics Bureau at Police Headquarters in Wanchai. I was not told why, only to turn up at a specific time in civilian clothes and not to speak to anyone about it. While being redeployed away from the unit for specialist work was all part of being a member of SBU, it was, at times, frustrating. It was also dangerous. The unit's main task at the time was anti-smuggling work. I believed that redeploying either Joe or myself was asking for trouble. High-speed chases at sea in total darkness required innumerable on-the-spot decisions. Every operation was finely balanced. The chances of collisions were high. Leaving these night-time ops to junior officers worried me enormously. I felt it my responsibility to confront Jack Devereux on the matter.

"I know, Mr Bird," he replied. "You are correct. It is far from ideal. Also, with you only having recently returned from Tai Ah Chau duties, I argued against this NB attachment myself. But, for once, I can do nothing. It's out of my hands. This one has come from the commissioner himself. Joe Poon will have to manage the unit without you. Tomorrow, Police Headquarters, 0900."

The following morning, I was met at PHQ and signed in at the Bureau's offices by Chief Inspector Jon Robinson, one of NB's top investigators. I had great respect for NB. In recent years, they'd made major inroads into disrupting the importation of heroin from China, and Robinson had been at the fore in many of the cases. As we walked along the Bureau's maze of corridors we passed dozens of framed photographs of famous drug seizures. There were display cases filled with paraphernalia: opium pipes, special waistcoats designed to smuggle drugs, and even a drug smuggler's hollowed-out shoe.

"What's this meeting about, Jon?" I asked.

"We are in the middle of a major double-sting operation. It's a massive op, one of the biggest I've ever been involved in. It's been on-going for months. There are hundreds of officers involved, and it could prove to be the biggest haul of pure grade heroin in the history of the Hong Kong Police."

"So not your normal operation, then?" I glanced at him.

"You might say that. We are about to enter the final phase of this operation so everyone is on edge. When you meet the director, I advise you to just listen."

"Sure, understood. I am, however, curious as to why I'm here?"

Robinson shook his head. "Sorry, the director wants to brief you himself."

"Who else is in this meeting today?" I asked as we reached the director's office.

Robinson stopped. "Just you."

The Director of the Narcotics Bureau was a clean-cut Chinese man in his late forties. I recognized him immediately from his many TV news appearances. He was sitting at his desk reading as we walked in. He motioned for me to sit down opposite.

"Mr Bird, what you see and hear over the next few days is strictly confidential," he began. The director was dressed in a blazer and slacks. He smoothed his cricket club necktie down the front of his crisp white shirt as he spoke. "You will discuss this with no one outside of the specialist team that's been assembled for this case."

He gave me a look, checking that I was responsive to what he was saying. I nodded my understanding and he launched into the briefing.

"We have been tracking a large shipment of heroin, originating in Thailand, through China and into Hong Kong. The heroin is currently being kept in a warehouse in Kowloon City. The triad gang that is guarding it is heavily-armed. An informant, one of the gang members, has been relaying intelligence to us for the past month. As a result, over one hundred officers, in covert surveillance teams, have been tracking both the shipment and the gang members throughout Hong Kong. We also have surveillance teams deployed to monitor the movements of the syndicate's head man and the financier."

I nodded again that I was following the story, assuming I was soon about to be told why I was involved.

"The syndicate's plan is to transport the heroin on an ocean-going yacht to Australia where it will be offloaded by triad gangs in Sydney and sold on the streets. The quantity of heroin is not yet known, but intelligence suggests it is a very large amount with a street value in the hundreds of millions of dollars," said the director. "The yacht has been brought in from the Philippines."

He examined a file on his desk. "A Canadian national, a Caucasian male, has been hired by the gang to skipper the yacht. This man is aware of the yacht's intended cargo, so he is therefore part of the gang. The Canadian's first job, after he arrived in Hong Kong, was to hire a crew of experienced amateur sailors to work on the yacht. He did this by advertising the job as a straightforward yacht delivery. Their idea being that if this 'genuine' crew faced a customs or immigration check in Sydney, a bunch of amateur sailors without criminal backgrounds who also had no idea they were shipping drugs, would appear routine and not raise suspicions. The good news is we have been able to infiltrate this amateur crew with one of our undercover officers who applied for a position on the yacht and was accepted."

I sat up a little, impressed.

The director went on. "With one of our undercover officers on board as part of the crew, the yacht will be allowed to leave Hong Kong with its illicit cargo. This is where you come in." He looked at me and smiled. "We are planning to intercept the yacht on the open ocean, just before it leaves Hong Kong territorial waters, using a police sting vessel. And we want you to drive it."

"Sting vessel, sir?" I asked.

"Yes, I'll come to that in a second," he replied. "Once we have intercepted the syndicate's yacht out at sea, we will confiscate both the yacht and the drugs, while the syndicate members on board will be detained. Jon," the director nodded to Robinson.

"The interception of the yacht, as it leaves Hong Kong waters is quite delicate," said Robinson. "It is vital we approach it and get our officers on board before any of the gang members can send a message to their triad bosses back ashore."

I pictured the scene, a yacht on the open ocean. I began to consider the variables in this scenario. Was resistance by the crew of the yacht expected? Would they be armed? The state of the sea, and the visibility at the time would also be important factors. Robinson continued.

"The reason for this is that once we have overpowered the

gang and seized the yacht, we plan to produce an exact replica, an identical yacht, then sail it, together with a substitute cargo of 'drugs' down to Australia."

Now I really was impressed.

"Once we arrive in Sydney, our undercover crew will meet up with the triad gang there. Then, together with the Australian Federal Police, arrest them. While these arrests are going on in Sydney, we will be making arrests of the Hong Kong syndicate here."

Robinson smiled at the look on my face. He knew the list of questions I had was beginning to pile up. But before I could speak, the director was off once more.

"After we intercept the yacht here in Hong Kong, the whole operation will remain top secret, keeping the syndicate's hierarchy and other gang members in the dark. If we can achieve this, we have a chance to obliterate the two syndicates, internationally, in one go. Now, you have some questions?"

"Yes, sir, I do," I replied. "How do you plan to keep the syndicate members in Hong Kong from finding out what has happened to their yacht between the time you intercept it as it leaves Hong Kong waters and the time the replica arrives in Sydney?"

It was Jon Robinson who answered. "As we said earlier, we have an informant. He is telling us that only three gang members will be included in the crew. There will be him, the Canadian skipper, and one other triad member on board the yacht. The remainder of the crew will be the amateurs, which includes our undercover officer, of course. This means that once we make the interception and overpower the bad guys we only have to convince a total of two criminals that it's in their interests to play ball with us, rather than spend the next thirty years in prison."

"So part of the deal for this Canadian and the one other gang member is to remain on board for the journey to Australia?" I asked.

"Correct, they will form part of the new crew that will predominantly be made up of undercover officers."

"And sail into Sydney?"

"Correct."

I looked across at the director. "And my role again, sir?"

"Initially we considered requesting the services of your whole unit to do a rapid interception, in your high-speed pursuit craft," said the director. "But if the yacht leaves Hong Kong in broad daylight, on the open ocean, they might see you guys coming, realize the game is up, and have time to either ditch the drugs or even prepare to defend their cargo. And if they have their wits about them at the time, they could also get a quick phone call or radio message out which would ruin the Australian half of our plans. So we have ruled that option out. We have decided to try and fool them with a vessel in distress ploy."

The director studied me for a reaction. Knowing there was more to come, I waited.

"We have hired a motorized yacht, a big white thing about fifty feet in length. It's the sort of boat you see cruising around the islands at weekends full of partying expats, you know the sort of vessel?"

"Yes, sir."

"As I said before, we want you to drive it," he said. "We will put a four-man team of NB officers on board with you, led by Jon here."

Robinson took over once more. "We will be dressed in Hawaiian shirts and shorts, like a bunch of guys on a day out. Once the target yacht is out of port, out at sea and well away from the drug syndicate guys ashore, we will pass close by and send out a distress signal from our yacht, shoot up a red flare and then request assistance from them. We think this is the best way to get really close without raising suspicions. Once close in, we will cross over and overpower their crew."

Now I had a lot more questions. But the director hadn't finished.

"We are calling this Operation Seagull," he said with a slight smile. "We get these code names from Op's Wing. There's a list of approved names. The Director of Operations thought it quite an appropriate title, all things considered. Jon, show Les the list of individual code names and call-signs for this op."

Robinson pulled out a single sheet of paper from a pink-colored hard-backed file and handed it to me. Under the words *Operation Seagull – Strictly Confidential* I read that the drug smugglers' yacht was to be referred to as *Seagull* while our vessel's call sign would be *Buzzard*. Robinson's personal call sign was *Broadsword* and a Chief Inspector Knowles, who was the undercover amateur on board Seagull, would be *Danny Boy*. If it was necessary to refer to the police informant over the air, his code name was *Popeye*.

"You are immediately relieved of your normal duties," said the director. "I have, this morning, spoken with your commanding officer, so a story of your absence has already been circulated. Your second-in-command—" the director looked down at his notes "—Inspector Poon," he said looking up, "will assume command of your unit until you return. We expect the sting to go down in the next five days. Now, the first thing for you to do is to inspect our vessel, *Buzzard*. Take her out for a spin. See how she handles."

The director looked first at Jon, then at me.

"Gentlemen, this is a major sting operation. Six months of hard work have gone into setting it up. There is a lot riding on this next phase in Hong Kong. There is no room for error. If we apprehend the syndicate here and seize the drugs as planned, that will also give the Australian Federal Police a very good chance to break up the triads in Sydney. Good luck. That will be all."

"I have lots more questions," I said to Robinson as we left the director's office.

"I am sure you have. Let's go into my office."

"Where did you find the undercover officer that has got himself recruited as a crew member?" I asked.

"It's Chief Inspector Greg Knowles. Do you know him?"

I shook my head.

"We have been really lucky here as Greg just happens to be an experienced ocean-going yachtsman. What's also brilliant about this is that he has been an undercover NB officer for some years and already comes with shoulder-length hair and a bushy beard, so he is ideal for the role as a backpacking amateur sailor looking for work. Greg had no problems in getting the crewing job and has already got quite close to the Canadian and begun passing us information."

From Robinson, I learned that members of the gang on the yacht could be carrying firearms, which meant it would be critical to get the team of police officers onboard fast. "Knowles will be carrying a police firearm concealed in a compartment at the bottom of his personal luggage. And of course we will also be armed."

"Having an undercover officer on board *Seagull* will certainly help during the interception phase," I said. "Where is the yacht now?"

"It's moored up in Sai Kung Marina in the New Territories. We have it under surveillance."

"Do you think this will work?" I asked. "I mean, assuming we intercept the yacht, overpower the crew, and you find the drugs on board. There's the confidentiality factor, isn't there? The triads in Hong Kong are going to be keen to know the progress of their shipment. How are you going to maintain the charade during the three-to-four week trip on the identical yacht with the substitute drugs?"

"As the director just said, we will convince the skipper and the others on board that it is in their interests to cooperate. Thirty years in prison is pretty strong leverage."

That afternoon, Jon and I drove over to The Royal Hong Kong Yacht Club in Causeway Bay. Jon led the way around the pontoons to a white cruiser docked at an end-berth where we found NB Inspector Ben Eccles on the lower bridge busying himself with a large kit bag.

Eccles looked up and smiled. "Just filling the fridge with beers," he said. "We need to look like a bunch of expats on a day out, right?" He was wearing a pair of khaki shorts and a scarlet Hawaiian shirt. "Just getting into the part," he added, glancing down at the green parrots and bright yellow pineapple print on the shirt front.

"Don't drink all those damn beers," Robinson said. "We haven't even started this part of the operation yet."

I entered the bridge and looked around. As I suspected might be the case, our cruiser was not equipped with radar. "Jon, there's no radar."

"Radar? Do we need one?"

"What if *Seagull* leaves at night and we need to locate them?"

"Well, they should be easy to spot, right? I mean it's a big white yacht. Should stick out like a sore thumb?"

"Well no, not really. At sea, it gets dark at night, you know? Can we change this for one equipped with a decent radar system?"

"No way. It's taken me weeks to get the funds approved and

to get this one sorted. It's too late to change now. This is it."

Jon's large Motorola handset burst into life, interrupting my proposed maritime lecture. He looked at the portable phone and raised a hand, "Sorry Les, hang on, let me take this call."

As Jon went out on deck, I decided to inspect *Buzzard*. I found the logbook on the bridge. She was listed as a fifty-five-foot, twin-engine, motor cruiser. After a quick walk-around, I hauled up the stern deck hatch and took a look inside. I estimated that the two eight-hundred-horsepower diesel engines would give her a top speed of about thirty knots in good conditions. The engines themselves looked reasonably clean and well-maintained. Back up top, there was a flying bridge from where the yacht could also be driven. Visibility from this flying bridge was good, but the steering position was very exposed. I did a quick check of the electrics, tried all the lights and started the engines. The fuel and water gauges read full. Down below, there were two cabins, a toilet and shower plus a small galley. It was adequate for a few days. I located the life-saving gear, life jackets, small anchor, buoys, and coils of rope in a stern locker. I dragged everything out, spreading the gear out on deck. Everything was in order.

While I understood that confidentiality was critical to the success of this operation, I felt that a rapid interception, using RHIBs from my unit, would have been a far better option than using this pleasure cruiser, which was in no way designed for such a job. There were so many unknown or untested factors involved in using this vessel in a police intercept scenario. But NB thought otherwise. And now it was too late to change.

"There's movement," Jon said, appearing from the bow. "Our surveillance teams inform us that the drugs are now being moved by road up to Hebe Haven Yacht Club in Sai Kung. They left about half an hour ago. Currently there are only three people on board *Seagull* at the jetty waiting to receive the shipment: Popeye, an as-yet unidentified Chinese male, and another man who appears to be Asian in appearance but is certainly not Chinese. Our guys are working on putting IDs on these other two now."

I looked at my watch. 1515. Realistically, they could be ready to set sail sometime tonight. We needed to get a move on with our preparations.

A few hours later, I drove across Hong Kong Island to Marine HQ to collect my gear from the office. As I drove, I thought of Maria. She would be expecting me home tonight. I knew someone from headquarters would contact her, spin her a line about me being detained at work on some highly confidential case, telling her I was fine, giving her the usual story. I also knew she would ask questions, which the officer making the call wouldn't be able to answer. As usual she was going to worry. She would not be able to sleep without knowing more. She would contact some of my colleagues from the unit. She would phone Joe. They wouldn't be able to help. I felt bad and for a second I considered calling her myself, just to tell her I was okay and not to worry. But then I recalled the director's warning about confidentiality and the months of work by hundreds of officers.

As I was parking the car at Marine HQ, I prayed I would not bump into anyone who wanted to chat about work. Divisional staff were always pressing me for stories or information about the unit's work. Today was not the day.

I climbed out of the car and headed for the office.

"Hello stranger," said Don Bishop from the front seat of his car, parked a few spaces away.

Bugger, I thought. *Sod's Law.*

Upon the conclusion of the Tai Ah Chau duties, Don had been posted back as Marine operational commander of the southern territorial waters, the waters through which *Seagull* would sail on its way out of Hong Kong. The place where the planned interception would take place. And Don was forever trying to find out what my unit was up to and where we were operating. I didn't need him sniffing around and getting in the way at a time like this. Confidentiality was critical to the success of this operation.

"Don, how are you?" I replied. "You having a kip in your car or are you on stakeout?"

"Less of your cheek," he began, edging himself out of his battered Merc. "I was listening to the final bars of Land of Hope and Glory," he said. "And where are you swanning off to anyway? Fancy a beer in the Mess?"

"No, Don. I'm a bit busy at the moment, just popping into the office to collect some kit." I knew full well that he wouldn't settle for that.

"Ah, sneaky beaky time, is it? What have you got on tonight then, young Leslie?"

"Nothing special, Don. As you well know, we are working up north, up in Mirs Bay, and I need some stuff from the office. Now, I must be away, I'll catch you later for that drink."

Before he could probe any further, I was off through the front doors and out of his clutches. I hadn't told Don a complete lie, the unit was actually deployed up on the border that week. I just neglected to tell him that they were doing so without me.

After collecting the gear I needed, I had just enough time to grab a Hawaiian shirt, one I thought would give Ben Eccles a run for first place in the loudest shirt on *Buzzard* competition, and headed back to the marina. By 2000, I was back onboard and running through the final pre-operation checks when the four-man narcotics team turned up. In addition to Jon Robinson and Ben Eccles there was also Inspectors Justin Kennedy and Barry So. They were carrying sacks of gear: personal kit plus bags of radios, chargers, binoculars, and a couple of night vision devices which cheered me up considerably. On board, Jon and the other guys were checking their handguns and ammunition. Earlier, while collecting my personal gear from the office, I had withdrawn a standard service revolver and twelve rounds of ammunition from the Marine armory. I now had the gun secured under my shirt in a holster tucked into the small of my back.

It was just after 2100 when we cast off and motored out of the Royal Hong Kong Yacht Club basin. I steered *Buzzard* slowly through Victoria Harbor heading west. The yacht handled quite well but, as suspected, she felt light and rolled easily in the swell of the harbor waters. That was worrying. If things got a bit hairy during the interception, being on a vessel that is unstable is far from ideal. I felt much more at home on something sturdier, more responsive, and more powerful.

The reflection of Hong Kong's iconic skyline lit up the water as we went. The harbor was always busy. Sampans jostled through the swell thrown up from ocean-going freighters. I maneuvered *Buzzard* past the Star Ferry concourse, the sounds of one of the world's most vibrant cities mixed with the boat engines and harbor wash as it slapped against our bow.

Circumnavigating Hong Kong Island that night was a simple job. The lights of the city as we passed through the harbor provided good visibility and, as I'd hoped, the sea was relatively calm. We motored east through the Lamma Channel, hugging the coast, towards the mooring spots I had identified earlier. Once out in the open sea the swell, originating from the east, became heavier so I turned to port and headed for a secluded mooring in Stanley Bay. We could tie up there and wait for news of *Seagull*.

As we secured *Buzzard* to a mooring buoy in the bay, I listened to Eccles carrying out radio and telephone checks with the police operations room. All seemed in order as call signs were coming through loud and clear. At midnight, Jon called everyone around in the lower cabin for an update.

"I have just been told that the shipment of drugs has been put on board *Seagull* at Hebe Haven Yacht Club," he began. "Apparently, the syndicate took several hours to secure it, so I guess it will be well-hidden. The yacht remains moored at the jetty and the crew appear to be sleeping." Jon looked down at his notes. "The two guys who were at the pier earlier with Popeye are still on board and appear to be part of his crew. They brought a lot of personal kit with them."

"IDs?" asked Eccles.

"Yes, one is a Hong Kong Chinese male. He is a triad society member with plenty of form – drugs, wounding, assault occasioning actual bodily harm, resisting arrest, etcetera. A nasty piece of work. The other is a Filipino national who was part of the crew that sailed *Seagull* up from the Philippines. The gang must be keeping him on for his sailing skills." Jon lowered his notes. "The hired amateurs, including Knowles, have not yet shown up, so it doesn't look like they are moving just yet. I suggest we get some rest."

The night was uneventful. I tried to sleep on top of my sleeping bag down in one of the cabins. I thought of Maria at home. She would be waiting for the phone to ring. I felt guilty for putting her through all this.

At dawn, I got up and wandered around *Buzzard*. Jon looked as though he'd been up all night. "Any news?" I asked.

"Nothing. No one is moving." He shuffled off.

It was a clear, sunny morning, so I sat out on the forward deck with the others. Justin Kennedy had appointed himself as ship's cook and was busy in the galley rustling up some food. We were killing time, laying around, when Jon's Motorola burst into life. He disappeared up onto the flying bridge to take the call.

Seconds later he was back. He smiled and nodded. It was on.

Jon told us that more crew members had arrived at the marina and were loading equipment onto *Seagull*, and that they looked like they were preparing to sail.

I took a look at the Admiralty chart on the bridge of *Buzzard*. I calculated that once the yacht was underway, it would take them most of the day to reach the waters south of Hong Kong where we would attempt to board. As feared, this meant the boarding would take place during the hours of darkness. This, compounded with the fact that our attempted intercept was going to be along the southern boundary, an area exposed to the Pacific Ocean and known for its turbulent weather, was cause for concern. I started to worry about the capabilities of our vessel and how she would handle in rough seas.

Several more times, Jon went over the interception and forced boarding plan, which was to take place two nautical miles north of the international boundary. Jon asked if anyone had questions. I raised my hand.

"It's not a question," I said. "I just want to make everyone aware that this looks like it may take place at night, which means our Hawaiian shirts and weekend looks now mean nothing, as those on board the yacht will not be able to see us. Also, the boarding will take place in total darkness, which means things might get a bit hairy, so just be mentally prepared for that."

"Good points, thanks," replied Jon. "We will be putting up flares of course, as though we are in distress."

By 1730, the sun was resting on the hills over Lamma Island to the west. At this rate I calculated that *Seagull* should be nearing the southern boundary sometime between 1900 and 2000 hours, in total darkness.

I climbed up to the flying bridge and started both engines. Plumes of smoke billowed from the stern. We eased out of the bay at five knots. No hurry. As we went, I drew my service revolver, did a final check and secured it back under my shirt.

Jon and the other guys sat down on deck and enjoyed the sunset. All four were dressed in colorful casual clothes and really did look like a group of good mates out on a day's sailing.

As we continued slowly south, a breeze picked up from the east, followed by a cold gust. I sensed a storm further out. I looked down at the guys. Ben Eccles was setting up his night vision device, his shirt flapping in the wind.

"Best get into the lower cabin," I shouted down to Jon and the others. "It's going to get a bit lumpy soon and I don't want anyone going for an unscheduled swim."

As the guys edged around the side of *Buzzard* and into the cabin, our launch rolled in the increasing swell.

"I think that's it," shouted Eccles from below. "Just there, moving slowly this way." He pointed out to sea and then looked up at me. I could just make out the shape of a vessel about one nautical mile away, its silhouette against the lights of Hong Kong Island. "Okay, let's move around a bit and see if we can confirm that," I replied. I turned *Buzzard* and headed further south towards the darkness of the southern boundary.

As I was adjusting *Buzzard's* speed, there was a sudden loud crack from the control panel and the revolutions of our starboard side propeller shot up to maximum. *Buzzard* swung violently to port and I had difficulty remaining upright. My immediate reaction was to pull back on the throttle, thinking that someone on the main bridge below had pushed forward on the controls. As I did so, the first large wave struck the side of *Buzzard* with an almighty thwack and we rolled wildly once more. I could hear shouts from the guys down below who were sent sprawling across the cabin, their equipment clattering and crashing around after them.

I tried correcting *Buzzard's* turn by ramming the starboard side throttle into reverse. Nothing happened. We continued veering to port, pitching and tossing in the increasing swell. What the hell was going on in the wheelhouse below? Who was interfering with the controls? I hung over the side. There was no one anywhere near the console.

Realizing we had a serious mechanical problem, I yanked the keys out of the starboard side engine socket and the veering immediately stopped. The starboard side telegraph cable had snapped, leaving the throttle jammed in the full-ahead position. With *Seagull* almost upon us, there was no time to get down to the engine compartment and disengage the engine, which was now as good as useless. I cursed to myself as we were sideswiped by yet another large wave. This loss of an engine, combined with the strong wind and deteriorating seas were now making this far more difficult than it needed to be. And *Seagull* was now visible, about half a mile away.

"Piece of shit," I muttered to myself.

"What's going on?" yelled an anxious-sounding Jon Robinson from below.

"Oh, nothing special," I replied. "It's great fun up here."

"Well, have your fun some other time. *Seagull* is almost here."

Ben Eccles came out of the lower cabin and positioned himself against the bulkhead. He held up a flare in his hand to show me what he was about to do. There was a flash of light and a crack as he shot the red distress flare high into the air above us. Jon began waving his arms above his head giving the international distress signal, hoping the Canadian skipper could see him. But *Seagull* slowly turned away.

"They are ignoring us," shouted Jon looking up at me. "He's ignoring a vessel in distress. For all he knows, we could be sinking in this storm."

There came another loud crack, this time from the direction of *Seagull*. The sound of a single gunshot.

"Jesus, they're shooting at us!" Jon shouted, quickly disappearing back inside the cabin and taking cover.

Up on the flying bridge, I decided it was time to put an end to this case as speedily as possible. Engaging our one good engine to full speed, I grasped the wheel with both hands and prepared to hang on. In the following heavy swell, we shot forward. I was now flipping the wheel left then right in my attempts to keep a straight course towards *Seagull*, but with an eight-foot high wave ebbing and flowing directly into our stern, our speed was fluctuating wildly. We were, in effect, surfing in a fifty-five foot cruiser towards our target.

From up on the flying bridge, I now had a clear view of *Seagull* and could see people scrambling around on the rolling deck. They must have been very confused as to what was going on as *Buzzard* came bearing down. I was still seething from being shot at and was very much aware that those on board the yacht had a clear view of me on *Buzzard's* flying bridge.

It had been my intention to maneuver *Buzzard* alongside *Seagull* at speed, give the yacht a hefty nudge, then kill the speed and hopefully be able to hold her steady long enough for our team to jump across. But on one engine, in these heavy seas, this was not going to be easy. I braced for the impact.

The collision between the two vessels was nothing less than spectacular. Finding it impossible to hold our angle of approach, we rammed *Seagull* far harder than I had intended. There was an almighty crash from the impact, which sent everyone on the deck of the yacht sprawling. Slamming our one working engine into reverse and spinning the wheel inwards towards the yacht I was able to hold *Buzzard* alongside *Seagull*, just for a second. As the yachts touched I screamed at the NB guys, "Jump now!

Jump!"

And they did, as one, landing and colliding with each other onto the deck of *Seagull*. It was hardly an impressive arrival, but they somehow made it.

Using our one working telegraph to reverse away, I half-expected its single cable to snap under the strain. But it held, and the boats quickly separated. *Buzzard* and *Seagull* now rolled and pitched in the darkness.

I quickly aimed a spotlight onto *Seagull's* decks to see what was going on. Although both boats were being tossed around in the dark waters, and rain arriving in gusts, I could see someone at the helm, but I couldn't make out who. Then he turned, giving the thumbs up. It was Danny Boy — Greg Knowles. I also saw Ben Eccles clambering back up on deck from the lower cabin area. He waved and held his hand up to his ear signaling I should grab the portable radio pack-set I had slung against the console.

"*Buzzard*, *Buzzard* this is *Seagull*," came Eccles' voice. "All secure, we have control."

I later learned from Knowles that after we fired the distress flare, there was panic on board *Seagull* and an argument broke out between the Chinese triad, who insisted they turn away and ignore the signal, and Greg Knowles who tried to persuade the Canadian skipper to go closer to respond to the 'vessel in distress.' It was at this point that the Filipino began to remove something from his kit bag. Knowles, suspecting it maybe a firearm, tackled him from behind and knocked him out with a blow to the head. Knowles then jumped on the Canadian skipper and shoved him to one side where he went tumbling across the deck. With the skipper floored, Greg managed to get hold of *Seagull's* wheel and keep her steady, allowing us to get close. It was at that point that I crashed into *Seagull*, sending everyone sprawling once more.

While this was going on, the Chinese triad managed to crawl down through the hatch and disappear below. Ben Eccles, who was the first of the boarding party to get to his feet, followed. It didn't take Ben long to overpower him.

Back on *Buzzard* I wiped the rain from my face and took stock. The consequences of the collision could have been much worse. We could easily have lost someone over the side during the boarding.

As things seemed to be settling down on *Seagull,* I reversed *Buzzard* a little more and took a look at the damage I'd caused. Our deck planking was cracked and broken, but I couldn't see the hull. I hoped there was no structural damage and that it would hold for now. The radio burst into life once more. It was Jon.

"We need to get to sheltered waters as soon as possible. Can you escort us?"

"Heading due north at slow speed towards Hong Kong Island. Follow me."

In the lee of Stanley Bay, I helped the others secure *Seagull.* Soon, a much larger party of NB officers arrived and began the systematic search of the seized yacht. In addition to the Canadian skipper, there were only two other members of the drug syndicate onboard, the young Hong Kong Chinese male and the Filipino. The remainder of the crew consisted of our man Knowles plus three innocent recruits. These guys were, quite understandably, terrified.

It wasn't long before the haul was found. Large packets of heroin, each the size of a house brick, were sealed inside the yacht's water tanks. Brick after brick were lifted out and stacked inside the yacht's cabin area. An hour later, there was a mountain of the stuff.

"How much is there?" I asked Jon.

"There's about eighty slabs I think," he said, sitting down and rubbing his shin. "Did you have to smash into the yacht so hard? I almost broke my bloody leg."

"So how much is one brick worth on the street?" I asked.

"Oh, it's about half a kilo of pure grade I think, so over forty kilograms altogether. On the street here in Hong Kong, I'd say that could fetch between two hundred to three hundred million dollars." He looked up at me. "But in Australia, the triads would have cut it down and distributed it to middle men, then sold it on to pushers on the streets. Who knows how much it would have fetched down there. This is the biggest haul of pure grade I have ever seen. Probably the biggest haul we have ever had."

"During the search did your guys find the gun that fired that shot at us?" I asked.

"No, nothing," Jon shook his head. "And Knowles told me that as far as he was aware, no one fired a gun during our approach. It's very strange, I was sure the explosion we heard was a gunshot."

"Winston Churchill said there's nothing more exhilarating than being shot at and not being hit," I smiled.

"I don't think the director is going to feel much exhilaration when he sees the bloody great hole you made in the side of the yacht. The last thing he said to me before we headed out was, 'Don't damage that boat.'" Jon got to his feet and limped off.

Once the forensic officers had completed their work and the evidence was secured, I was left with the task of driving the damaged *Buzzard* back to the Royal Hong Kong Yacht Club inside Victoria Harbor.

On one engine it was a slow journey, during which I had time to reflect on what had just happened. We had been lucky during that boarding. In those conditions and with only one engine, I had been very fortunate to get in close and alongside *Seagull*, let alone hold our position long enough for our team to jump across.

They too had been lucky not to end up in the sea between the two rolling vessels. Someone could easily have been killed.

The sun was coming up as I gingerly maneuvered *Buzzard* back into her mooring slot at the yacht club. I thought of Maria, who had been at home for two nights not knowing where I was or what I had been doing. I suddenly realized I was very tired.

A total of forty-three kilograms of pure grade heroin were found on the yacht which, at that time, was the largest single seizure of heroin in the history of the Hong Kong Police, and would have been the largest seized shipment into Australia had it got that far.

In the days following the arrest, information was passed to our Australian colleagues. Six weeks later an identical '*Seagull*' sailed into Sydney Harbor. It was skippered by the Canadian and crewed by undercover Hong Kong police officers, plus the Chinese triad and the Filipino. Two kilograms of the seized heroin, together with forty-one kilograms of a synthetic substitute, was packed into the yacht's water tanks.

Days later, twenty-four people were arrested in simultaneous operations in Australia and Hong Kong. These included the respective syndicate heads, the middle-men, and the financiers. Both gangs were, in effect, wiped out.

At its conclusion, this was the most successful narcotics operation for both the Royal Hong Kong Police as well as the Australian Federal Police. At every stage, it was essential there was seamless cooperation between both forces and that strict confidentiality was maintained for almost six months. And it worked. In the weeks that followed, Jon Robinson invited me back to Police Headquarters for the operational debrief. It was there that I was told that the Canadian skipper was the NB informant.

"So what did he get in return for providing the information

and for his cooperation?" I asked.

"Immunity from prosecution, a new identity, and four million Hong Kong dollars."

"Four million, that's a lot." I thought about it for a second. "But I guess he will need that to help facilitate a new identity. I am sure whichever triad gang lost forty-three kilograms of top-grade heroin will be very keen to have a word with him. What about the other two?"

"The Chinese triad guy and the Filipino made full confessions. It was a critical part of the case that these two also agreed to act as part of the crew on the replica *Seagull*, as the triad gang in Sydney were aware of the identities of the crew out of Hong Kong."

In a high court case in Hong Kong the following month, the Chinese and Filipino gang members both received prison sentences of nine years. The Canadian skipper simply disappeared.

One evening, about a week after the case became public, I happened to stop by the Mariners Rest for a drink.

"Well, well, well, look what the cat's dragged in," announced Don Bishop from the far end of the bar as I walked in. The Mess was full and it was obvious that Don had been there for some time. I made my way through the crowd and settled down on a stool next to him. He placed a cold beer in my hand, then leaned forward and winked.

"That's the beer I said I would buy you a couple of months ago, remember?"

"What?"

"Oh, you know," he whispered, "the night you went sailing down south." He winked again and chuckled. "Don't worry, your secret is safe with me."

22

DEADLY GAME
亡命遊戲

Since the days of the Opium Wars, Hong Kong has been on the trading route between East Asia and the rest of the world. Its strategic location made Hong Kong a financial and economic gateway to China. It also made it the ideal platform for illegal trading and smuggling between the colony and China.

By the late 1970s, China had started to open its doors to foreign investment. By the mid-1980s and early 1990s, its economy was developing rapidly to the extent that there was a surge in the number of wealthy Chinese with money to flaunt. The desire for high-end luxury goods, from cars to clothes and jewelry, especially from Europe and America, continued to grow. At the top of the must-have list of the new elite in China were cars and also electronics, such as video recorders and TVs. High taxes and duties in China meant these products were still in short supply.

At the conclusion of the *Seagull* case, I was assured by Jack Devereux that there would be no more redeployments of either Joe or myself.

"I want you to focus on getting to grips with this cross-border smuggling," he said. "I have spoken with the Commissioner, and he agrees. This is now the priority."

In the few months I had been away, the volume of goods

crossing the border by illegal means had grown significantly. To meet an increased demand, the gangs had upped their game by manufacturing bigger, faster speedboats. Speedboats in which they could pack much more cargo, and stay ahead of the new high-speed pursuit vessels of the Marine Police. They were sixty-foot-long, grey molded fiberglass speedboats fitted with as many as five powerful 250 or 300 horsepower engines, which gave them top speeds of up to eighty knots (ninety mph), and they soon picked up the nickname *daai fei*, literally 'big flyer'. The open cargo compartment of the *daai fei* was big enough to accommodate a luxury car or four hundred VCRs. Because the *daai fei*s were purpose-built for illegal activity, they also came with defense and escape capabilities. To protect the crew from gunfire, the coxswain's position was surrounded by metal plating, and the bow section was reinforced with an armored tip which could be used to ram anything or anyone that got in its way. In a press article at the time, Jack Devereux described the *daai fei* as 'a death machine, a military tank with the acceleration of a Ferrari.'

By the end of 1990, smuggling by *daai fei* was a multi-million-dollar operation, and our job was to stop it using whatever means we could devise.

"You just watch yourself, Leslie-boy," advised Don Bishop one afternoon at Marine HQ.

"Thanks, Don," I replied. "I assume you are referring to the nocturnal activities of my unit?"

"I am indeed, dear lad. I saw one of those *daai fei*s the other day. Death traps. Those smugglers are ruthless. They'll stop at nothing to avoid arrest. And I mean nothing."

Don fixed me with one of his one-eyebrow-raised stares then turned and stomped off. It was good advice. Arrest-avoidance tactics by these mainland-based gangs was something never too far from my thoughts.

Another feature of these syndicates' activities was the luxury car 'steal to order' business. Anyone in China with the ready cash could place an order for a specific make, model, even color, of vehicle. The Hong Kong-based members of the syndicate would then simply go out into the streets and steal one. The operation was slick and professional. After stealing the ordered vehicle, it would be driven immediately to a prearranged loading point, a secluded jetty in the rural areas of the New Territories, where a mobile crane and crew were waiting with a specially-designed sling to winch the car into the waiting *daai fei* alongside a pier. The road-to-boat transfer took no more than sixty seconds to complete. The *daai fei* with the stolen car on board would then accelerate off into the night on its way to mainland China. The profit on this few hours' work was, of course, one hundred percent of the selling price of the car in China. In 1990 alone, 660 luxury vehicles, mostly Mercedes Benz, were reported stolen and never recovered. We suspected that all 660 ended up in China.

It was almost all night-time operations for the unit. The syndicates that operated their fleets of *daai fei*s preferred the cover of darkness, for obvious reasons. Our food, rest and sleep were taken during the day at our forward operating base in Tolo Channel. Our home lives, what there was of them, remained tense.

"Kitty is on my case again," said Joe one morning after returning to the base. We had had a long, cold, fruitless night. Joe and I were in the locker room. He was peeling off layers of thermals. Joe had by now overcome his one-man crusade against certain mainland coxswains. He was seeing things clearly once more.

"She is still asking me how long I am going to continue with the unit. Her two main points are always the same. It's the danger and the unsociable hours. She also says she has hardly seen me

A SMALL BAND OF MEN

in the past six months and that when she does I am always too tired to talk. And, of course, I keep getting the 'and every night I can't sleep with worry in case you get hurt, or worse!' lecture."

Despite the unsociable hours and the occasional brush with danger, SBU had a very low turnover of staff. I actually cannot recall any officer ever asking for a transfer out. We were seen as an elite unit, and there was a long list of Marine officers wanting to join. We were, understandably, very selective about who we took. We frequently had to rely on each other in close-quarter situations so it was important to have the right man standing next to you.

Tolo Channel is a ten-mile-long narrow body of water on the north-east tip of Hong Kong's New Territories. It connects, at its most inner point, the towns of Sha Tin and Tai Po and, at its outermost point, the open sea and the Chinese coast beyond. The Chinese name for the mouth of Tolo Channel is appropriately Chek Mun, or Red Gate.

Tolo Channel was a smuggler's dream. Not only did it connect two large towns with the open sea and the China coast, there were also twelve remote piers and jetties scattered along both sides of the channel, offering secluded loading points. All had good, quiet, roads leading to the urban areas. On a moonless night, the channel was dark, making it easy to go undetected. And being a channel, its waters were invariably calm. This was an ideal location for high-speed vessels to operate.

On the night of June 3, 1990, our unit was busy preparing their kit for the evening's patrol. That day, we had been moored at the Marine Police base inside Tolo Channel. Our engineers had been fine-tuning our outboard engines, while our deck crews had been doing running repairs. By early evening, everyone was focused on that night's task, checking and rechecking equipment — boat engines, weapons, communications – as well as coordinating

278

map references and timings. Everything needed to be checked and double-checked.

Information had been received from our lookouts along the channel that there was quite a lot of motorized sampan movement around Sam Mun Jai Cove on the northern side of inner Tolo Channel. These sampans were the syndicate's lookouts, their eyes and ears. It was the lookouts' job to try and spot police movements and report in to their controller via either a shortwave radio or mobile phone. The controller would then decide on which loading points his *daai feis* would use that evening.

I found Joe Poon talking to a group of NCOs. We walked out of the briefing room and onto the pier. It was a moonless night. We stared out across the calm waters of the bay, into the darkness.

"Sir, there's a message for you." It was Joe's radio operator, Billy Lee. He came running along the pier and handed me a scrawled handwritten note. "There's information there could be a loading within the hour," said Billy in his usual way before I could read it. He smiled and adjusted his glasses. I could see he was excited by the news. We had a chance of an arrest and the seizure of a *daai fei*.

"Thank you, Billy," I said.

Joe took a glance at his watch, "I suggest we move into Sam Mun Jai covertly, as soon as possible and see what's happening."

I agreed. "Don't forget, if we can get a clear view, and there is *daai fei* activity, we must wait for the loading to be complete before we move in. We need evidence of the act of smuggling in order to make the case stand up in court."

"Let me lead," Joe said, a firm tone in his voice. "I will use NVGs and wait until I have visual evidence, then I'll illuminate the bay with flares. We can move in, fast, and make arrests before the *daai feis* have time to shoot off."

I turned to Billy. "Tell Mr Kwan to come and see me now, we need to get the unit ready."

Billy was already on his way before I could finish my sentence.

Our aim, as always, was to get as close to the jetty as possible without being detected by any of the syndicate lookouts. We needed to wait until the *daai feis* had cast off from the jetty with a full load before we moved in to make arrests. If they were moving, they were then, in the eyes of the law as it stood at that time, in the act of exporting unmanifested cargo.

But with this strategy there came a high degree of physical risk. Once underway, a *daai fei* can reach high speeds in seconds. It then becomes a very dangerous game to try and stop it. With the days of putting a warning shot across the bows now a thing of the past, we were left with little in the way of safe methods of stopping these high-powered, armor-plated, craft. Some *daai fei* coxswains were not averse to ramming police vessels in order to avoid arrest.

Marine Police Headquarters, realizing the dangers involved in trying to combat this new method of smuggling by *daai fei*, had made several representations to government for changes to the existing maritime legislation. Quite simply, we wanted the construction or use of vessels purpose-built for smuggling, to be made illegal. That way, we could seize these boats in circumstances that suited us, in the shipyards, and not at eighty knots during a high-speed chase in total darkness, as was currently the case. But the bureaucratic machine was slow.

That night, we knew the *daai feis* would make their way out of their home base on the Chinese side of Mirs Bay and down Tolo Channel shortly after dark. The syndicates wanted to utilize the whole night, or ten hours of darkness for each *daai fei*. Their first run therefore would be an early one.

At 1900, we set off for the outer waters of Sam Mun Jai

Harbour. It was pitch-black except for the dull lights of my console. I watched Joe's RHIB just ahead through my night vision goggles. It was usual for Joe to command the RHIBs that were going to attempt the arrest at the pier. His local knowledge of the bays and inlets and his ability to listen in to, and understand, the smugglers' Chinese radio chatter, made him the best man for the job. It was invariably a situation where split-second decisions and good reflexes were of paramount importance. No one was better at this than Joe Poon.

As the unit's senior officer, I placed myself in the role of pursuit commander. If one or more of the *daai fei*s were to make a break for it, a decision would need to be made very quickly as what to do next. Many of the coxswains employed by the syndicates were mainlanders, some former military. These guys in particular didn't want to be apprehended in Hong Kong waters, and would go to any lengths to avoid arrest.

I could see Joe just ahead. His RHIB was stationary so I maneuvered slowly alongside. We needed to maintain radio silence as we knew the syndicate lookouts had the means to monitor police radio channels. Joe was looking into Sam Mun Jai through his NVGs. We were careful to remain in the shadows, hugging the coast as we slowly approached the suspected loading area.

"What's happening?" I asked.

Joe pulled his radio earpiece out and pointed into the darkness. "Two *daai fei*s alongside the pier. A truck just pulled up and they are already transferring cargo into the boats. About ten to twelve men on the pier."

I pulled my night vision goggles out of the cargo pocket of my trousers and took a look.

"They will be ready to go in under a minute," I said.

"Yes," replied Joe, "see you later, good luck."

There was a sudden rev of engines and a pungent smell of petrol as Joe and his second RHIB took off for the pier.

I watched them move in. My sergeant, standing to my right, slung his Sterling submachine gun off his shoulder and checked the firing mechanism. He then flicked the action to automatic.

I watched as the men on the pier continued to carry boxes from the truck to the waiting *daai fei*. They worked quickly and efficiently, unaware that the fast police boats were approaching. Scanning back, I looked for Joe. The RHIBs were just a few hundred feet from the pier and closing in. Then all hell broke loose. Joe had been spotted. Within a matter of seconds, the two *daai fei*s were moving away from the pier, great plumes of grey smoke billowing from their massive engines as the coxswains hit the accelerator. On the pier, men ran in all directions leaving what was left of their cargo where it was. The delivery truck shuddered forward, its tailgate flapping at the rear, boxes tumbled out and crashed onto the road.

Joe's two RHIBs circled off the pier, but it was too late for a safe interception. The two *daai fei*s were already accelerating away: forty, fifty, now sixty knots. Joe and his second RHIB turned and attempted to get alongside, but the sheer speed of the bigger boats gave the policemen little chance.

I glanced left and right at the two RHIBs on either side of my own. With these two *daai fei*s heading in our direction we were entering into the second phase of the game. I radioed for our coxswains to hold position. I'd worked with these men in situations like this dozens of times before. I trusted them completely. But what we didn't need now was a sudden rush of blood to the head and someone trying to be a hero by blocking the channel with his RHIB. Now was the time to rely on this trust.

Joe put up a flare giving us a clearer idea of where everyone was and what was happening. Upon spotting our police vessels ahead, both *daai feis* swung away into Sha Tin Bay.

"What the hell?" I said to my sergeant. "Why have they gone in there? There's no other way out, they have boxed themselves in."

We watched as the two *daai feis* slowed down, their crews realizing their mistake.

"Mainland coxswains," Joe's voice came through my earpiece. "Looks like they left their local Hong Kong navigators on the jetty in the hurry to get away. They are disoriented, they are not sure of the way out of the channel."

We now had five RHIBs in the mouth of Sha Tin Bay, and we all knew what would happen next. Before anyone could speak the two *daai feis* did a 180-degree turn and accelerated towards us. I slammed the throttles of my RHIB into reverse and began moving out of the way, I motioned for the others to do the same. Those *daai fei* coxswains were not going to stop for anything.

They came out of the bay doing eighty knots. The high-pitched scream from the banks of five 300-horsepower engines was deafening as they tore past. The bow waves caught our small fleet of RHIBs and for a few seconds we were thrown all over the place.

Joe shot up another flare and the channel lit up once more. We could see clearly both *daai feis*, which seemed to have parted company, but were both heading northwards towards the mouth of Tolo Channel and the open sea. While we had little chance of catching them now, we swung our RHIBs in their direction and followed. There was always the possibility that one would encounter a mechanical problem or, possibly, without a local navigator, run aground on the rocks while still inside Hong Kong territorial waters. Then we would have something.

I followed the *daai fei* that seemed to favor the middle of Tolo Channel. Joe, and one of the other RHIBs, went after the other.

Possibly this coxswain believed that by running close to the coastline he had a better chance of finding the open sea and an escape route back to China.

"Sir!" screamed my NCO above the noise of our outboard engines. He was standing next to me and had been fiddling with his portable radio.

"Collision! There's been a collision!"

He was pressing on his earphones, trying to make out what was going on. I quickly throttled down to reduce engine noise and we came to a complete stop. The NCO looked up.

"A *daai fei* has rammed one of our RHIBs!" he shouted.

I felt my guts sink. I immediately turned our boat around and headed back towards Three Fathoms Cove.

The unit was easy to locate as someone had illuminated the whole area with a flare. As we approached, I could see three of our RHIBs moored together in the bay. There was no sign of a *daai fei* so I eased back on the throttles and we slowed to a couple of knots. Some of our guys were sitting down in their boats, one of our NCOs appeared to be receiving treatment. He was sitting on the deck of his RHIB with his back to the console. Another officer sitting in one of the other boats was completely soaked and had obviously been overboard. I could see Kwan kneeling next to him. I had a really bad feeling now. I then spotted Joe sitting on the balustrade of the middle of the three RHIBs. His head was down, arms tightly wrapped around his middle. He was staring at the empty deck just in front. I moored alongside one of the outer RHIBs and climbed across the raft of boats to where Joe was sitting. I was about to speak when I noticed the uniform boots in the shadows of the bow section. I froze. As my eyes became accustomed to the change of light I found myself looking at the shape of a crumpled body.

"It's Billy," said Joe without looking up. "It's Billy Lee. He took the full force of the armor-plated bow of the *daai fei*."

Marine Police Constable Billy Lee Kam-sing, age twenty-seven, lay dead on the deck in front of us. I felt the life drop out of me.

I can't recall how long I stood there looking at the crushed body at the bow. "Billy Lee?" I heard myself say.

"He was hit by the armored bow of the *daai fei*, at eighty knots," said Joe. "He's a mess."

I sat down next to Joe and looked out across the bay and the dark waters of the Tolo Channel.

Joe and Billy Lee's RHIBs had been tracking the second *daai fei* along the south side of the channel. As they passed Three Fathoms Cove, the *daai fei* did a 180-degree about-turn and headed directly for the two smaller police boats. Although the coxswain of Billy Lee's RHIB made several attempts to avoid the *daai fei* as it careered towards them, it smashed at full-speed into the starboard side of the RHIB. The momentum of this very heavy speedboat lifted it over the forward section of the police pursuit craft, and it hit the water on the other side. As it flew across the top of the police RHIB, it hit Billy Lee face on. He was killed instantly.

The physical impact of the *daai fei* colliding with the RHIB also flung the two other police crew members overboard. Joe Poon pulled them both from the sea seconds later. These two now sat on the deck trying to come to terms with what had just happened. Kwan was looking after them.

"They are both in a state of shock," he said. "Physically they seem okay, not seriously hurt." Kwan stood up and stepped over to Billy's body. He was silent for a while, "I'll get something to cover him up," he said finally.

I looked again at Billy's smashed body. This was a deliberate attempt by those onboard the *daai fei* to ram and render the police vessel inoperative. It was an act of murder.

Joe was the first to pull himself together. "I am going up the channel, to see if I can find the bastard," he said. "That *daai fei* may have experienced mechanical problems or even hit the rocks. If I find him. . ." Joe turned away.

As a sergeant covered Billy Lee's body with a plastic sheet I asked for a radio. I had to begin the process of reporting the death of a young officer killed in the line of duty — all over a boatload of VCRs. I thought of Billy's family, his parents. They would probably be at home, while I sat here in this boat with their son, crumpled on a metal deck under an oily tarpaulin, his life finished. I thought of my own wife at home, and the families of everyone in the unit. I had difficulty finding the words to make the report. It was going to be tough in the weeks ahead.

Joe returned two hours later looking tired. "Nothing," was all he said. He slumped down on the deck and put his head in his hands.

We all knew the risks of going up against the *daai fei* gangs, and we all suspected that one day it would result in something awful. But this was the first officer from the unit to be killed while on duty.

"Some of the younger ones," said Joe Poon next morning, after he and a few others had cleared away their gear, "are talking about taking the law into their own hands, by orchestrating some kind of revenge action. I suggest we send some of them home on leave. They are angry. They need time to cool down."

There were lots of messages of condolence. Jack Devereux came out to speak with the unit. Surprisingly, so did Don Bishop, to express his sympathy, a show of solidarity. I appreciated these efforts.

There was an inquiry into Billy's death. PHQ went through our operational tactics with a fine-toothed comb. Jack Devereux was summoned to see the commissioner, to explain. The old man went armed with a file full of letters requesting changes in maritime legislation. The ones he had been asking for, for over a year.

As a result of the enquiry into Billy Lee's death, the law was changed. It became a crime to construct, own or operate a vessel that was deemed purpose-built for smuggling. Within a matter of days, all known areas where *daai fei*s were manufactured, moored, stored or hidden were raided. Arrests were made and prison sentences doled out. Dozens of *daai fei*s were seized and before long, all Marine Police bases around Hong Kong resembled scrap yards, cluttered with grey hulls and large outboard engines. The Marine North Division base, located inside Tolo Channel itself, had so many speedboats piled up in its compound, it became known by the press as the '*Daai Fei* Graveyard.' Change had finally come - but it had come at a cost.

23

THE HANDOVER BEGINS
回歸序幕拉開

WITH THE CHANGES to Hong Kong's maritime legislation with respect to smuggling in place, illegal activity between the territory and China was dealt a severe blow — to the effect that the crime syndicates on both sides temporarily closed down their cross-border activity. But it didn't last.

No longer able to operate out of Hong Kong, the syndicates moved their shipyard operations to the southern ports of China. Here, these purpose-built speedboats were once more fitted with armor-plated cockpits and reinforced bow sections for ramming anything and everything that dared get in their way. The deadly game was back on.

In 1991, I was promoted to the rank of superintendent, which meant a transfer out of SBU to command one of the Marine divisions. I was sorry to leave the unit, but as I had recently become a father, to a girl, Chloe, I decided that a job with less frontline presence was for the best. Anyway, I didn't think Maria could take any more sleepless nights waiting for that phone call.

For the next four years, I headed Marine divisions in both the northern and the eastern waters of Hong Kong. This one-thousand-square-kilometer expanse of open sea, known as Marine Eastern Waters District, bordered the Chinese coast around Mirs Bay to the north, and the South China Sea to the east. A Marine divisional commander's job is both operational and administrative, and it is up to the individual how operational, or how active, he wants to make it. After those three years in SBU, during which sleeping in my own bed at night had become something of a luxury, I was comfortable to leave the frontline work to my assistant commanders, all of whom were experienced operational officers. I felt that being responsible for five hundred Marine Police officers, a headquarters building and a dozen patrol launches, I had enough on my plate. I no longer needed to spend my nights sitting in an open boat waiting for the bad guys to show up.

In the same year as my promotion to superintendent, Joe was promoted to chief inspector and, for a time, commanded SBU himself before also returning to divisional work. I caught up with him from time to time, usually in Marine HQ.

"Do I need to call you sir now?" he asked with a slight smile one morning shortly after I'd received the news of the promotion.

"Of course," I said. "As does Don Bishop."

Joe cracked up laughing at the thought.

It was an odd sensation being senior to Don, particularly when I thought back to those early years. Fifteen years before, I'd been his 'bag man,' in the days when he was feared by all. Ordered to go out drinking with him, and often having to help carry him home. But Don had mellowed somewhat with the years. He'd even made an honest woman of the Lady Angelique, which surprised everyone, and she was now expecting their first child. How times had changed. But we still saw that old fire from time to time, especially after he'd had a drink. On one occasion, I popped into the Mariners Rest early one Friday evening to find Don alone at the bar a little the worse for wear. He'd already switched from beer to whisky, so I knew he was on a mission. As

I walked into the Mess, Don stood up from his chair, thrust out his chest and saluted.

"Senior officer in the Mess!" shouted Don at the top of his voice, "Atten. . .shun!" He stamped one large foot next to the other. I managed to calm him down a little and even persuade him to drink a glass of water before I pushed off, leaving him alone to his single malt.

In June 1995, just two years before Hong Kong was to be handed back to the People's Republic of China, I was called to a meeting with Jack Devereux. In past years, being summoned to the old man's office had always led to some lively venture or other. So it was with more than a modicum of trepidation that I fronted up on this occasion.

"I want you for a special job," he began.

I'd been here before, of course so I suspected the worst, and I got it. I was to be reassigned. The role was to help form the new Hong Kong Government Liaison Committee on Cross-Border Security. It was a job no one wanted.

The committee had been established to meet with our Chinese counterparts to ensure the successful transition of police powers during and after the handover. In the Joint Declaration, the contract drawn up between Beijing and London, it stated just how the territory would be managed after the change of sovereignty. It included how the policing of Hong Kong waters would remain the responsibility of the Hong Kong Marine Police for a minimum of fifty years. In the coming months, members of Hong Kong's land police units, Marine Police, Customs and Excise Department, Immigration Department, and the Government Secretariat were going to be redeployed to form this new committee to meet with the Chinese. Our goal being to agree on the maritime terms within the Joint Declaration and how they would be implemented. It was a massive operation to transition all the departments, especially those responsible for the border areas. In the Marine Police, we knew who our Chinese counterparts were. At the best of times we found them to be a stubborn bunch.

"With all due respect sir, that's an awful job. Can't you find someone else?"

With all that had happened over the past seven years, combating Chinese syndicates, some of which we suspected had official mainland connections, I wasn't really in the mood to play games with our chums from across the border. Devereux thought otherwise.

"That's exactly why I want you on the committee, Mr Bird. Your experience on the frontline in our fight against smuggling, and the fact that you have been a Marine commander of the border divisions makes you the ideal choice from our side."

"From a cast of how many, sir?"

"Enough. It's done. Your name has been presented as our lead officer in these negotiations. Now, you will need to take two other senior officers with you to the first meeting in Shenzhen. Any suggestions?"

"Chief Inspectors Joe Poon and Don Bishop."

"Bishop!" Devereux practically exploded. "You must be joking. He's too much of a loose cannon. There's no way you are taking him. Not a chance."

The ear-bashing went on for several minutes. Devereux wanted our committee to impress upon the Chinese that the *daai fei* smuggling syndicates that were still operating from their side would be their problem after July 1, 1997. "We need diplomats, not pirates like Bishop to persuade them into action."

I tried again. "Sir, the mainland Chinese forces who control the southern borders are unorthodox themselves. Some of them behave like crime lords rather than civil servants. We need a show of force. The rest of our committee will be made up of pencil pushers from Customs and Excise, Immigration, and the Secretariat. They will be terrified about going into China at this time. There's no way Don Bishop will allow the Chinese to bully our delegates into terms we don't want. We need some muscle to balance the team."

"Muscle! I'm not sending you to a goddam bar brawl, Bird!" Devereux shouted. "The whole world is going to be watching this handover. Can you imagine what the governor, the prime minister even, will say when they open *The Times* at breakfast to find photographs of Don Bishop dragging some Chinese official across the negotiating table by his lapels. 'A Royal Hong Kong Mess' would be a good headline don't you think?"

"I'll do all the talking, sir. Bishop will be there purely as show. You know how these mainlanders think. It's all about face. We need to look the part, to look tough in order to gain a modicum of respect from them."

Devereux went quiet for a minute. "Maybe you have a point," he said, deep in thought. "Okay, fine. But it's on your head, Bird. You understand me? And for God's sake keep him away from the booze. That's an order."

I called Don that afternoon. He took the news better than expected.

"No way. You can stick that suggestion where the sun doesn't shine, Leslie-boy."

The line went dead, but after three more attempts to reach him he picked up the receiver.

"Listen, Don, just listen. It's in our own interests to eyeball these guys, even if we suspect they don't play on the level."

"We know they don't play on the level, young Leslie, sir," he grumbled.

That was actually the first time he had ever called me sir

without following it with some expletive or other.

"No, Don, we suspect they don't. That's different. As I said, it's in our own interests that we take this chance to meet with them and point out why, in the lead-up to the handover, it is in their interests to help put a stop to crime in the waters of Hong Kong."

"Bah, and how do you propose we do that? You can't reason with these people."

"I don't intend to reason with them, Don, I plan to threaten them."

"Ha! I always suspected that when someone was promoted to superintendent in the Royal Hong Kong Police there was a requirement to have their brain removed. You've just proven that, young Leslie. Have you lost your marbles, sir? You can't threaten these people. They'll feed you to the pigs. Threaten them! You will be shipped back to Hong Kong in a pine box, lad. I mean, sir."

I let it go. I knew this would be Don's response, but that was what I wanted. He was on board and he would be at the first meeting at his belligerent best. Joe Poon, on the other hand, was going to be a more difficult proposition.

I felt Joe was a good choice. Joe thought otherwise.

"Absolutely no way, sir."

"Excuse me?"

"Sorry, sir, but no, I can't. It's not possible for me to go to China. They know who I am. You know what's gone down over the years. I have been having run-ins with the PLA along the northern border for twenty years. I have been the Chinese face in every major operation we have done. After you left SBU, I had several altercations with their *Gung On*. There have been some pretty delicate situations. You know me, I don't back off. The authorities in southern China are none-too pleased with CI Joe

Poon of the 'British' Royal Hong Kong Police. Once I cross that border. . ."

"They can't touch you," I said. "You will be a member of an international delegation. This is our chance to meet with these people formally, face-to-face. It's in our own interests too, if we can get them to help us finally eradicate this *daai fei* racket. I need your eyes and ears, and your views. You see and hear things that I will miss, you know that."

"No, I am sorry. There will be an accident. They will arrange something for me. They have their ways."

"Joe, they have also been coerced into meeting with us. They will also be kicking and screaming about being part of this joint committee. And their directive will come with a warning from Beijing about behaving themselves. It will be the mainland officials that are for the chopping block if anything goes amiss on their own turf. They will be too preoccupied with all their politics to give the health and wellbeing of one Joe Poon a second thought."

Joe sat in silence for a while and thought this through. "Yes, there is that," he replied, doubt in his voice.

"Come on, Joe. It will be a laugh, going across the border on official business. Who would have thought it, twenty years ago, you, me and Diamond Don Bishop, going into China to eyeball their hierarchy?"

There was silence on the other end of the line. I could tell he was weighing up his options.

"You are going to die someday, Joe," I reminded him. "You might as well be doing something worthwhile when it happens."

"You're all nuts," he said exhaling. "Okay, I'm in."

Within the month, I received word of the first meeting. The location was to be Shenzhen Municipal Government Building, some twenty miles across the border on the Chinese side. The plan was for Don, Joe, and myself to meet with the other Hong Kong government representatives at the border crossing at Lowu on the Hong Kong side. There we would clear immigration into China and be met by their officers who would escort us to the meeting venue.

On the morning of the first meeting, I met Don and Joe at Marine Police Headquarters in Tsim Sha Tsui, Kowloon, where a car and driver were waiting to take us to the border crossing. We were dressed in civvies for the meeting after the powers-that-be from both sides deemed it inappropriate for uniforms and badges of rank.

When I arrived, Don was leaning on the bonnet of a large police saloon, his hands in his pockets and a stuff-this look on his face.

"Morning, Don. Ready for our little excursion?"

"Bah, waste of time this is. You have got a lot to answer for, Leslie. I hope for their sakes they serve some cold beer with lunch."

Don was wearing a police tie complete with silver Royal crest pin set just below the knot. His way of making a statement. We stood in the shade of the headquarters building, out of the morning's scorching sun, and waited for Joe Poon.

He came sprinting around a corner. "Sorry gents, just checked my personal issue into the armory. I don't think the Chinese immigration and customs would take kindly to me carrying a firearm."

"Pity," Don said. "We should all be carrying."

With that, Don climbed into the front seat of the car and slammed the door.

About an hour later, we met the other members of our delegation at the border.

"God help us," Don said under his breath as we approached

the gathering of Government Secretariat men, who all wore identical-looking suits with bland ties. "Pencil-neck there looks like he needs a good feed. Look at these blighters. The Chinese are going to think we are a pushover."

"It's a meeting, Don, not a fist-fight," I muttered as I extended a hand to our team leader.

After clearing formalities on the Hong Kong side, we were met by a mainland Chinese gentleman dressed in a suit who bowed gracefully, smiled, and introduced himself as the secretary of the Chinese delegation. It was his responsibility, he informed us, to ensure our safe passage to the meeting. The secretary was flanked by two immaculate People's Liberation Army officers who stood motionless behind him. I found it odd to be so close to the PLA. Don gave them his infamous one-eye-half-closed stare. The first time I had been on the receiving end of that stare, I had felt like a rabbit caught in the glare of oncoming headlights.

The Chinese arranged a bus to take us to the center of the town of Shenzhen. Building works on both sides of the road dominated the entire trip. The whole of southern China was on the move, new roads, new towns, new everything, one massive building site. The older members of our party discussed how the place had changed since the last time they had visited. A time when southern China was a sleepy backwater of paddy fields and ox carts.

Shenzhen itself had been transformed from a village into a town, that was well on its way to becoming a city. Every building seemed to be either in the process of being demolished or built. Dust blanketed everything. The sounds of jack-hammers thumping through concrete echoed from all directions. Hundreds of workmen in overalls, safety hats and muddy boots clambered like ants over the structures as we zigzagged our way along new highways through the grey landscape.

Shenzhen Municipal Government Building was a featureless three-story block in the center of town. Concrete walls and an iron grill fence surrounded the grounds. The gates were guarded by uniformed PLA soldiers. I glanced at Joe as the gates were closed behind us. He didn't look happy.

Once inside we were escorted down spotless corridors which had a recently-washed smell of disinfectant. After being ushered into a large meeting room, our guide told us to take our seats. He then closed the door and left us alone.

The room was simple. Tiled floors, white walls, a large Formica-topped table with rows of plastic chairs on either side. A few portraits of dull-looking government officials hung on the wall opposite.

"It's bloody freezing in here," said Don, as he maneuvered his ample frame onto a flimsy plastic chair. "So that's their plan, to freeze us to death." He folded his arms across his chest, the stuff-this expression still firmly planted on his face.

After about ten minutes, the Chinese delegation entered. They were a mix of older government men and younger, hard-looking, military types. Introductions were made from both sides by the respective delegation leaders as green tea was served from porcelain tea pots into small, handleless, china cups. Don's cup disappeared inside his mitt as he sipped his tea. I thought I heard a grunt and caught his eye. I knew what he was thinking.

On the Chinese side, the older ones did all the talking while the younger military-looking ones remained silent. They stared across the table at us, an indifferent look on their faces. Don stared straight back, a defiant look on his. Our team included a couple of interpreters, who simultaneously translated the Chinese side's Mandarin into both Cantonese and English.

One by one, the various departments had their say until it was maritime security's turn. The leader of the Hong Kong delegation began by reading out the relevant part of the Joint Declaration where it states that the Hong Kong authorities would be responsible for policing the waters of the territory after the handover. Before he could go any further with his introductory speech, the leader of the Chinese side raised a hand to stop him.

"I am fully aware of this statement," he announced.

Don moved in his seat and leant forward across the table. "And," continued the Chinese chairman, "you have my word that we will adhere to this to the letter. You can rest assured, gentlemen, that our military patrol craft will not enter the waters of the Special Administrative Region of Hong Kong unless requested to do so by the authorities of Hong Kong, or by prior agreement between your government and our own."

The Chinese chairman looked across the table and smiled.

I looked at Joe, who had remained silent throughout the meeting. He stared, expressionless, across the table directly at the Chinese chairman. The head of our delegation nodded with approval. He thanked the Chinese chairman for his statement and quickly made some notes. He then looked towards me and raised his eyes, giving me the chance to speak.

"Thank you, Mr Chairman," I began. "That is very reassuring. However, there is one other maritime matter that I hope you will be able to assist us with." I looked across at the Chinese. "I refer to the current illegal import-export situation that exists between Hong Kong and the southern coastal areas of Mirs Bay and Bias Bay."

I was careful not to infer that smuggling was a Shenzhen-specific problem, more of one controlled by persons from the provinces in the far-away south. I felt it was important not to try and link the current smuggling with anything to do with central government agencies. Not if we hoped to make any progress.

The Chinese chairman listened patiently as I outlined the

current smuggling-by-speedboat situation.

"I am sure, like us," I continued, "that you are eager to see an end to this illegal activity. With the handover of sovereignty of Hong Kong rapidly approaching, it is, I am sure you agree, in everyone's interests that this high-profile crime does not remain an issue for either government."

The chairman shifted in his seat as he listened.

"I have information here relating to the current smuggling-at-sea trends we are dealing with," I continued. "I would like to pass this information to you today and ask you to suggest ways in which we, together, can put a stop to this." I picked up a thin file I had prepared prior to the meeting and waited for a response. The Chinese chairman nodded.

"I am sure we can offer support," he replied smiling directly at me. "Please let me see the file."

I pushed it across the table and he flicked through it. I felt sure he knew everything that was in this file. What he would be most concerned about was if there was any suggestion — or worse, proof — that the smuggling was condoned by someone with links to the government agencies. Which there was not. What was included in the file were close-up photographs of crew members of the speedboat smuggling syndicates. In the months prior to the meeting, helicopters from both the RAF and Hong Kong's own Auxiliary Air Force had been assisting Marine Police with gathering information. They had obtained quite a number of clear, close-up photographs of the crews caught in the act. I was sure that certain members of the Chinese delegation would be able to positively identify some of these smugglers.

Without changing his expression, the chairman closed the file and looked up. "Anything else we can help you with?" he offered.

"Yes there is," I replied. "Recently there has been a spate of thefts of Mercedes Benz saloon cars in Hong Kong. Almost all of the cars stolen are new, and are of the larger variety. We believe these cars are being smuggled out of Hong Kong by sea, across the border and into Shenzhen. They are being stolen to order."

Joe Poon sprang to life. "These stolen Mercedes Benz cars are all right-hand drive," he added. "Because we drive on the left-hand side of the road in Hong Kong. So your officers should easily be able to spot them on the roads here, as cars in China are all left-hand drive. These stolen ones would almost certainly be the only right-hand drive cars in Shenzhen," he concluded.

The Chinese chairman smiled. "Of course, I will see what I can do," he replied. He turned and spoke to an aide who was standing to the rear.

"Now gentlemen," he continued. "I think that brings an end to this first meeting between us. From our side, I can say that this has been very productive, and I will ensure your requests are considered. I hope you too have found this meeting useful and constructive. I look forward to meeting with you all again in the near future. Have a safe journey home. Until the next meeting, goodbye."

And with that he stood up, bowed and left the room. His delegation members each did the same.

"Oh, that's it then," said Don. "No scabby dog for lunch?"

Our guide returned and offered to escort us back to our transport at the rear of the building.

"Not as painful as I thought," Don said as we began to file out. "But there's still enough time for them to put a bullet in the back of your head, Joe, bah!" He laughed and prodded Joe on the shoulder.

Joe turned and gave Don an evil look. "We are not home and dry yet, Don, don't relax. They might miss me and hit a much larger target." Joe jabbed Don in the stomach.

Out in the courtyard, there was no sign of our bus. Waiting, in its place, was a fleet of black limousines.

"Well, this is more like it," declared Don as we watched the members of our delegation being ushered into the waiting cars. "It's about time we received a little respect. This one's ours, I guess," he said pointing at the limo pulling up in front of where we were standing.

A smartly-dressed driver jumped out and came around the rear of the car and opened the doors for us. Inside, the air conditioning was running and this time the cool air felt good. There were no complaints from Joe. "We should be back at the border within the hour," he said, as he settled into the back seat.

Once everyone was comfortably seated, the convoy of five identical black Mercedes Benz saloon cars pulled out of the government compound and headed through the busy streets of Shenzhen. "Well, have you noticed yet?" asked Joe to an already-dozing Don Bishop.

"What? Noticed what?" replied Bishop barely opening his eyes.

"Which side of this car the driver is sitting on," replied Joe.

Don blinked and squinted at the driver.

"It's the same for the limo in front," continued Joe, "and for the one behind," he said, turning to look out of the rear window. "In fact, all five of them," Joe said with a smile. "The Hong Kong delegation on cross-border security is being driven through China, and back to the border crossing, in five right-hand drive Mercedes Benz. The cheeky buggers."

24

GOODBYE AND ALL THAT
1997
再見亦是朋友

As was the norm these days, the Mariners Rest was empty. Despite it being a Friday afternoon not a single soul was in the place, not even a barman. The days of the Marine Police Officers' Mess being packed to the rafters seemed to have evaporated as the handover approached. It was as though everyone was afraid of the future. Afraid to do anything that could, after July, be cast in a negative light. Things such as getting smashed in the Officers' Mess, which was certainly a big no-no these days. Or, maybe there wasn't much cause for celebration. It was a time of uncertainty as to what the future had in store. I'd arranged to meet Joe in the Mess as he was now working at headquarters as a staff officer. I tried to imagine Joe driving a desk. Square peg in a round hole, which was the reason for the meeting. I wanted to hear how he was getting on. I wanted to see if I could help him find a more suitable job.

The Mess that afternoon was spotless. It looked like it hadn't been used in weeks. Probably the only person frequenting the place that day had been the cleaner.

I went behind the bar and pulled a beer from the cooler and signed for my drink. The Mariners was a trust bar. No barman, just help yourself and sign a chit. Pouring the beer into a glass, I walked around to a cluster of empty armchairs and plonked myself down. It was twenty years ago that I first came into the Mariners Rest, on that Friday afternoon, my first day in the Marine Police. There must have been more than a hundred officers in here on that day — policemen and civilians, locals and expats. Friday was always socializing day. Some of the old boys would say they got more work done in the Mess on a Friday than during the rest of the week put together. Not anymore. You rarely saw a senior officer these days. I sipped my beer and stared out over Victoria Harbor. The heavy footsteps on the polished wooden floorboards brought me back to the present.

"Fancy seeing you in here," Don said as he made straight for the bar. He grabbed a beer and cracked it open. "It's not often there's another living, breathing entity in here," he continued as he held up a glass, examining its condition.

"I was just thinking about the very first time I came in here, Don. I met you for the first time on that day."

"Really?" Don said as he dropped into the armchair opposite. "Mid-1970s or something like that, wasn't it?"

"Almost. 1977. My first day in Marine. You introduced me to an odd group of blokes including a French priest and Hong Kong's last hangman."

Don chuckled into his beer. "That old rogue, Lucas Remington. What a card he was. He's long gone, you know, died in 1985, I think."

He fiddled with his beer mat, taking great care to position his glass directly in the center. As he leant forward, I studied the top of his enormous bald head. Back in the 1970s, when I first met him he must have been in his mid-thirties, but I had always assumed Don was older. He certainly looked it, and acted it. He was one of those officers who had always looked and behaved older than he actually was.

"So," I said looking directly at him. "Have you decided what you are going to do?"

All expatriate officers serving on permanent employment terms in the Royal Hong Kong Police had been offered an early retirement package in the lead-up to the handover. The offer included a commuted pension, calculated in accordance with the number of years the officer had served, plus a one-off loss of earnings payment to compensate for the years of employment lost, if one chose to leave the force before the change of sovereignty. After all, it was the employer not the employee who was leaving town. It was such a good offer that some said it was as though our soon-to-be lords and masters in Beijing actually wanted us to go.

My question to Don was the one many of us were asking each other these days. Accept the early retirement package or stay on after the handover and serve until retirement which, for most, was fifty-five.

"Let's examine some of the relevant issues about a post-handover police force first then, shall we, Leslie, sir?" Don said, seemingly amused at my interest in his future. "If you don't mind, I will use your predicament as an officer on permanent and pensionable service."

I shrugged and nodded for him to continue.

"Item one to consider is the Royal title. For the whole of your twenty-plus years you have served in the *Royal* Hong Kong Police, correct?"

It was a rhetorical question. I nodded again.

"And this 'Royal' title will disappear on July 1. Possibly you don't mind that. I don't know?" Don looked for a reaction, but he didn't get one, so he continued. "Then there is the small matter, the obvious one, of course, that Hong Kong will cease to be a

British territory and become a special administrative region of the People's Republic of China. If you stay you will be working, indirectly, for the Chinese government, in Beijing."

Don stared at me again, waiting for a response. He didn't get one.

"Item three," he continued. "In the rank of superintendent, the crowns on your shoulders will be replaced by Bauhinia flowers," Don coughed and grinned to himself. "Whereas in my case," Don lowered his voice, "the three pips on my shoulders will, if I stay, be replaced by three Chinese stars. Our uniforms will change too, quite drastically I would think. I read somewhere that our military style caps will go, and yours with all that braid." Don shook his head and tut-tutted. "The police force preference in headgear will probably be some type of baseball cap I can imagine."

None of what Don was saying was news to me. Everyone knew there would be changes after the handover, but I was quite enjoying his little performance.

Don shifted in his seat then took a drink of beer before replacing his glass back in the middle of the beer mat. He adjusted it slightly, satisfied it was dead center.

"So, that's just the uniform, Don," I said.

"There's more to this post-handover than the uniform of course," he continued. "There's also the flag, isn't there? You will be required to salute the red Chinese flag as it flies over this building. You okay with that?"

I shrugged. He still was yet to answer my question about his own intentions, but I decided to let him prattle on.

"Then comes the more important issue of job satisfaction. It makes sense to put the young Chinese officers in frontline jobs. They will need the experience, to take over the command of a whole division, from chaps like you. Yes?"

I nodded. "That makes sense."

"And this will happen sooner rather than later methinks, Leslie-boy. Sooner rather than later. And when it does, what are they going to do with you for the next, what, ten years? You have been a divisional commander for the past eight years, and before that, you commanded SBU. Will they be putting you out to pasture for the remainder of your career? A desk job? Pushing paper? Waiting for your retirement date, waiting for your pension, counting the days, glancing at the desk calendar every morning before you put yet another red line through one more day. If you stay on after 1997, how many years will you need to serve before you can touch your pension?"

"It's eleven years actually, Don," I replied.

"Eleven years," spluttered Don. "You, nine-to-five, in a back office, closed doors, signing files all day. Like that lot." He pointed to the door of the bar. "Eleven years — that's a lot of days. Bit like a prison sentence, eh?"

I shivered at the thought. "I asked you what you were going to do, Don," I reminded him.

"Ah, sorry, yes. But let me just finish your scenario first. What about future promotion? Again, it makes sense to promote the local chaps, the younger ones who are going to be in the force for the next twenty years. Not a white man rapidly nearing the age of retirement. A man crossing off the days on his desk calendar."

I nodded in response.

"Also..." he hadn't finished "...take a look at this place," Don waved his hand around. "It's dead, there's no spirit, no atmosphere, where's the esprit de corps? Where's the camaraderie? Where's the comradeship? You have lots of good friends in the force, don't you? Local and expats?"

I stared back at him.

"Those friendships were built on trust, I'll wager.

306

Comradeship, camaraderie. Yes?"

I nodded again.

"It's gone already. We are already just going through the motions. It's a grim picture, don't you think?"

I sat back in my chair and took a drink. "That's quite a speech, Don, and quite a picture. Thanks. But what about you? I asked what are you intending to do?"

"Oh, I'm staying," he laughed as he emptied his beer.

I just stared back at him. I was speechless. At first I thought he was joking. But then I realized he wasn't.

Don sat back in his chair and began fiddling with his glass, avoiding eye contact. He was waiting for my response. But I was so taken aback by what I'd just heard that I didn't know what to say. Don looked up. "You see, I have nowhere else to go, old sport. Who else would put up with Diamond Don Bishop?"

As Don spoke, there were more footsteps on the wooden floor by the door. I glanced over to see Joe come in. He nodded and went behind the bar to get himself a drink.

"You are staying?" I asked Don, finally finding my voice. "*You* are staying!" again. "*You* are going to wear the three Chinese stars on your shoulders and salute the red flag? Chief Inspector Donald Bishop of the Royal Hong Kong Police is going to salute the red flag?"

"Oh yes, Leslie, sir. You see I honestly have nowhere else to go. There's no question of me going back to England. I am a dinosaur and I know it."

Don stood up and walked across the room towards the bar. I was lost for words. The last person I expected to stay on after the change in sovereignty and serve the Chinese government, albeit indirectly in his mind, was Diamond Don Bishop.

"Well, say something, for God's sake," said Don as he rummaged around behind the bar.

"Did you say you are staying?" asked Joe, finally grasping what was going on. "After the handover?"

"Yes, I am. You locals are not getting rid of me that easily. I quite enjoy terrorizing the natives, you know."

"Don, I am a little surprised to hear your news," I said.

"Yes, it surprised the hell out of Police Headquarters, too, when I told them. This early retirement package was designed to tempt people like me to go before the handover. You see I am a bit of an embarrassment to today's hierarchy. I represent the old school, the old colonials. I think they want me well and truly out of the way by July 1, bah. But I ain't going."

"Yes, I am sure the hierarchy at PHQ were shocked when you told them, no offense."

"None taken." Don huffed, and opened a cupboard behind the bar, producing a bottle. "Ah, here it is, my own single malt." He held it up for Joe and me to see.

"You really are staying on? After the handover?" Joe shook his head in disbelief. Don smiled, took three tumbler glasses from a rack, poured sizable measures and handed them around.

"A toast," he declared. "Here's to the last twenty years together. And…" he hesitated for a second "…here's to the future, whatever it may bring – *post tenebras spero lucem.*"

We drank, *yam sing*, down in one. It was good stuff. Don held up his empty glass and smiled. Then he shook his head and made a sound like a horse - one that had just lifted its head out of the trough. Bah!!

ACKNOWLEDGEMENTS

I'M FOREVER indebted to three former Marine Police colleagues for encouraging me to write this book. To Mark Ogden, Bill Bailey and Bruce Venables, I thank you for your motivation and unflagging support during the research and the writing process. I am also beholden to my oft-partners in crime, Frankie Poon Tze-chung and Jackie Ling Wai-po. Working alongside you two inspired me to write much of what is here. To Kit Ha and Fraser Morton, who gave me invaluable advice and encouragement during the development phase of this story, I express my utmost gratitude.

No one has been more important to me in the pursuit of this work than my family. This book, quite literally, would not exist without the resolve of May Anne, Catherine and Victoria, who were with me throughout. Thank you, girls, for providing unending inspiration.

About The Author

Les Bird was born in 1951 in Staffordshire, England. After leaving school he travelled extensively through Africa and Australia before joining the Royal Hong Kong Police in 1976. He served in the Force for over two decades before moving into the private security business world. Bird is a founding member and chairman of Asia's Rhinos Rugby Football Club. He is married with two daughters. He still lives in Hong Kong.